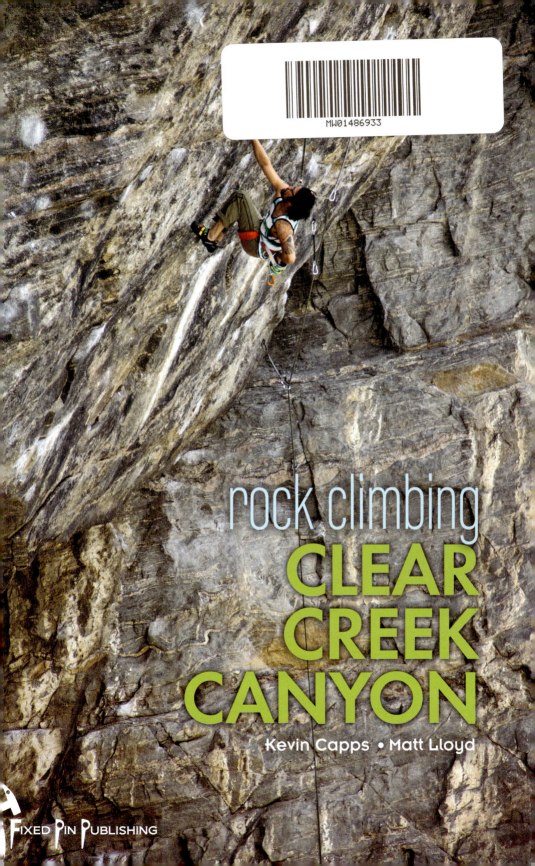

rock climbing

CLEAR
CREEK
CANYON

Kevin Capps • Matt Lloyd

FIXED PIN PUBLISHING

Rock Climbing Clear Creek Canyon

Authors: Kevin Capps, Matt Lloyd

Uncredited photos: Kevin Capps, Dan Gambino, Jason Haas, Matt Lloyd
Cover photo: Daniel Woods on *Mourning Glory* (5.14c), p152. photo: Keith Ladzinski
Opening page photo: Jamie Gatchalian on *Kinky Reggae* (5.14a), New River Wall, p81. photo: Keith North

International Standard Book Number:
ISBN 978-0-9895156-3-4

Library of Congress Catalog in Publication Data:
Library of Congress Control Number: 2014944283

Fixed Pin Publishing is continually expanding its guidebooks and loves to hear from locals about their home areas. If you have an idea for a book or a manuscript for a guide, or would like to find out more about our company, please contact:

Jason Haas
Fixed Pin Publishing
P.O. Box 3481
Boulder, CO 80307
jason@fixedpin.com

Ben Schneider
Fixed Pin Publishing
P.O. Box 3481
Boulder, CO 80307
ben@fixedpin.com

WWW.FIXED PIN.COM

Acknowledgments

Without these wonderful climbing partners, this guidebook would have not been possible. We would like to thank everyone who shared a rope with us during this process.

Laura Capps
Jason Haas
Luke Childers
Jason Baker
Dan Hooley
Bethany Lukens

Sam Norris
Cerri Norris
Jay Samuelson
Sevve Stember
Dan Gambino
Kevin Meurer

Dan Cornella
Amie Bergeson
Tom Sciolino
Bill Brandenburg
Keith North

Foreword

Unleashed from the Rockies, Clear Creek rushes down its canyon like a stampede of wild horses. I was captivated by this energy early one morning as I traversed a steep hillside on my way to work on a new route. Above me, a harem of thirty bighorn sheep lay and watched me pass, though I was halted. A large ram approached from behind as if he followed me in, hooves scraping the dirt and tilting his full-curled horns. On the hill, another found a stance in front of his flock, gazing down on the contender while the ewes remained still during the ensuing rumble. The warriors rose to their hindquarters and repeatedly charged into each other. Their heads reverberated like the crack of a gunshot, so close to me I could feel the power of each blow deep in my chest. If only for that moment, I felt like I belonged with those canyon climbers.

Superficially, Clear Creek Canyon provides a noisy casino speedway and ski-traffic bypass. However after 15 years of exploring and climbing in this urban canyon, I was proud to call it my home crag. My memories have the cathartic sound of whitewater rapids, a buzz of a distant rotary hammer, or try-hard battle cries of fellow climbers.

This was the nearest midweek escape from my white-collar reality. The first tunnel became an event horizon as I drove into the canyon. I felt pulled into each tunnel as if were a black hole, just to choose my own adventure on the other side from over 50 crags and rock formations. More often than not, I conveniently approached them in flip-flops, armed with a rack of draws and a gri-gri, because they have been tamed for our bolt-chasing pleasure.

You will find that the crags of Clear Creek host a variety of climbing styles as diverse as the composition of its metamorphic stone. Experiences range from first leads to first ascents, 5.11-heaven to some of the state's hardest lines. Chase down the trendy clip-ups or discover trad obscurities reserved only for the Clear Creek veteran. Test yourself with benchmark projects or tie-in to a handful of multi-pitch outings that will take you to surprisingly extraordinary positions, exposed scenarios, and lofty perches high above the water. These are the training grounds for the local weekend warrior while visiting climbers queue for their chance to chalk up for the most sprayed upon classics.

Even with its relatively short climbing history, every decade since the eighties saw an influx of a couple of hundred new routes, established by the growing campaign of devoted Clear Creek Crusaders. After the dust cleared, their rampage yielded some of the canyon's best and obvious lines. It was the shoulders of these giants on which we stood. Fortunately, some real gems had been overlooked, but we had to work harder for them. By scheming shenanigans, excavating choss, and stepping off the talus path, we pillaged our own legacy routes.

My earliest escapades in developing new routes were inspired here. One of which Casey Bernal and I climbed in the middle of winter. Dodging falling ice, swinging around on a web of fixed lines, and sharing smokes on the Ashtray Ledge, we hand-drilled the bolts together. We felt as if we were a thousand feet up even though we were only about a hundred. But we didn't care; we were young pioneers.

I spent years refining my modern 'hook or crook' first ascent techniques, and mustering good ol' school ground-up courage; doors opened to more self-expression and adventures with great friends. I had the honor to top out with Derek Lawrence after establishing the canyon's longest trad route as a farewell tribute to our fallen "Big Brother." I looked forward to Tuesday night at the crag with Dave Montgomery as we continually threw ourselves on our bromance proj'. I dream to someday see a grin from my son while I belay him above the Creekside tyrol. The next generation will hopefully have even easier and safer access to this climbing resource with the eventual addition of the Clear Creek Canyon Park segment of the Peaks to Plains Trail.

Clear Creek Canyon has become a hot climbing destination and a modern guidebook is essential to fully appreciate its unique character and color. This fresh edition highlights hundreds of new routes, with updated information of the entire stretch of the canyon, as well as new crags not documented on the Internet. Magazine quality photographs truly capture the canyon's spirit. Experienced climbers Kevin Capps and Matt Lloyd have not only painstakingly explored almost every route in this guide first-hand, but have each authored many new high end routes of their own. Kevin's passion and skill as a mountain guide and instructor is evident with the book's practical interface. And while Matt is known as a fearless Jack of All Trades, I consider him a master of the Canyon.

Potential is high for the next generation of aspiring developers and first ascentionists. I am convinced there are easily another couple of hundred more routes locked away in the rugged hillsides and the Crusade will march toward them.

~ Darren Mabe
Author of *Clear Creek Canyon Rock Climbs* (2008)
Flagstaff, AZ
February 20, 2014

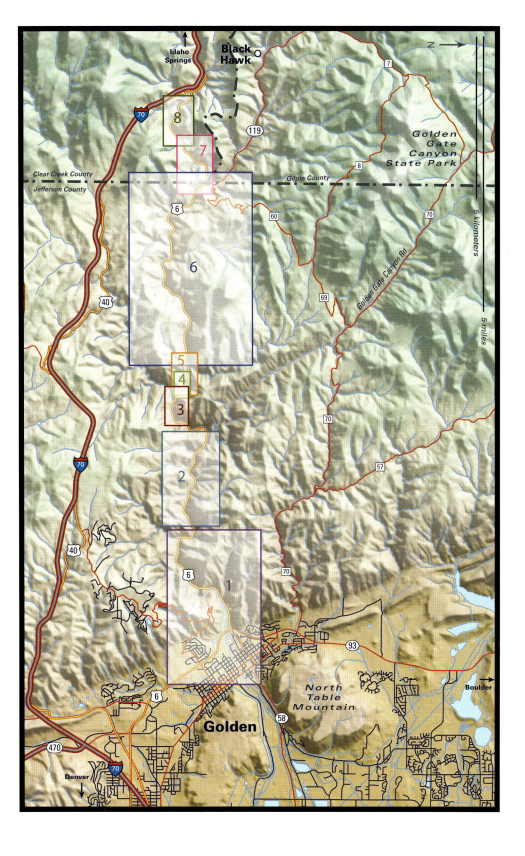

TABLE OF CONTENTS

Introduction

Getting There

Clear Creek Canyon is located in Golden, Colorado, 20 minutes west of Denver, and 30 minutes south of Boulder. This guidebook has a variety of detailed maps for getting to the crag, each of which is equipped with mileage up the canyon, where to park, and trails to the rocks. All of the distances to the crags are measured from the stoplight at the intersection of Highways US-6, CO-93, and CO-58 in Golden; zero your odometer when passing under this light. This marks the base of the canyon and just beyond this intersection to the west on the left (south) side of the road is the main meet up spot for climbers looking to carpool up canyon, which runs along U.S. Highway 6 as it makes its way west towards Idaho Springs, making a left at the intersection of CO-119 and US-6 instead of continuing on to Black Hawk or Central City. Be advised that this road may see an abundance of traffic from people commuting to the mountains for skiing, hiking, gambling, etc. on the weekends.

Getting to the Crags and Parking: Each chapter is laid out into the most obvious sections of the canyon, including a wider spectrum of areas up until Tunnel 2. A lot of the climbing in the canyon is divided by the tunnels, as well as parking either on the east or west side of those tunnels. Each crag has a detailed description of where to park with mileage and a picture. Mile markers are referenced when they are the most useful landmark. With the canyon's growing popularity, it is very important to park in the parking areas in an efficient way to fit as many cars as possible in the pull offs. Parking areas for High Wire and Wall of the '90s are oftentimes full on busy weekends. Also, it is very important to LOCK your car when leaving for the crag. It doesn't happen often, but there have been incidents of break-ins in the canyon.

Ratings

Quality Ratings

This guide uses a four-star system to denote the quality of each route. We've given our best effort to establish conservative and unbiased star ratings, and have consulted many other climbers during the research. Many factors inform a climb's quality and hence its star rating, but the main considerations are: quality of movement, quality of rock, positioning and exposure, general aesthetics, and the overall quality of the line (Is it an obvious line or is it forced/contrived? Does it follow a proud feature? etc.).

★★★★   A consensus Clear Creek classic. These are the must-do routes in the canyon. They are the classics that leave you coming back for more day after day. Clear Creek classics are regarded as some of the best and most popular routes in Colorado.

★★★   A great rock climb. These routes feature excellent climbing, but aren't quite the best in the canyon. Still, they are highly recommended.

★★   This is a good route with fun, worthwhile climbing that you'd recommend or repeat in the future. For certain areas in the canyon, climbs will get a maximum of two stars due to crappy approaches or bad belay stances.

★   A route with one star is OK, but it's not a route that you would do a bunch of times. It might have some redeeming quality about it such as, maybe it's a fun warm up, is long and sustained but contains some chossy rock, or if it's a fun route but might be manufactured.

No stars: Bottom line: climb something else. The route is plagued with vegetation, poor rock, is overly contrived, or simply too uninteresting to bother with.

Difficulty Ratings

The goal was to create a consistent rating system throughout the whole canyon. In order to do that, we had to climb every single route to form proper opinions. However, we also used the consensus from www.mountainproject.com to help solidify our opinions and match those of the community.

Many visiting climbers try and compare Clear Creek Canyon ratings to Rifle or even Eldorado Canyon, but the truth is that all of the climbs in this book are rated when compared to other climbs in Clear Creek Canyon and not to a climbing area that is four hours away. There have been a few adjustments to books in the past, but our intentions are to gain a consistency from Tunnel 1 to Tunnel 6. It is important to take into consideration that grades are highly influenced on your strengths and weaknesses. We tried to write whether a route is going to be reachy, crimpy, powerful, slopy, technical, or awkward in the descriptions. Keep this in mind, for instance, if you're short and want to try a reachy route as you should be prepared for it to feel slightly harder for the grade.

Abbreviations

FA: First Ascent
TR: Toprope

FFA: First Free Ascent
SR: Standard Rack

FKA: First Known Ascent
P1, P2: Pitch one, pitch two, etc.

Line Colors on Route Description Photos

Routes are color coded by difficulty rating: ⬤ Purple represents routes rated 5.8 and under. ⬤ Turquoise is for all the 5.9s in the canyon, ⬤ while yellow means 5.10. ⬤ 5.11s are color-coded red ⬤ and 5.12s are illustrated in green. ⬤ Orange represents the 5.13s ⬤ while hot pink is for 5.14. ◯ Any route outlined in white means it is a project, regardelss of what grade it will end up being redpointed at.

Equipment

For the large majority of the climbs in the canyon, a 70-meter rope, 14 quickdraws, and a belay device are the essential materials. While a 60-meter rope will get you up and down most of the climbs in the canyon, you will be limited at walls like Cat Slab, Little Eiger, and even Creekside.

• 60 or 70-meter rope
• Helmets are highly recommended, especially for multi-pitch climbs
• 12-18 quickdraws; read route descriptions. If there are 12 bolts, and a 2-bolt anchor, then bring 14 quick-draws.
• Slings or Runners: Some routes will specify whether or not slings are necessary to reduce rope drag, although, in general three or four slings are nice to have regardless.
• Stickclip: These are nice to reduce the danger of a few hairy first or second clips. There are a few routes in the canyon that require them and we tried to note it in the route descriptions.
• Trad Climbing: The gear for all of the trad climbs are listed Black Diamond Camalot sizes. Many old school sport routes will even have optional gear, at times, like the runout finish to the classic, *Balkan' Dirt Diving* at Sports Wall.

Fixed Quickdraws on Sport Routes

Is it ok to leave fixed quickdaws or equip a route with permadraws? This has been at the center of many de-bates over the years and will continue to be. There are walls like Primo Wall, New River Wall, and even the Wall of Justice where there has been fixed gear for years. There have been doz-ens of accounts of quickdraws being stolen off of projects on Anarchy Wall, Primo Wall, the Armory, and even New River Wall. Please do NOT take these quickdraws, they are not booty. On the other hand, it is important to take into consideration the visual im-pact we are making on other people enjoying the canyon such as fisher-man, or other outdoor enthusiasts, or even motorists for that matter. Also, if you don't want a thief, especially the Smith Rock leprechaun, stealing your draws, then don't leave them up.

Darren Mabe works his *Double Stout Extension*, Wall of the '90s, p102.
📷 Kristen McIlrath

Bailing on a Route

Having a bail biner or a 3/8" Quick-link in your pack at all times is nice for those days when the summer storms come in or if you don't have enough juice to make it to the top. However, if there is dangerous lightning coming in fast, then it is quickest and probably best to just lower off of a quickdraw and come back the next day to retrieve it.

Climbing Safety in Clear Creek Canyon

Safety is of the upmost importance when it comes to climbing and longevity in the sport. Not much changes in terms of climbing safety in Clear Creek compared to other areas. However, there are a few specific things for visiting climbers or newer climbers to pay attention to and observe. It is also important to mention that there are new cell phone towers installed in the canyon as of 2012, but as of 2014, Verizon is the only provider that gets full cell phone reception in the canyon. Other providers may receive service at areas like Canal Zone, or higher up at areas like Primo Wall or Creekside.

- Always knot the ends of your rope whether you're rappelling or lowering a climber. You do not want to lower yourself or your partner off your line.
- There are many routes in the canyon that require a 70-meter rope; be sure and refer to the route length for that requirement. Depending on how much the route meanders, typically 105 feet is the absolute limit to any 60-meter rope when stretched. If routes are over 105 feet, use a 70-meter rope or prepare to down climb.
- Communication is key – always know how to communicate with your climber/belayer, and more importantly, learn how to communicate when verbal communication is not possible.
- Every year in Clear Creek there are a handful of accidents due to miscommunication while cleaning a route. Never take your climber off belay when you shouldn't!
- Please do not toprope through the anchor as it adds unnecessary wear and tear.
- There are two types of tyroleans in Clear Creek; steel cable and rope. In both situations, it is important to anchor yourself in with a primary and a back up line. Carabiners are required for the rope tyroleans and steel pulleys or steel carabiners should be used for the steel cable by Mission Wall. Please use caution when assessing the safety of the tyroleans, and note that when the rope tyroleans are wet, they stretch and are much more strenuous to maneuver across.
- When wading the creek to get to a wall like New Economy Cliff or even Primo, a pair of waders and a long stick for balance are nice to have. Use extra caution during high water, which happens in late spring through summer as there have been incidences of people being swept away. The water is always much stronger than it looks.

Chris Barlow never thought *Y2K*, 5.12c, Wall of the '90s, p101, was something to fear. How about you? Adam Sanders

Welcome to Clear Creek Canyon Park!

With numerous crags sprinkled along the flanks of US Highway 6, Clear Creek Canyon has had a long history of unencumbered climbing access. Jefferson County Open Space manages the majority of the crags in the canyon, from the mouth of the canyon to the intersection of US-6 and Hwy-119 and has long been present in the canyon, though many climbers may just now be becoming aware of the fact that they are climbing in an Open Space park. As the popularity of climbing continues to grow and the Denver Metro area continues to expand, it is incredibly important that climbers are conscious of their impacts at the crags. With a few exceptions, climbers in the canyon have done a good job of limiting avoidable impacts. Avoidable impacts include human waste, litter, and off-leash dogs. Please help continue this trend by carrying a wag-bag in your pack, packing out all trash, and ideally leaving Fido at home. With the majority of the routes in the canyon being fixed hardware routes, discussion around management of fixed hardware does come up from time to time. To ensure that climbers continue to have access with limited restrictions, climbers wishing to add to the already astounding number of routes in the canyon should keep a few key things in mind as they eye the next new crag.

- <u>Erosion and vegetation loss are one of the biggest concerns that exist around the development of new routes.</u> Consider what will happen to the slope that you're walking on when hundreds of feet start walking up it. Also, use restraint when considering making improvements in the form of trails and staging areas. Open Space has begun working to improve climbing access trails at some of the more popular crags in the canyon. Consider contacting Open Space to discuss the best ways to mitigate your impacts and consult the Jefferson County Open Space Climbing Management Guide (http://jeffco.us/parks/climbing/climbing-management-guide/) before you sink your first bolts.
- <u>Encroachment on wildlife habitat, especially cliff-nesting birds is a big concern.</u> If you are eyeing a new cliff and see evidence of nesting activity, it may be best to move on. While seasonal closures can address certain impact concerns, ask yourself if your new line(s) are worth drawing the attention of Open Space staff that monitor nest sites throughout the canyon.
- <u>Not every cliff needs a line of bolts ascending its face.</u> The nature of the rock in Clear Creek Canyon has played a significant role in limiting the hap-hazard bolting of less than worthy lines. With that said some small, one and two-star cliffs have been developed in recent years. Trends such as this make land managers nervous about resource impacts. And if every vertical face in the canyon starts to see bolts sprouting out of them, it is likely that Open Space will have to re-examine its climbing management strategy in the canyon.

Thanks for taking the time to consider the land manager's perspective. If you ever have a question, please don't hesitate to contact Open Space at (303) 271-5925. Working in partnership towards a common goal of providing the best recreation experience possible, which includes preserving the environment, is a far better path than one that pits recreating climbers against land managers. Climb safe and enjoy what Clear Creek Canyon has to offer!

– **Mike Morin**
January, 2014

Guiding Service

For some, hiring a guide to bring you out for a day of climbing is an excellent and safe option. If you are new to climbing, looking to learn how to set proper anchors for toproping, want to further your ability levels, learn how to lead climb, or even learn how to mulit-pitch climb, Denver Mountain Guiding is the premier and local guide service for the canyon. Owner, Kevin Capps, has been guiding the canyon for years and is also the author of this book, along with DMG guide and co-author Matt Lloyd. The guide's at Denver Mountain Guiding have more experience in the canyon than any other guide service out there (denvermountainguideing.com). Give them a call at (303) 884-2755 or email at info@DenverMountainGuiding.com.

Weather

Summer: During the summer months you might expect the temperatures to be anywhere from 60 degrees at night and mornings to the upper 90s in the heat of the day. Clear Creek Canyon has over 300 days of sunshine per year, but one should note that in the summer there are dangerous and fast moving electrical storms. Getting an early start and checking the forecast are often the best ways to avoid afternoon storms. Many local climbers will wait until it cools off in the late afternoons to climb as well. When there is heavy rainfall, the canyon roads are not the safest places to be due to potential and occasional rock fall/slides.

Spring and Fall: These are often the most beautiful times to climb in the canyon and offer the best climbing temps, from the upper 40s in the morning to the 60s or 70s in the day. It is important to note that the mountain winds are much stronger this time of year.

Winter: The winters in the canyon can often be mild, and Highlander is one of the most popular crags due to its all day sun. There is plenty of snowfall each year in the canyon, so take this into consideration if planning to climb in the shade or start a long approach that might be wet and muddy. Also, many ice bridges form in January making access to areas like Primo Wall much easier. However, it is important to check to make sure the ice is solid before attempting to cross.

Leave NO Trace

Clear Creek Canyon has shown a growing popularity in the past several years by climbers, kayakers, fisherman, and even hikers and trail runners. There has also been a growing amount of erosion taking place on the trails, and a large amount of trash that has been left behind by climbers. Please stay on trails and pack out trash, even if it's not yours.

Dogs

If you bring your dog to the crag, please be considerate of other climbers. You are responsible for its safety and the safety of others that interact with your dog. Please note that many approaches and crags in the canyon are not suitable for dogs due to exposed ledges, loose scree fields, or even creek crossings. Also, most of the crags are on Jefferson County Open Space land, who requires dogs be on a leash at all times.

Camping

Unfortunately there isn't any free camping around Golden (or the Front Range for that matter). Golden, and the surrounding Denver metropolitan area, have a plethora of hotels to choose from. For those looking for something a bit more economical, there are a few pay camping options. The Clear Creek RV Park, (303) 278-1437, is owned by the city of Golden and is located near the west end of 10th Street. Despite the name, there are also a few tent campsites on the premises. The sites are open around May 1 through October and as of 2014 were $25.80 a night for two people. The Jefferson County Fairgrounds, (303) 271-6600, is located close to US-6 and I-70. Tent campsites are available April through October for $25.00 a night. Chief Hosa, www.chiefhosa.org, (720) 913-0766 is a little further away and is located a bit further east along I-70 than the JeffCo Fairgrounds (exit #253). However, it is the cheapest option at $23.00 a night for up to two tents and four people. It is open May through September.

VOLTA 9.2

Tie in to a new level of performance.

9.2 mm multi-standard lightweight rope.

The VOLTA 9.2, part of Petzl's completely redesigned rope line, is the cord for the most demanding users. Lightweight yet durable, and rated for use as a single, half, or twin, it provides for exceptional performance at the crag and in the mountains.

Learn more about our all-new line of ropes on www.petzl.com/ropes

Daniel Woods shows he's an *Animal*, V9, when it comes to first ascents. 📷 Keith Ladzinski

Bouldering

There is a plethora of quality boulders in the canyon. The three most popular areas are below; be sure and bring crash pads and spotters.

• *Mile Marker 268*: Park by mile marker 268, cross to the north side of the road and take the drainage uphill as if going to 268 Wall (p41) to find different quality boulders including the classic *Maverick* (V5).
• *New River Wall Bouldering*: Use the same approach as for New River Wall (p82) and find a deep cave with a low roof at the base of the wall. *Dark Waters*, V13, is found in this area.
• *Catslab Boulders:* These boulders are found 20 meters downhill from Catslab (p158). They are tall, beautiful, and house a variety of problems ranging from V0-V7, including the classic *Into the Light* (V7).

The City of Golden

Golden is one of the greatest towns in America, with a rich history in gold mining, western culture, and of course, Coors beer. It also offers great restaurants, many fantastic microbreweries, and great rest day activities. The people in Golden are as good as they get; if you are ever looking for a suggestion on where to go then just ask a local. To access the main drag from the canyon, take CO-58 east, then take a right and drive down Washington Avenue. There is an abundance of shops, restaurants, and bars that are great for locals and tourists alike down this road. If you're thirsty, take a free tour of the Coors factory where you see the large copper kitchen along with being rewarded with three free beers....did we mention that it's free! If you have a more sophisticated taste for beer, head over to the Mountain Toad or Golden City Brewery, the two local hang outs.

Once you arrive in Golden, you will notice the American Mountaineering Center at 10th and Washington, which holds a nice climbing history museum. It's also the American Alpine Club and Colorado Mountain Club head-quarters. Just south of the museum is Clear Creek, where there is often a flurry of summertime activities. From May to September, many colorful groups of locals gather here for tubing down the creek, kayaking, fishing, grilling, and sun bathing. The water is often a bit chilly, it feels great in sunny conditions. Lyons Park is a great base camp for swimming in the creek, kayaking, or tubing. On a side note, alcohol is no longer permitted in the park.

If you need gear, head over to Bent Gate Mountaineering. It's right next door to Woody's Pizza, with the pizza buffet, and the Sherpa House – two great places to go for a bite to eat. Another fun place to go with live music in the summer time is the creek side restaurant, Bridgewater Grill.

TUNNEL ONE AREA

SEVVE STEMBER CUTS LOOSE ON SHADOWPLAY, 5.11C, TWILIGHT ZONE, P.23 JASON HAAS

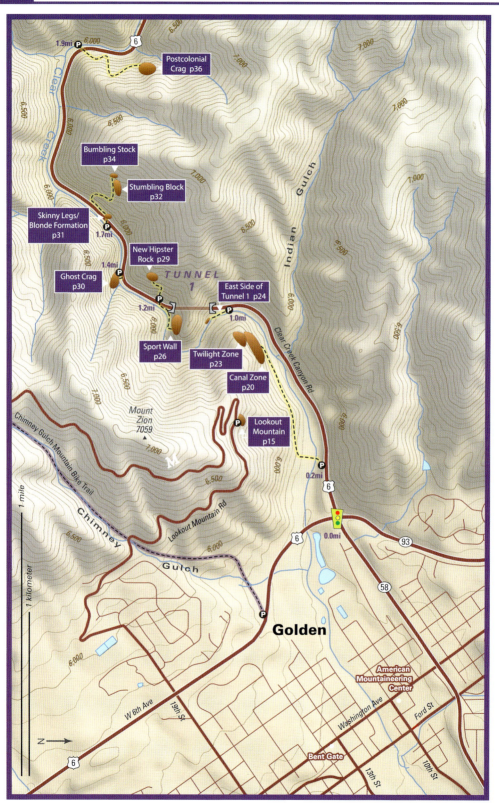

Postcolonial Crag p36

Bumbling Stock p34

Stumbling Block p32

Skinny Legs/ Blonde Formation p31

New Hipster Rock p29

Ghost Crag p30

East Side of Tunnel 1 p24

Sport Wall p26

Twilight Zone p23

Canal Zone p20

Lookout Mountain p15

Mount Zion 7059

TUNNEL 1

Clear Creek

Indian Gulch

Clear Creek Canyon Rd

Chimney Gulch Mountain Bike Trail

Chimney Gulch

Lookout Mountain Rd

Golden

American Mountaineering Center

Bent Gate

W 6th Ave

Washington Ave

Ford St

19th St

13th St

10th St

1 mile

1 kilometer

1.9mi

1.7mi

1.4mi

1.2mi

1.0mi

0.2mi

0.0mi

6,000

6,500

7,000

Lookout Mountain Crag

39°44'56.25"N 105°14'33.24"W

 5min

MOST OF
THE DAY

P.M.

9 Routes

≤5.8 5.9 5.10 5.11 5.12 5.13 5.14 proj

Crag Profile: This is a very popular crag in Golden as it has easy toprope access and moderate climbing. This wall offers a variety of slab and crack climbs on beautiful metamorphic rock, although most of the routes are guarded by a small roof towards the top, which makes for some fun and challenging finishes to the climbs. There are six toprope anchors, making it very easy to set up a rope. However, be aware that some anchors are over the edge of the cliff, so use caution when setting up ropes. This is a north-facing wall that sits in the shade most of the day.

Approach: From the intersection of US-6/CO-93/CO-58, head southeast on US-6 (away from Clear Creek Canyon) for 1.0 miles and turn right onto 19th Street. Follow the main road as it turns left and then heads up the windy hill, becoming Lookout Mountain Road. After 1.8 miles up (west) Lookout Mountain Road, park on either side of the road. From the parking area, there are trails just north/downhill of the road. The toprope access is about 50 yards from the road. The approach trail to get to the base is on the left (west) side of the wall. Be careful of rattlesnakes.

park on either side of the road

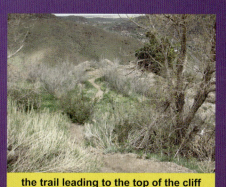
the trail leading to the top of the cliff

Bethany Lukens at Lookout Mountain Crag. Dan Gambino

Bethany Lukens on *Right Face*, 5.9, next page. 📷 Dan Gambino

1 **5.6 Face** 5.6 ★★
Meander up the slab on the left side of the wall. The holds become smaller the further right you move. Use a standard rack for leading the left side of the face. Otherwise set up a toprope from the leftmost bolted anchor. *Standard rack (55')*

2 **5.7 Dihedral** 5.7 ★
Launch up the prominent dihedral on the left side of the wall. Toprope from the leftmost anchor.
Rack to #3 Camalot, 2-bolt anchor (55')

3 **5.7 Arête** 5.7 TR ★
Climb the slabby arête on the left side of the main wall. Fun slab climbing leads to easier terrain, or for a harder finish, climb over the bulge. This route is to the right of the dihedral. *Use an anchor on the far left side of the wall (55')*

4 **Left Face** 5.10a TR ★★
Located on the face to the right of the arête and to the left of the crack. Interesting slab climbing leads to a crux pulling over the overhang to gain the top of the cliff just below the second or third anchor from the left. *2-bolt anchor (55')*

5 **Into the Void**
5.9 ★★
This is the leftmost crack on the main wall. Climb the slabby, protectable crack that leads to a tough and committing sequence pulling over the small roof. Climb to the anchor on your right. *Rack to #3 Camalot, 2-bolt anchor (55')*

6 **Center Face**
5.10b ★★★
After some easy climbing to the high first bolt, continue up the slab to a tricky roof crux via positive holds.
6 bolts, 2-bolt anchor (55')

7 **Thin Fingers** 5.10a ★★★
A thin, but very protectable crack on the slab leads to a few good gear placements in the bulge before having to pull the crux. This thin crack is located between the two bolted lines on the wall. *Rack to #1 Camalot, with extra small pieces, 2-bolt anchor (55')*

5.7 Dihedral

8 **Right Face** 5.9 ★★
Thin and technical face climbing down low leads to a roof move that's not as bad as its neighbors to the left. It's also the rightmost bolted line on the wall. *4 bolts, 2-bolt anchor (50')*

9 **5.8 Crack** 5.8 ★
Good jams on almost vertical rock make for a protectable and fun lead with a challenge at the end. This is the rightmost crack on the wall.
SR, 2-bolt anchor (45')

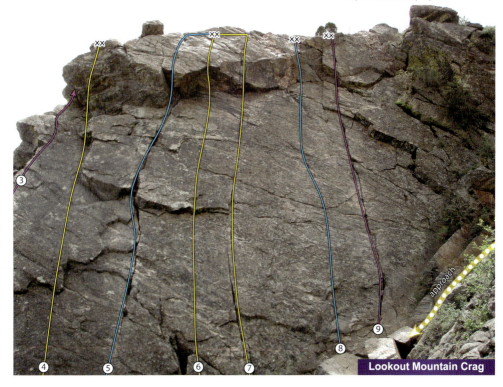

Lookout Mountain Crag

Tiers of Zion

 15min

 P.M.

≤5.8 5.9 5.10 5.11 5.12 5.13 5.14 *proj*

8 Routes

Crag Profile: This wall has been a hidden gem for years and hosts a handful of fantastic slab routes on great stone. When you approach this wall, you may see a number of deer, elk, or even mountain lion. Lush trees surround the start of the routes and the wall is also north-facing, which makes it a great summer time hang out. The wall receives a bit of late afternoon sun in the summer, but that's about it.

park here for Tiers of Zion

Approach: Tiers of Zion is located just past Lookout Mountain Crag on Lookout Mountain Road. To get there, drive 2.2 miles up Lookout Mountain Road past the stoplight at Sixth Avenue. After making a few sharp, hairpin turns, locate the parking area on the east side of the road (there is a metal trash can in the pullout). From the parking area, find a trailhead on the west side of the road and follow it up to the left;

the trail

do not continue downhill. You should be continuing on faint deer trails as you traverse the hillside to the southwest. Locate the wall and pass through some trees to get to the base of the crag. The easier slab routes are up to the left.

Tiers of Zion

approach

Note: To get to the first two moderate slab routes, take an immediate turn uphill to the left, following a gully, when you get to the wall.

❶ Irie 5.7 ★★

Start to the left of the large pine tree growing near the wall. Angle left on slabby terrain to a short vertical section with juggy holds.
6 bolts, 2-bolt anchor (55')
FA: Josh Pollock, Steve Grigel 2013

❷ The Burning Bush 5.7 ★★

These thin, interesting moves are more consistent than its neighbor. Start just right of the large pine tree growing near the base of the wall.
7 bolts, 2-bolt anchor (60')
FA: Josh Pollock, Lindsay Huck Clark 2013

❸ Zion Train 5.10a ★★

Climb past the anchor on *The Burning Bush* for three bolts to get into an alcove to belay. The *Zion Train* pitch climbs out of the alcove toward the roofs above, aiming for a bright yellow lichen streak. Dodge the first roof on its left side, stem and lieback to work over the larger roof above.
12 bolts, 2-bolt anchor (90')
FA: Josh Pollock, Steve Grigel 2014

Buffalo Soldier

Tiers of Zion

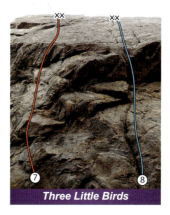

Three Little Birds

4 Buffalo Soldier 5.10c ★★ ☐☐
When you approach the wall from the trail, this is the first bolted line you will see on the wall to the right. Climb the resistance moves in the crack with ok rock until pulling over the small bulge 20 feet up and then bust out right to meet up with the following route. *7 bolts, 2-bolt anchor (65')*
FA: Chuck Fitch 2013

5 Lyin' Like a Lion, in Zion
5.10c ★★   ☐☐
This route begins directly to the left of a tree touching the wall and pulls a boulder problem at the start before gaining the moderate slab above.
8 bolts, 2-bolt anchor (65')
FA: Josh Pollock, Steve Grigel 2013

6 The Belay Brothers
Bounce Back 5.8+ ★   ☐☐
Starts just right of the previous route and place gear up to a #1 Camalot at the start to get to the fun bolted slab on the second half. *4 bolts, rack to #1 Camalot, 2-bolt anchor (70')*
FA: Josh Pollock, Jake Waples 2013

7 Old Pirates 5.11a ★★   ☐☐
A challenging start with a tensiony undercling crimp move lets you stand up into a nice hand jam below the bulge. Pull over and enjoy moderate climbing to the top.
7 bolts, 2-bolt anchor (70')
FA: Chuck Fitch 2013

8 Three Little Birds
5.9 ★★★★   ☐☐
This is a treasure for the moderate climber, and one of the best 5.9s out there. It has it all; a tough pull at the start, excellent climbing in the thin crack, and fantastic exposure.
7 bolts, 2-bolt anchor (65')
FA: Adam Huxley 2013

Canal Zone

Mile Marker: 271.5 10-15min

 MOST OF THE DAY P.M.

 **20 Routes**

≤5.8 5.9 5.10 5.11 5.12 5.13 5.14 proj

Crag Profile: Located next to an old concrete canal, Canal Zone is a great wall with a lot to offer if you like climbing 5.8 to 5.11 on great stone in the shade on a summer's day. This vertical to sometimes slabby wall has some great moderates in a great location but is often extremely busy, especially on a weekend. It is north-facing and has shade most of the day with late afternoon sun in the summer.

park here for Canal and Twilight Zone

Approach: From the stoplight at the intersection of Hwy-58, Hwy-93, and US-6, drive 0.2 miles west up canyon to the first pullout on the left (south) side of the road. The crag is located about a half mile upstream on the south side of the river. From the pullout, walk south and down the steep and loose hill below the parking lot to a wide dirt path. Head right and walk up canyon for a short ways to the nice new pedestrian bridge. Walk across the bridge, and once just beyond it, turn left onto a trail. Hike a short ways and then turn right on another trail that leads uphill to the old aqueduct. From here, turn right again and walk west along the aqueduct for a few minutes until you reach the cliff.

1 Cut Loose 5.11a ★★
The furthest left route on the wall. Easy climbing leads to a reachy roof move that is worthy of its namesake, which is easier for tall people.
7 bolts, 2-bolt anchor (70')
FA: Kirk Miller, Adam Schrader 2009

2 Bear's Choice 5.10b ★
This route shares the first two bolts of *Cut Loose* and continues straight up to the small roof where you will find yourself at the start of the crux. You can bust right at the roof for an easier finish.
8 bolts, 2-bolt anchor (70')
FA: Kirk Miller, Justin Winger 2009

3 Box of Rain 5.8 ★★
Powerful pulls on underclings and layback moves gain a rest ledge. Continue climbing along a shallow crack system through interesting climbing to an exciting finish.
8 bolts, 2-bolt anchor (75')
FA: Kirk Miller, Ryan Mayer, K. Turner 2009

4 Ripple 5.8 ★★
Fire up a black bulge on good holds and rounded laybacks to a rest stance. From here, push on to a final rest ledge before climbing the super fun left-hand laybacking seam corner. Challenging for the 5.8 leader.
9 bolts, 2-bolt anchor (70')
FA: Kirk Miller, Lindie Brink 2009

5 Venice Beach 5.8 ★★
Move up to a large lefthand, mini ledge and pull up onto it. Follow the rolling sections of stone to a ledge where you find different ways to finish. The direct option moves up through a v-slot past two bolts, while the other option is more to the right past two bolts using the face and arête. *9 bolts, 2-bolt anchor (70')*
FA: Kirk Miller, Kirk Raney

6 Holiday Road 5.8 ★★★
As you approach the Canal Zone on your left, before the retaining wall and *Beasto*, you'll find a break in some trees leading to rocky patio that lends access to climbs #1-6. *Holiday Road* will be the first line you'll see. Climb perfect stone through intermittent ledges and scoops to a final rest ledge below the last two bolts. Bring your friction skills to finish this one.
9 bolts, 2-bolt anchor (75')
FA: Kirk Miller 2009

7 Beasto 5.10a ★★★
Tackle the initial boulder problem past the first bolt and head up the bulging arête on jugs to a ledge with a tricky and fun crux heading left around the arête and back to the prow to finish. For extra points, go straight up at the seventh bolt instead of going left around the arête.
11 bolts, 2-bolt anchor (70')
FA: Kirk Miller 2008

8 Turkey Jerky 5.10b ★★
Pull the initial crux stemming through the overhanging dihedral to the first bolt, and chase the right-leaning seam to jugs at the bulge. Head straight up the arête to anchors. Sustained. *11 bolts, 2-bolt anchor (80')*
FA: Kirk Miller, Alex Duran 2008

9a Snake Eyes 5.11c ★★
This three-bolt variation starts on *Turkey Jerkey* and trends right to link-up with *Walking with a Ghost*, creating a harder start for *Walking*.

9 Walking with a Ghost 5.11c ★★★★
Classic! Thin, technical, and sustained face climbing that is in your face the whole way. One of the best routes at the Canal.
8 bolts, 2-bolt anchor (55')
FA: Kirk Miller 2008

10 Ivy League 5.9+ ★★
Start in the orange-streaked rock and head slightly left to a right-facing crack with jugs above. Continue on sloping ledges through the slabby pink rock. *7 bolts, 2-bolt anchor (50')*
FA: Kirk Miller 2008

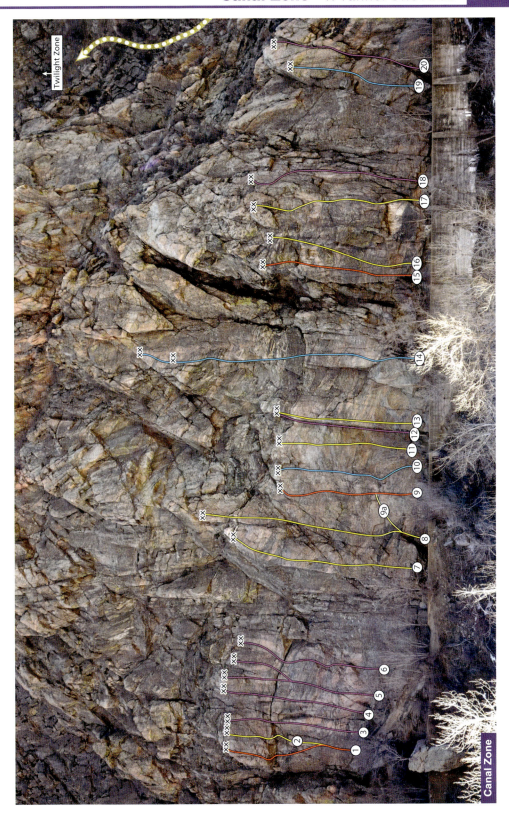

11 Panama Red 5.10a ★★★
Brilliant, dynamic moves past jugs and ledges will get you most of the way, but expect a more technical approach near the anchors. Well rounded and fun.
7 bolts, 2-bolt anchor (55')
FA: Kirk Miller, Ken Trout 2008

12 Route Canal 5.8+ ★
Climb the crack located in the corner of the left-facing dihedral to a shared anchor with *Gondolier Arête*. Fun and straightforward. *1 bolt, rack to #2 Camalot, 2-bolt anchor (50')*

13 Gondolier Arête 5.10a ★★
Climb juggy holds and sidepulls up the arête to a ledge at the sixth bolt. Clip the seventh bolt and enjoy the reachy crux to gain a jug to clip the anchor.
7 bolts, 2-bolt anchor (50')
FA: Kirk Miller 2008

14 Made in the Shade 5.9- ★★★★
This must-do route features amazing face climbing all the way to the final anchors. Start on a left-facing crack/corner with closely spaced bolts and climb up onto a sizable ledge before continuing onward. There are two anchors on this route, whichever anchor you choose to use please tie a knot in the end of your rope; it's a rope stretcher.
To First Anchor: 17 bolts (100')
To Second Anchor: 3 more bolts (125')
FA: Kirk Miller, Kirk Raney

15 Aretnophobia 5.11a ★★★
Start in the dihedral left of the arête and move around to the right side of the arête past the first bolt. Climb the face above using good face holds and the arête to a jug at the base of the roof. Figure out how to pull the crux bulge to gain increasingly better holds. A long draw on the sixth bolt will help with rope drag.
9 bolts, 2-bolt anchor (65')
FA: Todd and Kristin Felix 2008

16 Batso Canal 5.10c ★★
About five feet to the right of the arête, a bouldery start leads to climbing up and right, over a corner.
8 bolts, 2-bolt anchor (55')
FA: Kirk Miller 2008

17 Lambada 5.10b ★★
Climb up to the right of a small roof by bolt two. More face climbing brings you over a small bulge towards the top. *7 bolts, 2-bolt anchor (60')*
FA: Kirk Miller, Bruce Hildenbrand 2008

Laura Capps on *Batso Canal*, 5.10c. Jason Haas

18 Levada 5.8+ ★★

Fun and super-protected face climbing on various sidepulls and pinches leads to 20 feet of a 5.6 runout from the last bolt to the anchors. An optional #2 or #3 Camalot can protect the last bit of climbing, but is not necessary. *9 bolts, 2-bolt anchor (80')*
FA: Bruce Hildenbrand, Dale Haas

19 Buckets of Rain 5.9 ★★

Find the rightmost bolted route on the cliff about 20 feet right of *Levada*. Follow a right-arcing bolt line up a slab over a small bulge. Move back left and climb up near the left-hand arête. It's 5.10a if you climb straight up from the last bolt instead of sneaking way around left on the arête. *7 bolts, 2-bolt anchor (50')*
FA: Mike Morin, Jason Haas 07/13

20 Lame Line 5.8

This unremarkable trad line lies just right of *Buckets of Rain*. Finish in the groove/low-angled corner.
Rack to #3, optional #6 Camalot (60')
FA: Jason Haas, Mike Morin 07/13

Twilight Zone

Mile Marker: 271.5   20min   MOST OF THE DAY   SOMETIMES P.M.   **6 Routes**

| ≤5.8 | 5.9 | 5.10 | 5.11 | 5.12 | 5.13 | 5.14 | proj |

Crag Profile: Welcome to the Twilight Zone! If you have made it this far, then you will notice you are surrounded by an amphitheater of featured rock. The climbs here are categorized as Canal Zone's ugly sister because of the rock quality. It is recommended that belayers and climbers wear helmets. That being said, some of the climbs here have fantastic movement and are worthy of the hike uphill. This is high in the canyon and faces north. The only time it gets blasted with sun is in the summer afternoon.

Approach: Use the same approach as Canal Zone (p20). Hike about 50 feet past Canal Zone to find a faint trail leading uphill to the left, hidden in the bushes. Hike up switchbacks in the center of the gully until you reach the base of the cliff. Be very mindful of loose rock on this approach so you don't drop any bombs on the climbers at the Canal Zone.

1 Desperado 5.12c ★★★

A testpiece for the area. Desperate jamming in the crack on the steep wall brings you into a final hard boulder problem to get over the lip.
7 bolts, 2-bolt anchor (50')
FA: Kevin Capps 01/14

2 The Mind and the Matter 5.11b ★★

Climb into a fun roof on suspect jugs. Wander right and left to a contrived but fun finish above the final roof. Use long draws to avoid severe rope drag. *12 bolts, 2-bolt anchor (90')*
FA: Kirk Miller, Eric Schmeer 2008

3 Freedom Fries 5.11b ★

Located in the left corner of the cliff. Climb up the slab to a dihedral with two easily visible bolts. Continue through some bad rock to fun face climbing above.
13 bolts, 2-bolt anchor (90')
FA: Bruno Hache, Kirk Miller 2008

4 Shadow Play 5.11c ★★★

A slab leads to an overhanging bulge with a tough sequence. More vertical climbing culminates at a crux up high that guards the anchor.
11 bolts, 2-bolt anchor (90')
FA: Ryan and C. Laird 2008

5 Execution 5.11c ★★

This is one of the best routes on the wall. Climb through the overhanging start to a great kneebar at the lip and technical underclings and sidepulls above. One of the cleaner routes on the wall. *11 bolts, 2-bolt anchor (90')*
FA: Kirk Miller, Eric Schmeer 2008

6 The Chaser 5.11a ★★

The rightmost route. Pull past a small, broken roof by the fourth bolt to cleaner and more fun climbing above. *9 bolts, 2-bolt anchor (75')*
FA: Kirk Miller, Eric Schmeer 2008

Twilight Zone

East Side of Tunnel One Crag

Just Before Tunnel One 1min **3 Routes**

A.M.   MOST OF THE DAY   ≤5.8   5.9   5.10   5.11   5.12   5.13   5.14   *proj*

Crag Profile: This wall offers a few moderate trad climbs/topropes/highballs. However you climb them, they are short and kinda fun. Being so close to the road and creek, this is a hot spot for the locals to hang out and swim, so don't expect to be alone even if you are the only climbers at the wall. All of the routes start directly on the trail. The wall faces east and rarely gets sun, just a little in the morning.

Approach: This wall is on the east side of Tunnel One. Park just east of Tunnel One at 1.0 miles on the south side of the road and hike few hundred feet south on a trail to access the cliff. The trail will bring you to the base of the cliff on the right where you will be able to see a set of anchors about 50 feet up. At this point, you will be at the start of *Graffiti Face*.

1 Creekside Slabs
5.0-5.6 ★
The slabs are about 50 feet to the left of *Graffiti Face* and are most commonly toproped from the variety of two-bolt anchors at the top of the wall. To access the top of the wall, climb the third class terrain to the right of the slabs that leads to a ledge with the anchor.
2-bolt anchor (50')

2 Creek Corner 5.6 ★
This gear-protected route climbs the corner with broken cracks up and to the right until you reach the left-facing dihedral; follow the dihedral to the two-bolt anchor. Start about 10 feet to the left of *Graffiti Face*.
Rack to #3 Camalot, 2-bolt anchor (50')

3 Graffiti Face 5.10c R ★★
A fun, spicy start on polished holds leads to easier and more protectable terrain about 20 feet up. Start in the thin seam that climbs up the polished face with faded graffiti on it. It's very hard to protect the start of this climb, but there is a very thin, blocky seam that accepts small gear about 10 feet up. Once you establish yourself above the seam the climbing gets easier and meets up with *Creek Corner*. *Standard rack with extra thin cams, 2-bolt anchor (50')*

East Side of Tunnel 1 Crag

Laura Capps on the ultra-classic *Balkin Dirt Diving*, 5.12a, Sports Wall, p27.   Kevin Capps

Sports Wall

Just After Tunnel One 10min

A.M.   MOST OF THE DAY

14 Routes

| ≤5.8 | 5.9 | 5.10 | 5.11 | 5.12 | 5.13 | 5.14 | proj |

Crag Profile: While it doesn't look like much from the road, Sports Wall is a great wall that offers some classic lines on solid rock. This is one of the older walls in the canyon and often times you will climb past some old pins and bolts, or even find that a route doesn't have an anchor. Not to worry though, on the south/right side of the cliff there is an access trail that takes you back to the base of the wall. There is a mix of sport and trad

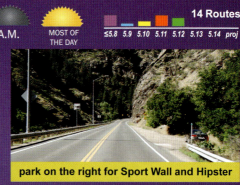

park on the right for Sport Wall and Hipster

climbs here, including *Balkan Dirt Diving*, one of the best 5.12s in the canyon. The wall faces west, gets sun most of the day, and is a great wall to come to for sun on a winter day.

Approach: Drive 1.2 miles up canyon, going through Tunnel One at 1.0 miles. Park at the first pullout on the right (north side), roughly 200 yards west of the tunnel. Cross to the south side of the road (by the creek) and walk east back down the canyon along the road for 200 yards until you see a prominent dirt trail leading uphill to the wall.

Sports Wall

1 #5 Crack 5.8
This is the leftmost route on the cliff band and starts in a right-facing corner. Begin to the right of a painted "5" on the wall and climb through a broken crack system with poor rock quality. Build an anchor at the top of the route at a tree.
Standard rack, tree anchor (60')

2 Slabtastic 5.8 PG-13
Work up the thin seam on the slab about 10 feet right of *#5 Crack*. This route is not very protectable and mostly done on toprope. Build an anchor at the tree.
Standard rack, tree anchor (60')

3 The Happiness of Pursuit 5.10c PG-13 ★
Climb the slightly overhanging face that leads to a fixed pin below two bulges. The climbing above the pin is not hard, but optional gear is recommended.
2 bolts, 1 fixed pin, 2-bolt anchor (40')

4 My Generation 5.11c ★★
This route is a harder, direct start to *Generation Gap*. Climb four bolts of challenging sequences to link up with *Generation Gap*.
8 bolts, 2-bolt anchor (65')
FA: Kevin Capps 2013

5 Generation Gap 5.11a ★★
A challenging move right off the ground leads to jugs and a ledge rest. From the ledge, the route continues up and left for a juggy finish.
9 bolts, 2-bolt anchor (65')
FA: Ken Trout 1992

6 Don't Go Chasing Waterfalls 5.12c ★★★
This route shares the first three bolts with *Generation Gap*. Once you leave the ledge above the third bolt, climb up and right through powerful tiered roofs with a hard-to-clip last bolt. Use *Balkan Dirt Diving*'s anchor. An optional 0.5 Camalot can protect the easier climbing going to the anchor.
7 bolts, 2-bolt anchor (65')
FA: Hill, Peavy, Peters 2011

7a Balkan Variation 5.11c ★★
This variation starts on *Balkan Dirt Diving* for the first two bolts and veers left for one bolt before joining up with the third bolt of *Generation Gap*. This variation climbs part way through the crux before busting left and is an easier alternative to *Balkin*.
9 bolts (65')

7 Balkan Dirt Diving 5.12a ★★★★
A classic, with a crux that hits you right off the deck. Climb the beautiful, thin seam and try to control the barn door, before entering a shallow dihedral that leads to a rest where you can assess the next few challenging sequences. An optional 0.5 Camalot can protect the climbing going to the anchor. *7 bolts, optional gear, 2-bolt anchor (65')*
FA: Ken Trout 1992

8 Pet Cemetery 5.11b ★★
Fun and thoughtful stemming leads to a powerful roof move. Optional gear can protect between the spacious bolt placements. *6 bolts, rack to #2 Camalot, 2-bolt anchor (65')*
FA: Ken Trout 1992

9 Coffin Crack 5.9+ ★★★
A fun and protectable route that climbs the obvious crack system to the left of *Rufus' Roof* to reach the coffin-like stem box in the rock. *Rack to #3 Camalot, 2-bolt anchor (65')*

10 Olaf's Roof 5.11b PG-13 ★
Start in the unprotectable dihedral on the left side of *Rufus' Roof*. Climb an easy crack to a thin seam in the upper roof. Bring extra small cams for protecting the upper roof.
Rack to #1 Camalot, tree anchor (65')

11 Rufus' Roof 5.12b
Climb the big roof on the right side of the wall. A long move leads past the fixed pin in the seam on the roof. This route is typically done on toprope, set up at the top of *Olaf's Roof*. (20')

12 Climbing Sports 5.10a ★
Start on the following route to climb past *Rufus' Roof*. Continue up cracks that lead to a steep dihedral.
Rack to #4 Camalot, tree anchor (65')

13 Changing Corners Dihedral 5.7 ★
Start on the changing corners dihedral and climb to the right of the big roof. Follow the big dihedral to easier climbing at the top.
Standard rack, 2-bolt anchor (65')

14 Beginner Sports 5.5 ★
Clamber up ledges on the right side of the wall to a bulge at the top. Climb to the left of the bulge for a protectable 5.5 or go to the right of the bulge for a slightly harder variation. *Standard rack, 2 bolt anchor (55')*

5 **Hip Hip Hurray** 5.12c ★★ 　　 ⬜⬜

Start on the ledge and climb the face to the right of the corner. Big moves on crimps leads to a decent rest about halfway up before climbing into one of the most awkward and challenging mantels you will ever find!

5 bolts, 2-bolt anchor (40')
FA: Mark Tarrant, Richard Wright 2007

Climber: Kevin Capps 📷 Jay Samuelson

New Hipster Rock

Just After Tunnel One   10min   A.M.   P.M.   **7 Routes**

≤5.8 5.9 5.10 5.11 5.12 5.13 5.14 proj

Crag Profile: This wall is not just for old geezers with hip replacements or even just young hipsters. In fact, this wall has a variety of great climbs on solid stone, including *The Hipster* and *Hip Hip Hurray*, that will test your sport climbing strengths. A lot of the climbs here are a little harder than they look, but if you are climbing anywhere close to the 5.12a range, you should get on *The Hipster*. New Hipster Rock is tucked in the south-facing hillside by Tunnel 1 and gets some much-deserved afternoon shade, but gets direct sun in the morning. Note: The first ascent of all six routes was done by Mark Tarrant and Richard Wright in 2007.

park on the right just past the tunnel

Approach: Drive 1.2 miles up canyon, going through Tunnel One. Park at the first pullout on the right (north side), roughly 200 yards west of the tunnel. This is the

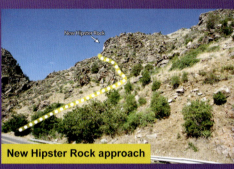
New Hipster Rock approach

same pullout as for Sports Wall (p26). Pick up a steep trail on the north (right) side of the road. Take this uphill for about 100 yards until it cuts left and goes past a rocky ridge. Follow the trail uphill from here until you reach New Hipster. Watch for rattlesnakes on the approach.

1 Hip-or-Campus 5.10a ★
Climb *Hip Service* to the first bolt, then continue straight up instead of traversing out right.
4 bolts, 2-bolt anchor (50')
FA: Chris Anthony, Kristen Waldvogel 2014

2 Hip Service 5.11a ★★
This is the leftmost route on the wall. A high first bolt leads to a thuggy undercling traverse for three bolts to the right before meeting up with *Hypnotherapy* and an easier finish.
5 bolts, 2-bolt anchor (45')

3 Hypnotherapy 5.11d ★★
Climb the arête on the left side of the wall. Compression climbing on the arête delivers a solid pump for the first half of the route before easing off. *6 bolts, 2-bolt anchor (45')*

4 Hippersnapper 5.11a ★
Face climbing on the left side of the big corner moves up and left, and even uses a couple holds around the arête up higher.
5 bolts, 2-bolt anchor (45')

5 Hip Hip Hurray 5.12c ★★
See previous page.

New Hipster Rock

6 The Hipster 5.12a ★★★★
One of the coolest arêtes in the canyon! Climb the bolt line just right of the beautiful overhanging arête. Cruxy climbing on the first half leads to a pumpy finish.
5 bolts, sketchy anchor (40')

7 Hip-Op 5.11b ★★
Climb the blocky corner five feet to the right of *The Hipster* until reaching pumpy face climbing on smooth pinches. *5 bolts, 2-bolt anchor (45')*

Ghost Crag

0.3mi Past Tunnel 1 5min

ALL DAY

1 Route

| ≤5.8 | 5.9 | 5.10 | 5.11 | 5.12 | 5.13 | 5.14 | proj |

Crag Profile: This is a small, overhanging crag by the creek that holds a solitary but quite hard sport climb.

Approach: To access this wall, drive 1.4 miles up canyon and park on the south (left) side of the road in a large parking area at a big curve. Wade the creek directly over to the route as the small bridge a few hundred feet east/downstream from the parking area is private property and is closed to the public.

parking for Ghost Crag

1 Ghost 5.13d ★

This tiny route has been a bit of a roller coaster. Originally thought to be 5.14a, it was then repeated and called 5.13b with a new hold discovered. That hold then broke, leaving us with the original beta and close to the original grade. *Ghost* climbs better than it looks from across the road; it's basically a 20-foot boulder problem with 20 feet of stout moves. Enjoyable.
4 bolts, 2 bolt anchor (20')
FA: unknown

Ghost Crag

Matt Lloyd in full guidebook mode and about to find out there's not a lot of nice on *Gneiss Cleavage*, 5.11b, Stumbling Block, p32. 📷 Jason Haas

Skinny Legs/Blonde Formation

Mile Marker: 270   2-5min
A.M.   P.M.   **3 Routes**

≤5.8 5.9 5.10 5.11 5.12 5.13 5.14 proj

Crag Profile: These roadside climbs must be climbed with care so no rocks get tossed onto the road. Of the climbs, *Skinny Legs and All* is the best and easiest approach, avoiding the steeper and looser belaying spots of the other climbs. The rock quality on the climbs is actually quite good, it's finding a good spot to belay from on the Blonde Formation that is hard to do.

Approach: Drive 1.7 miles up canyon and park at a long pullout on the left next to mile marker 270. These few roadside routes are on the right (north) side of the highway. You will be able to see the Blonde Formation a few feet off the road after parking. The Skinny Legs Formation is about 50 yards west on the road. Hike to a large tree, then pick up the steep approach trail leading up behind it.

Blonde Formation

To Skinny Legs & Stumbling Block

long pullout on the left at mm 270

Skinny Legs Formation

1 **Skinny Legs and All**
5.12b *
Balance your way up the thin seam through some long pulls to a break in the rock. Rest up and climb your way through the featured rock to the top. Harder for short people.
6 bolts, 2 bolt anchor (55')
FA: Fred Knapp, Brett Ruckman 1991

The Blonde Formation

2 **The Blonde Leading the Blonde 5.11b** *
Just a few feet from the road, climb up onto a small ledge and continue straight up, pulling through thin sequences and finishing right before a ledge and a bush. Would get more stars if it wasn't so close to the road.
5 bolts, 2 bolt anchor (45')
FA: Fred Knapp, Dawn Packard 1991

3 Blonde Man's Bluff 5.11a **
Scramble up the loose hillside and start on a left angling ramp to get to the first bolt. Sustained, technical climbing that will challenge your footwork. The belay position kinda sucks.
6 bolts, 2 bolt anchor (45')
FA: Fred Knapp, Brett Ruckman 1991

Skinny Legs...

The Blonde Formation

Stumbling Block

Mile Marker: 270 20min

A.M.   P.M.

10 Routes

≤5.8 5.9 5.10 5.11 5.12 5.13 5.14 proj

Crag Profile: While a fairly obscure area, *Naked Kill* is one of the best hard trad lines in the canyon. The loose, steep, hard-to-follow trail makes this area a poor choice for kids and dogs.

Approach: Drive 1.7 miles up canyon and park at a long pullout on the left next to mile marker 270. Walk west up the canyon past the Blonde Man's Bluff area (p31) and find a large tree with a steep, rocky climber's trail leading north up the hill.

Blonde Formation

To Skinny Legs & Stumbling Block

long pullout on the left at mm 270

1 Gneiss Cleavage 5.11b
This very odd climb is located on the far left side. Spot the two fixed pins in the horizontal seam about eight feet off the ground, and start just right of the pins in a shallow left-facing corner. Traverse hard left past the pins and follow it as the incipient crack arcs up to a ledge. Easier climbing above leads to another ledge. Build an anchor and downclimb off left.
2 fixed pins, rack to #2 Camalot (50')
FA: Brett Ruckman, Jack Roberts 1990

2 Décolletage 5.12c ★★
Tough slopers on solid stone is what makes this route worth climbing. Located on the obvious vertical wall above a ledge, this sloper testpiece is best done on a cool winter day. Bring a finger-sized cam for the top.
5 bolts, .4 Camalot, 2-bolt anchor (60')
FA: Brett Ruckman, Jack Roberts 1990

3 Stumbling Block Crack One 5.7 ★★
Stem and jam the corner to an off-width finish. Belay on the ledge.
Rack to #5 Camalot, No Anchor (40')

4 Sabaki 5.11b ★
Climb the sustained prow between the two corner cracks to the ledge. Two high bolts help identify the route.
2 bolts, standard rack including RPs, No Anchor (40')   *FA: Brett Ruckman, Marco Cornacchoine 1990*

to Bumbling Stock

walk off

Stumbling Block

⑤ Stumbling Block
Crack Two 5.8 ★
Boulder up onto a ledge and then jam a hand crack in the corner. *Rack to #3, (2) #1 - #2 Camalots, No Anchor (40')*
Variation: 5.8 R
From the initial ledge about 10 feet up, move up and left onto the face and follow it to the main ledge.

⑥ FP Chimney 5.7
Head into the depths of the deep chimney and emerge on the main ledge. Someone should continue up the chimney system to the top of the wall, although adding some bolts is advised. *No gear, No Anchor (40')*

⑦ Naked Kill 5.12d R ★★★★
This sustained trad testpiece is the flared splitter just right of the chimney. The route is in your face from the beginning, with techy jams, techy gear, long reaches, and a potentially bad landing if you botch the start. Many people seem to bail at the bolt where the angle breaks, but the route really ends at the *Razor Blade* anchor. The upper slab goes at 5.9+ and the corner goes at 5.8.
Rack to #3 Camalot, (2) sets of RPs (80')
FA: Brett Ruckman, Jack Roberts 1990

⑧ Razor Blade Titillation
5.12a ★★
Follow a seam in the shallow dihedral to get to a nice rest before the roof. Clip a fixed pin above the roof and execute a fun and committing sequence on small holds. A little reachy on the upper headwall.
8 bolts, 1 fixed pin, 2-bolt anchor (75')
FA: Brett Ruckman, M Cornacchoine 1990

⑨ Battle's End 5.12d ★★★
A fantastic line that is reminiscent of the Clear Creek classic, *Anarchitect* with its hard, back-to-back sequences on sloping holds. Actual climbing holds appear on this route in cooler temps. *11 bolts, 2-bolt anchor (85')*
FA: Richard Wright, FFA: Alan Nelson 1997

⑩ Lips Against Steel 5.11c ★★
Climb the thin, right-angling seam that shares the first three bolts with *Battle's End*. After pulling the crux while clipping bolts, go straight up and a little to the right to get to the wide flaring crack.
3 bolts, rack to #4 Camalot, 2-bolt anchor (80')   FA: Brett Ruckman, Jack Roberts 1990

Darren Mabe on the first ascent of *Crack a Beer*, 5.10d, next page. 📷 Adam Peters

Bumbling Stock

Mile Marker: 270   25min   A.M.   P.M.   ≤5.8 5.9 5.10 5.11 5.12 5.13 5.14 proj   **3 Routes**

Crag Profile: Tucked in on the hillside just a few hundred feet west of Stumbling Block (p32) is Bumbling Stock. On the left side of the wall you will see overhanging, tiered roofs with project anchors high up and to the right (and left), a sport climb, and a splitter offwidth. This wall is southeast-facing and gets morning sun with peaceful afternoon shade. Beware of poison ivy along the base of the cliff.

Approach: Drive 1.7 miles up canyon and park at a long pullout on the left next to mile marker 270. Walk west up the canyon past the Blonde Man's Bluff area (p31) and find a large tree with a steep, rocky climber's trail leading north up the hill. Once you gain the Stumbling Block, turn left and walk a few hundred yards west to this small cliff.

Bumbling Stock

1 Desiderata 5.11c ★★
Despite the intermediate anchor, this is best climbed as a single pitch. Several holds have broken on the lower section and most would argue has become the crux of the whole route. *13 bolts (including the intermediate anchor) (105')*   *FA: Darren Mabe*

2 Crack a Beer 5.10d ★★
A true offwidth - there's no cheating the crux on this one. Thankfully the business is short lived. Run up an easy, but poorly protected slab a bit right of *Desiderata* (5.7 R). Clip the intermediate anchor on that route, and then head for the distinctive offwidth above. Stacks or deep fists will get you through the steep start and into the easier terrain above. *Rack 0.4 - #2, (2) #4 - #5 Camalots (105')*
FA: Darren Mabe

3 Break a Bottle 5.8 TR ★★
There is a clean slab to the right of *Crack a Beer* with an anchor above a ledge. Accessing it is a little tricky, but this would make for a nice lead if bolts were added.

Matt Lloyd on the first ascent of *The Marble Man*, 5.13b, Postcolonial Crag, next page. Scott Clark

Postcolonial Crag

A Little Past mm270   15-20min   A.M.   P.M.   **4 Routes**

≤5.8 5.9 5.10 5.11 5.12 5.13 5.14 proj

Crag Profile: This wall has two really fun (although short) sport climbs and a couple of highball boulders or heady trad leads. The rock is very reminiscent of granite you might see in Joshua Tree with its bullet hard stone, sharp crimps, and smeary feet. This wall will feel much better with colder temps or shade, and is in the shade in the afternoon. Postcolonial Crag was originally put off from bolting for years because of attempts to boulder the

Parking on the Left at the Curve

routes, but high and difficult cruxes on both *The Marble Man* and *Stonewall* proved to be better suited as sport routes.

Approach: Park in the large pullout on the south (left) side of the road 1.9 miles up the canyon at a big curve. Walk across the road to find a faint trail with a small cairn that switchbacks up steep and sometimes loose terrain. Be very careful not to kick off any rocks that might hit the road. You can see the small wall up the hill from the parking area, use that as a reference because the trail is often hard to follow.

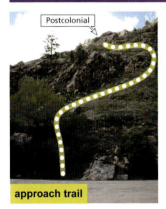
Postcolonial

approach trail

1 The Marble Man 5.13b ★★
As you approach the cliff from the trail, you'll see the beautiful and short arête that is *The Marble Man,* which features fantastic climbing on excellent stone. If it were longer it would be an uber classic.
3 bolts, 2-bolt anchor (30')
FA: Matt Lloyd 2013

2 Stonewall 5.13a ★★
Climb the first two bolts of *Marble Man,* then traverse up and right on thin crimpers and terrible feet. This is very comparable to *Chaos* on Anarchy Wall. *4 bolts, 2 bolt anchor (30')*
FA: Kevin Capps 2013;
Equipped by Matt Lloyd

3 Wench 5.11c/V3 R ★
To find the start of *Wench,* walk about 50 feet to the right of *The Marble Man* to find a boulder with an arête on the right side of it. Climb up the slopey rail until reaching the crack traverse about halfway up with difficult moves high on the boulder. This is where you can start to place gear. This route is more of a highball boulder problem than a route.
A light rack with a couple of thin pieces or a few crash pads, no anchor (25')
FA: Bjorn 2010

4 Hagseed 5.10c
Climb the hand-to-fist sized crack to the right of *Wench.*
Rack to #3 Camalot, No Anchor (15')
FA: Bjorn 2010

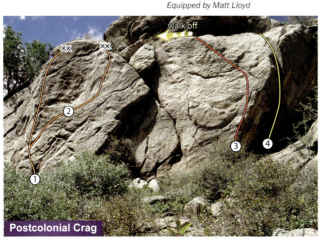
walk off
xx   xx
2
3
4
1
Postcolonial Crag

Lover's Leap on Beaver Brook

3.4mi up Lookout Mountain Rd 40min

ALL DAY

≤5.8 5.9 5.10 5.11 5.12 5.13 5.14 proj

4 Routes

Crag Profile: This cliff rewards you for the long approach with some beautiful scenic views and often times nice seclusion from the large crowds in the popular parts of the canyon. While the approach is from Windy Saddle, nestled between Mt. Zion and Lookout Mountain in Golden, this little crag is still technically in Clear Creek Canyon. It hosts a number of fun slab moderates and at least one or two routes that will give you a bit of a harder challenge.

Parking

The wall faces north to northeast and receives an abundance of shade with the tree cover.

Approach: From its intersection with US-6, drive 3.4 miles up Lookout Mountain Road (going past the pullout for Lookout Mountain Crag (p15)) and park on the west side of the road in an established parking area at a spot called The Windy Saddle. From the parking lot, take the Lookout Mountain Trail west for 0.2 miles to get to the Beaver Brook Trail. Hike an additional 1.6 miles west on the trail (just past a 1.5 mile marker sign), to find yourself at the top of the cliff to the right/north side of the trail. Scramble down the west side of the crag and around to the east side to find the slab with the bolted sport routes.

Lover's Leap is below

approach trail

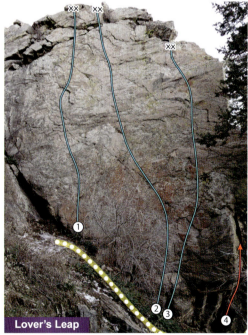
Lover's Leap

1 BB Gun 5.9 ★★★★
The leftmost line on the wall involves thin and technical slab climbing. **9 bolts, 2-bolt anchor (60')**
FA: Kirk Miller, Janice Sakata, BJ Nash 2010

2 BB King 5.9+ ★★★
Enjoy excellent face climbing on the slightly less than vertical terrain. Start to the right, then traverse up and left in a seam to the upper face.
10 bolts, 2-bolt anchor (70')
FA: Kirk Miller, Ken and Marsha Trout 2010

3 BB Brain 5.9 ★★
Some face climbing down low brings you through a tricky mantel about halfway up, then more moderate climbing leads to the anchor. **7 bolts, 2-bolt anchor (50')**
FA: Kirk Miller 2010

4 Lover's Bulge 5.10d ★★
Climb up the featured face just left of Black and Blue. A few difficult sequences up the steep wall brings you to a lower angled slab at the finish. **7 bolts, 2-bolt anchor (50')**

5 Black and Blue 5.10c ★★ ☐☐

This is currently the rightmost bolted line. A tricky start and sequence using an optional and painful kneebar that lives up to its namesake brings you to an easier finish up the northwest slab of the formation.
7 bolts, 2-bolt anchor (50')
FA: Kirk Miller, Jared Hostetter 2012

6 Bed and Breakfast 5.8 ★ ☐☐

Start on the northwest face behind a large pine tree. Follow the crack past a bulge and a bolt to the lower angled climbing above. *1 bolt, rack to #2 Camalot, 2-bolt anchor (50')*
FA: Kirk Miller, Jared Hostetter 2012

Lover's Leap - right side

Mark Anderson on the FA of American Mustang, 14a, CCC: P. Adam Sanders

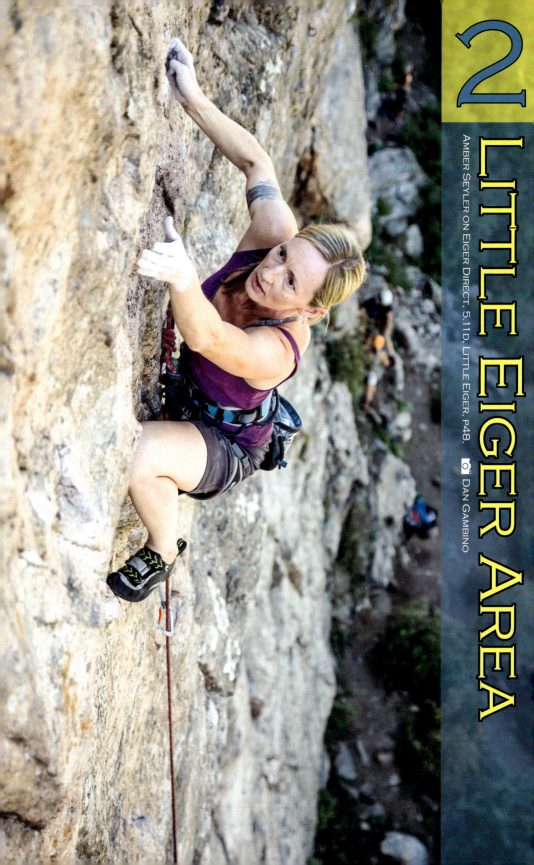

LITTLE EIGER AREA

AMBER SEYLER ON EIGER DIRECT, 5.11D, LITTLE EIGER, P48.

○ DAN GAMBINO

268 Wall

Mile Marker: 268   30min   MOST OF THE DAY   **3 Routes**

≤5.8 5.9 5.10 5.11 5.12 5.13 5.14 *proj*

Crag Profile: While there isn't much at this wall, it does offer a little bit of adventure (in the approach mostly), and also some solitude on a busy Clear Creek day. Bring a crash pad and break up the hike by bouldering on all of the cool boulders along the way. *The Metal* (5.12c) is a beautiful line and is worthy of the extra effort to hike uphill. The wall is mostly north-facing and is shaded, especially during the second half of the day.

Approach: Expect a long bushwhack uphill. Drive 3.6 miles up the canyon and park on the south (left) side of the road in a large dirt parking area at mile marker 268. Cross the road to the north and follow a faint trail up the drainage, staying slightly to the left. After hiking a couple hundred yards uphill, continue up and to the right to spot a wall with two large pine trees in front of it. Once you get close to the wall, walk around to the right side to get to the lower wall where *Welfare Crack* is located. To access *The Metal*, continue up and right of the lower wall and scramble up some fourth class terrain. Alternatively, walk around to get to the upper tier of the wall.

park on the left at mm 268

268 Wall
268 Wall Approach

1 **Welfare Crack** 5.11c ★★
This is a nice trad climb on the lower wall. Moderate climbing brings you to a ledge and the start of a gently overhanging and flaring finger to hand-sized crack.
Standard rack, 2-bolt anchor (50')
FA: Matt Lloyd, Josh Leininger 2009

2 **Unfinished Route**
This unfinished sport route is located on the upper tier of the wall and is the left of the two bolted lines. Feel free to finish this would-be 5.11 route. *4 bolts (35')*
FA: Started by Matt Lloyd 2009

268 Wall

3 **The Metal** 5.12c ★★
Climb the blunt arête on right side of the upper tier, which is defined by big, powerful moves. Stickclipping the first bolt is a good idea so you don't go tumbling backwards off the ledge. *5 bolts, 2-bolt anchor (40')*
FA: Matt Lloyd 2009

METOLIUS SUPER CHALK

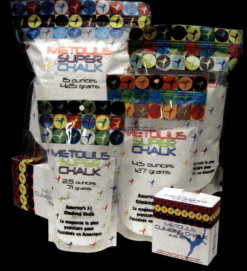

Jonathan Siegrist on Desdichado 13c Eldo - Photo Andy Mann

The Shield

Mile Marker: 267.5   10min

MOST OF THE DAY

A.M. in SUMMER

3 Routes

≤5.8 5.9 5.10 5.11 5.12 5.13 5.14 *proj*

Crag Profile: As you drive west up the canyon, you'll notice a short, dome-shaped wall on the south side of the road just before Little Eiger and Rainy Day Rock. This is the Shield. This isn't a destination wall, but it does offer a few short routes in the shade with a short approach. It faces north and gets an abundance of shade.

Approach: Park on the north (right) side of the road 4.4 miles up the canyon. This is just past the bridge that is shortly after the 267.5 milemarker sign. Take the trail on the left side of the road near the bridge (east of the Little Eiger trail). Follow the creek-side trail for a few hundred yards downstream (going past Rainy Day Rock) before seeing the cliff uphill to the right. Scramble through the

The Shield

The Shield approach

loose, bushy hillside to the base of the crag. There is not a clear, visible trail up to the cliff.

1 Widget 5.11a ★
This is the leftmost bolted line on the wall. A challenging start brings you past the third bolt and easier climbing above. The fourth bolt is hidden, but it's there.
4 bolts, 2-bolt anchor (45')

2 The Gladiator 5.11c ★★★
Climb the first two bolts of *Widget*, and then traverse up and right in a right-angling, layback seam. Best route on the wall.
5 bolts, 2-bolt anchor (45')

3 Turd Ferguson 5.12a
Start in a left-facing corner on the right side of the wall. Pull past some bad rock to a small shake before taking on the painful jams in the overhanging and constricting crack. Move up and right in the corner for a bit of an awkward finish.
4 bolts, 2-bolt anchor (40')

The Shield

Bronson MacDonald is good at making *First Impressions*, 5.9, Little Eiger, p48. 📷 Dan Gambino

Rainy Day Rock

Just After the First Bridge   5min   ALL DAY

7 Routes

≤5.8	5.9	5.10	5.11	5.12	5.13	5.14	proj

Crag Profile: This small overhanging wall offers decent climbing with some reprieve from the rain, should you get bouted by the weather. These climbs are short, powerful, and interesting considering their lack of height.

Approach: Park on the north (right) side of the road 4.4 miles up the canyon. This is just past the bridge that is shortly after the 267.5 milemarker sign. Take the trail on the left side of the road near the bridge (east of the Little Eiger trail). Walk downstream on the south side of the river for about 100 yards; the small wall will be visible to the right.

park on the right for Little Eiger, the Shield, and Rainy Day Rock

approach

Rainy Day Rock

1 Thunder Road 5.11b
The bolts have been removed from this route. *FA: Alan Nelson*

2 Lightning Rod 5.11a
Climb the left-leaning crack in the corner to the left of *Rain Man*.
Rack to #1 Camalot, 1-bolt anchor (30')
FA: Alan Nelson

3 Rain Man 5.11d ★
This is the first climb encountered from the trail. Climb the corner and flake past a scary third clip.
3 bolts, 2-bolt anchor (25')
FA: Alan Nelson

4 Slapaho 5.13c ★★
Start below the overhanging dihedral. Climb bouldery, powerful moves through the roof to a cryptic crux. It climbs better than it looks and is a boulderer's dream route.
5 bolts, 2-bolt anchor (25')
FA: Steve Damboise

5 Rainy Day Twelve A 5.12a ★★
Begin in a right-facing dihedral just right of the roof. Climb the difficult and technical dihedral to an easier finish. One of the better routes on the wall. *3 bolts, 2-bolt anchor (25')*
FA: Kurt Smith, Mike Pont

6 Swinging in the Rain 5.11b ★
Start just below the ledge at head height. Bust a hard crux mantel to easier climbing above.
3 bolts, 2-bolt anchor (25')
FA: Alan Nelson, Tod Anderson 1993

7 Your Brain on Rain 5.11d ★
The farthest right route on the wall offers some intense climbing on interesting holds. Powerful pulls lead to off-balance climbing and the anchors. Worth the effort.
3 bolts, 2-bolt anchor (25')
FA: Alan Nelson 1996

Little Eiger

Just Beyond the First Bridge 5min

A.M. in SUMMER | MOST OF THE DAY

28 Routes

≤5.8 5.9 5.10 5.11 5.12 5.13 5.14 proj

Crag Profile: The Eiger! If you're ready for over 20 tall and fantastic Clear Creek moderates, then Little Eiger is the place to go. Most of the routes are in the 5.10 range and push the 100-foot mark, with a few that require a 70-meter rope. It is a great place to come to for a quick pump after work, especially with its close proximity to the road and short drive up the canyon. If you do happen to have the whole day, go for "Little Eiger in a day" by climbing every route to get in over 2,000 feet of climbing! This wall gets a little bit of sun in the mornings and a touch of sun the late afternoon, but stays shaded most of the day.

Approach: Park on the north (right) side of the road 4.4 miles up the canyon; the trail will be directly across from you on the south side of the road. This is just past the bridge that is shortly after the 267.5 milemarker sign. A two-minute hike takes you to the base of the wall and the first route you see is the classic *Bush Administration* (5.10b). There is extra parking a few hundred feet away on the east side of the bridge.

Little Eiger

park on the right for Little Eiger, the Shield, and Rainy Day Rock

Little Eiger - overview

Little Eiger - left

1 Black Hole 5.11c R ★★
Climb the thin, left-angling crack that goes up the blocky right-facing corner on the left side of the cave. Thin, and kind of awkward crack climbing leads past a couple of fixed pins to an old anchor up and left on a ledge. *Rack to 0.75 Camalot, extra slings for the anchor (30')*   FA: Ken Trout 1985

2 Black Haul 5.10b ★
Around the corner to the left of *Bonehead*, find a small and overhanging alcove with two short crack climbs in it. *Black Haul* ascends the crack to the right, scaling the left-facing dihedral. This short route still delivers a pump, but a questionable sling anchor makes you cross your fingers. *SR with extra thin gear, 2-bolt anchor (30')*   FA: Ken Trout 1985

3 Delusions of Grandeur 5.12b R ★★
Just around the corner to the left of *Bonehead* is a blank face. Climb up the ramp to the face and a high first bolt that is typically stickclipped. A couple of powerful and crimpy moves lead past the second bolt and easier terrain. Shares anchors with *Bonehead*. *3 bolts, 2-bolt anchor (40')*
FA: Chris Deulen 2007

4 Bonehead 5.10c ★★
Start on the arête on the far left side of the main wall before entering the cave. Climb sharp and balancy sidepulls while staying focused on good footwork.
8 bolts, 2-bolt anchor (50')
FA: Alan Nelson, Ken Trout 1991

5 Conehead 5.11a ★★★
Fun face climbing leads to a juggy flake before starting a thin and technical sequence with tiny footholds that finishes on small/sharp sidepulls. After surviving the crux, easier terrain brings you over the bulge to the anchor.
7 bolts, 2-bolt anchor (50')
FA: Alan Nelson, Ken Trout 1991

6 Headline 5.10a ★★★
First led using traditional gear, this route now has six bolts, but is fun no matter how you decide to climb it. A quick sequence up the face leads to a juggy, left-leaning crack with good jams. If leading on gear, bring a standard rack with extra small pieces and a couple 0.75 Camalots.
6 bolts, 2-bolt anchor (50')
FA: Ken Trout 1988

7 Trouthead 5.10d ★★
A few different cruxes on this route, each with its own flavor and separated by a decent rest, lead to the anchor up and left.
7 bolts, 2-bolt anchor (60')
FA: Ken Trout 2003

8 Eiger Sanction 5.10d ★★
Climb through the closely spaced bolts on sustained terrain to a rest at the halfway mark. Save something for the technical and slabby topout. An additional bolt a few feet to the right of the tenth bolt allows for some variation finishes.
11 bolts, 2-bolt anchor (85')
FA: Ken Trout 1991

9 Eiffel Tower 5.10d PG13 ★★
Start about 30 feet left of *Herbal Essence* on the left side of the slab. Thin face climbing leads you past the third bolt and a 20-foot runout on 5.8 terrain. Once you clip the fourth bolt, rest up and get ready for some reachy moves through a zigzagging sequence. *7 bolts, 2-bolt anchor (80')*
FA: John Bissel 1991

⑩ Herbal Essence 5.9+ ★★★ ☐☐
A fun and sustained moderate slab leads to more vertical climbing through a right-facing flake and more varied climbing above.
12-bolts, 2-bolt anchor (85')
FA: Ken Trout, Kirk Miller 2006

⑪ Footloose 5.10a ★★ ☐☐
Easier face climbing leads to a difficult sequence pulling up and over the left-leaning, left-facing dihedral near the top. The anchors are up and left of the last bolt.
11 bolts, 2-bolt anchor (80')
FA: Richard Wright 1996

⑫ First Impressions
5.9 ★★★★ ☐☐
A great introduction to the wall as well as a wonderful warmup. Easy slab climbing leads to great stemming and liebacking in a prominent left-facing dihedral with a crux just before going to the chains.
10 bolts, 2-bolt anchor (80') *FA: Richard Wright, Anna Brandenburg-Schroeder*

⑬ Eiger Direct 5.11d ★★★★ ☐☐
Classic! After pulling a challenging exit move out of the bulgy dihedral, get a quick rest before the start of the business. Super balancy sidepulls with smeary feet are sure to challenge your footwork, route finding abilities, and stamina.
10 bolts, 2-bolt anchor (80')
FA: Richard Wright 1995

⑭ The Radometer in the Red Zone 5.11b ★★ ☐☐
Hard crimping on the upper half of this climb leads to a couple of balancy moves below the anchors.
6 bolts, 2-bolt anchor (60')
FA: Richard Wright 1996

⑮ TOO! 5.12b ★★★ ☐☐
There are three fun pitches and one scramble of a pitch, but at times it climbs through a few loose sections so be careful when the wall is crowded. Helmets are advised.
P1: 5.10d Moderate face climbing leads to an overhang about 40 feet up that starts with a big cross and a couple more big moves on super positive holds. Hit an anchor at 60 feet; to continue on to the top of the first pitch climb up and left. More sustained climbing brings you to a belay below some easy 5th class ledges. Slings are recommended to reduce rope drag. *First Anchor: 6 bolts (60'), Second: 12 bolts, slings (120')*
P2: 5.4 X This is a long scramble with a rope. Continue up the easy fifth class ledge system to an intermediate rap anchor by a tree, and then push on up a left-angling ramp in a short left-facing corner. Pass one bolt before reaching a small belay ledge. *1 bolt, 2-bolt anchor (100')*
P3: 5.11b Excellent and sustained! From the belay, climb up and right, passing a hanging belay anchor at the true base of the pitch and climb up to a crux towards the top. *10 bolts, 2-bolt anchor (100')*
P4: 5.12b Start out by making a sketchy traverse up and right for about 30 feet with one bolt to get to the base of the steep and exposed upper headwall. Fun climbing on positive holds brings you to a ledge where you can size up the crux above. Engage in the challenging sequence with a big and committing move out left to a good hold before traversing on small crimps to get back to the right. This pitch is easier if you're tall and can make the reach out left casual, but it's still a challenging onsight overall. *10 bolts, 2-bolt anchor (95')*
Descent: It's best to lower back down to your belayer at the top of P3 instead of belaying your follower up to the top of P4. From the top of the third pitch, rappel back down to the top of P2. Then either rappel to the anchor by the tree or to the top of the first pitch, if there is no one below you (this rap can dislodge some rocks). It's a 70-meter rappel to the ground from the top of P1. Otherwise use the intermediate anchor if you only have a 60-meter rope. Remember to knot your ends and watch for loose rocks. *FA: John Bissel, Matt Esson, Steve LaPorta 1993*

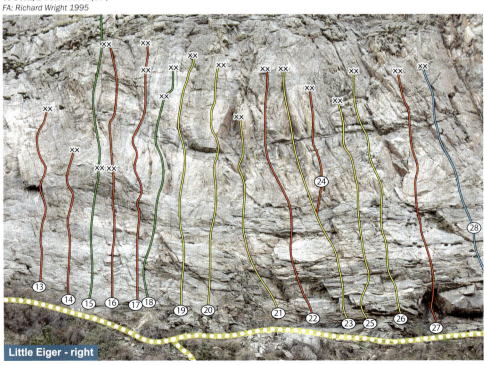

Little Eiger - right

95'
XX
100'
XX
100'
XX
XX
120'
XX
XX
15

Too!

16 The Nordwand 5.11b ★★
Most will stop at the first anchor and avoid the high, reachy crux over a bulge. Share the high anchor with *Too!*. *13 bolts, slings (120')*
First Anchor 5.10c ★★
A fun, mellow jug hual. *6 bolts (60')*
FA: Tod Anderson

17 Natural Selection
5.11b ★★
Moderate climbing leads to a delicate slab crux. The climbing to the first anchor is good, but it's not worth the extra effort to reach the second set of anchors. *First Anchor: 13 bolts (105'); Second Anchor: 16 bolts (130')*
FA: Tod Anderson 1992

18 Tierra del Fuego
5.12a ★★★
This is just to the left of *Bush Administration*. The thin and technical face seems to get thinner the higher you climb before culminating at one final, super thin, sequence past the first anchor. Keep going to the next anchor. *13 bolts, 2-bolt anchor (105')*
FA: Thor Kiesser
First Anchor 5.11b ★★★
Stop at the first anchor. *11 bolts (95')*
FA Extension: Gregg Purnell 2005

19 Bush Administration
5.10b ★★★
This is the first route encountered when hiking up the trail. Fantastic face climbing leads to a cruxy and steep corner three-quarters of the way up. *12 bolts, 2-bolt anchor (115')*
FA: Thor Kiesser 2004

20 Bush Gardens 5.10b ★★★
Be sure to use a 70-meter rope on this long route. The wall starts out a little less than vertical and gets steeper as you fight the pump and climb higher.
11 bolts, 2-bolt anchor (115')
FA: Thor Kiesser 2004

21 The Naked Hedge
5.10b ★★
Twenty feet right of where the trail meets the wall is this sport route, which ascends some ugly and loose terrain before getting better and climbing up the right side of a wide dihedral on a bit of an edge.
12 bolts, 2-bolt anchor (90')
FA: Thor Kiesser 2004

22 The Green Zone 5.11a ★★
Start on the small overhanging bulge with positive holds. Moderate climbing leads to a small rest before you have to crimp your way through the gently overhanging crux and busting up to a jug. There are a few loose blocks on this side of the wall; use caution. *16 bolts, 2-bolt anchor (110')*
FA: Thor Kiesser 2005

23 Persistent Vegetative
State 5.10a ★★★
Glorious 5.10 climbing the whole way leads to a stemming dihedral up high. Head left at the junction where *Free Up the Weed* goes up and right after the fifth bolt.
15 bolts, 2-bolt anchor (115')
FA: Thor Kiesser 2005

24 Free Up the Weed
5.11a ★★
Climb the first five bolts of *Persistent Vegetative State*, then bust up and right to some hard moves that take you through a stemming corner and a bulging arête on your right.
13 bolts, 2-bolt anchor (115')
FA: Thor Kiesser 2005

25 The Decider 5.10b ★
Easier climbing leads to a final crux bulge towards the top.
13 bolts, 2-bolt anchor (100')
FA: Stu Ritchie 2006

26 Misunderestimate
5.10b ★★
Moderate climbing leads to a stemming corner. Afterwards, go up and right over a small roof to encounter the more difficult upper half.
14 bolts, 2-bolt anchor (115')
FA: Thor Kiesser 2006

27 Tsunami of Charisma
5.11b ★★★
Start underneath an alcove roof on the far right side of the wall. Pull the roof to gain a slab. This is a fun route even though the finish is on some not so good rock.
15 bolts, 2-bolt anchor (115')
FA: Thor Kiesser 2006

28 Is Our Children
Learning? 5.9+ ★
This is currently the rightmost route on the wall and features plenty of ledges to rest on, making it a good warm-up. Be mindful of the steep drop off that will take you all the way to the highway.
13 bolts, 2-bolt anchor (115')
FA: Thor Kiesser 2007

The Red Slab

Just Before the First Bridge 10-15min MOST OF THE DAY P.M. 14 Routes

≤5.8 5.9 5.10 5.11 5.12 5.13 5.14 proj

Crag Profile: This is the red wall across from Little Eiger and hosts a variety of slab climbs that are sure to challenge your footwork and slab abilities. Some of the routes are definitely harder than they look and never seem to have a positive hold when you want them to. Because of the nature of the rock, there are a lot of smooth edges and sidepulls, which gives the impression that every jug has been replaced with a sharp crimp. The hardman's test piece, *Pink Slip* (5.12b), is a classic for the canyon, and has one of the best slab cruxes you'll find almost anywhere. Also, climbs like *Snakes for Snacks* (5.10a) and *Rattle and Scream* (5.10a) will test your composure as you make your way through the runouts. The Red Slab is south-facing and is a nice place to come in the winter or a summer evening. It will typically go into the shade around 4pm in the summer.

Approach: Drive 4.4 miles and park on the left (just before the bridge) as for Rainy Day Rock. This is just past milemarker 267.5. Locate a fourth-class approach on the north side of the road and just east of the bridge. After scrambling about 15 feet towards the cliff, the trail gets nice and easy. Be careful doing this approach in the rain. This is not a good crag for kids or dogs.

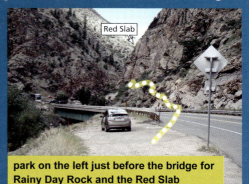
Red Slab

park on the left just before the bridge for Rainy Day Rock and the Red Slab

---

1 Slip It In 5.11a ★★

Just downhill and to the left of the main wall is this standalone route on a nice section of stone. A short boulder problem over the small roof gets you established on the wall. Moderate climbing brings you to a thin, balancy sequence going past the last bolt to gain the anchors.
4 bolts, 2-bolt anchor (50')
FA: Alan Nelson, Kurt Smith 1990

2 Bumblies for Breakfast 5.10a R ★★

The leftmost route on the main wall. The climbing is good but the route doesn't see much traffic due to its runout nature (especially between bolts three and four).
6 bolts, 2-bolt anchor (80') FA: Alan Nelson, Annette Bunge, Ken Trout 1990

3 Vapor Trail 5.9 ★★

This is a fun and exciting route that can feel heady at times. It has been described as devious, with good holds pointing the wrong direction.
7 bolts, 2-bolt anchor (80')
FA: Alan Nelson, Guy Lords 1990

4 Trundelero 5.10b ★★

Climb through the overhanging crack near the base of the wall. Don't be intimidated by the roof – it's juggy and fun, and the crux is much higher on the climb. *8 bolts, 2-bolt anchor (90')*
FA: Alan Nelson, Guy Lords 1990

5 Wicked Game 5.10d R ★★

Locate the hand crack in the roof just right of *Trundelero*. Great climbing up high is unfortunately only attained by climbing through lichen-covered, loose, and uninspiring terrain below. It's still a worthy adventure for those that don't mind some space between the bolts.
6 bolts, 1 fixed pin, 2-bolt anchor (90')
FA: Alan Nelson, Guy Lords 1990

6 Spring Fever 5.10c ★★

Start a few feet left of *Diamondback*, and pull a hard move through the small roof to easier movement above. While it's a spicy lead using just the bolts, optional gear placements are available. Lead it on gear like the first ascensionist with small stoppers up to a #2 Camalot.
6 bolts, 2-bolt anchor (85')
FA: Alan Nelson, C. Mearns 1990

7 Diamondback 5.10b ★★★

This is one of the best climbs at the Red Slab due to its sustained nature and fun edge pulling. Locate the left-facing dihedral and climb past the little roof to get onto the face above. A little soft for the grade.
7 bolts, 2-bolt anchors. (85')
FA: Alan Nelson, Guy Lords 1990

8 Pink Slip 5.12b ★★★★

A beautiful, thought provoking, and technical slab climb makes this a classic for the canyon. Start just right of the small dihedral. A couple of challenging sequences leads to a decent rest before taking on the smeary crux and meeting up with *Slip and Slide* after the fifth bolt. There is no powering your way through this test piece.
8 bolts, 2-bolt anchor (85')
FA: Alan Nelson, Kurt Smith 1990

9 Slip and Slide 5.10d ★★★★

Fantastic and sustained slab climbing the whole way makes this one of the best routes on the wall! Technical movement with holds that always seem to be a little worse than you think they will be mandates good footwork. *8 bolts, 2-bolt anchor (85')*
FA: Alan Nelson, Kurt Smith 1990

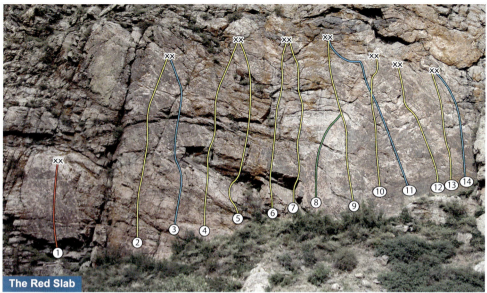

The Red Slab

10 Lounge Lizard 5.10b ★★ ☐☐
Fun face climbing through closely spaced bolts on thin holds.
9 bolts, 2-bolt anchor (70')
FA: Thor Kiesser, Stu Ritchie 2004

11 MK-'74 5.9 X ★ ☐☐
Begin in a left-leaning groove with light colored rock to the left of *Snakes and Snacks*. There is a small graffiti "MK-'74" at the base. Insecure slab climbing with few opportunities for gear is why this route is typically toproped. Finish up and left on *Slip and Slide*. *Rack to #1 Camalot, nuts, RPs, offset nuts, 2-bolt anchor (85')*

12 Snakes and Snacks 5.10a PG13 ★★ ☐☐
A fun slab climb with some spicy runouts. Start with some easier climbing on positive holds, then climb up and left onto bad, sloping holds that demand good footwork.
4 bolts, 2-bolt anchor (65')   *FA: Alan Nelson, Annette Bunge, Ken Trout 1990*

13 Rattle and Scream 5.10a PG13 ★ ☐☐
This is the rightmost bolted line on the wall. A challenging start with a high second bolt leads to more sustained and moderate climbing.
5 bolts, 2-bolt anchor (60')
FA: Thor Kiesser, Scott Bilyeu

14 And Now for Something Completely Different 5.9 R ☐☐
Toprope or lead the hard-to-protect face to the right of *Rattle and Scream*, using that route's anchors.
Standard rack with extra thin gear, 2-bolt anchor (60')

Jay Samuelson is known to *Slapaho*, 5.13c, p45, from time to time. 📷 Luke Childers

DENVER MOUNTAIN GUIDING

The Premier Guide Service for Clear Creek Canyon

Rock Climbing Courses • Private Instruction • Summer Camps • Summit the Flatirons

(303) 884-2755
info@denvermountainguiding.com
www.denvermountainguiding.com

DENVER MOUNTAIN GUIDING
GOLDEN, CO

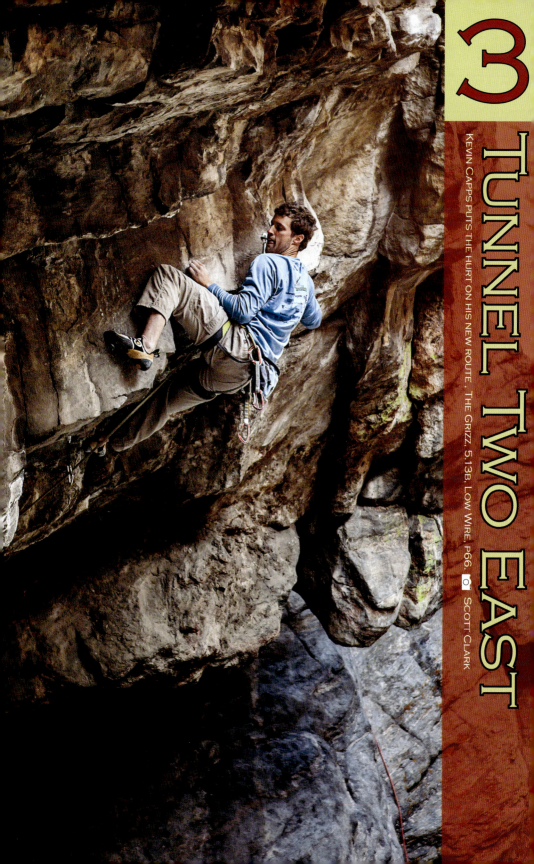

3

TUNNEL TWO EAST

KEVIN CAPPS PUTS THE HURT ON HIS NEW ROUTE, THE GRIZZ, 5.13B. LOW WIRE, P66. 📷 SCOTT CLARK

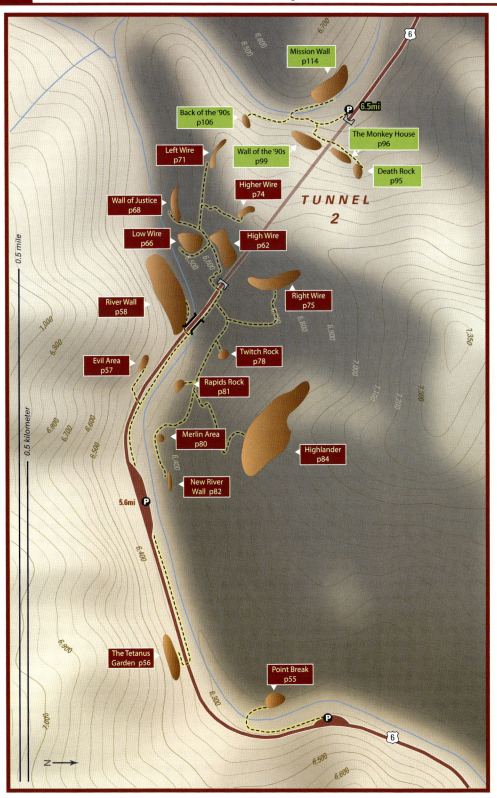

Mission Wall
p114

Back of the '90s
p106

The Monkey House
p96

6.5mi

Left Wire
p71

Wall of the '90s
p99

Death Rock
p95

Higher Wire
p74

Wall of Justice
p68

TUNNEL 2

Low Wire
p66

High Wire
p62

Right Wire
p75

River Wall
p58

Evil Area
p57

Twitch Rock
p78

Rapids Rock
p81

Merlin Area
p80

Highlander
p84

New River
Wall p82

5.6mi

The Tetanus
Garden p56

Point Break
p55

0.5 mile

0.5 kilometer

N →

Point Break

 10-15min

 A.M.   P.M.

7 Routes

≤5.8 5.9 5.10 5.11 5.12 5.13 5.14 proj

Crag Profile: The large, ominous roof on the north side of the road you see driving up the canyon before getting to Tunnel 2 is Point Break. An eager sport climber can't help but be drawn to this wall to take on the mighty overhanging prow and test their skills on *Laughing with God* (5.12c), *Bodhisattva* (5.12b), or even *Warchild* (project). There are also a handful of more moderate climbs ranging from 5.9 to 5.10d.

Approach: Park at mile 5.6 on the north (right) side of the road, and then hike down the hillside to wade across the creek in the shallowest part. The best times to cross are late summer through early spring. Occasionally ice bridges form in winter, which make it easy to cross. After crossing the creek, do a short hike up the hill and make your way to the base of the cliff. There is typically a fixed line closer to the wall. Be mindful on the steep approach.

wade   **Approach**

① **Surfing Can Save Your Life** 5.10d ★
Find the leftmost route around the corner from the *Warchild* roof. A challenging start leads to more relaxing climbing higher up.
5 bolts, 2-bolt anchor (45')
FA: Luke Childers 2010

② **Warchild** project ★★★
An ambitious project (5.13?) takes on the steepest part of the roof. Climb the bolted line to the right of the arête. *6 bolts, 2-bolt anchor (45')*
Equipper: Luke Childers 2010

③ **Laughing with God** 5.12c ★★
Begin in a corner below a roof on the right side of the wall. A big move going from an undercling below the roof to a crimp at the lip makes this route challenging and a bit reachy, yet still doable for shorties.
6 bolts, 2-bolt anchor (50')
FA: Jason Baker 2010

④ **Vaya con Dios, Brah!** 5.10d ★★
Start on *Laughing*, then cruise up and right avoiding the massive roof, and continue on the slab to the upper wall. *6 bolts, 2-bolt anchor (50')*
FA: Jason Baker, Rob Dezonia 2010

⑤ **Bodhisattva** 5.12b ★
Start underneath the overhanging bulge on the right side of the wall underneath the slab. It's harder than it looks, with a crux sequence moving past bolt two before easing up. Stick clipping the second bolt seems mandatory. *6 bolts, 2-bolt anchor (50')*
FA: Kevin Capps 2013;
Equipper: Jason Baker 2010

⑥ **50 Year Storm** 5.9+ ★★
Climb *Jump or Jerk Off* to the third bolt. Then cruise up and left for another moderate variation.
6 bolts, 2-bolt anchor (50')
FA: Jason Baker 2010

⑦ **Jump or Jerk Off** 5.9+ ★★
The rightmost route on the wall follows steep climbing on good holds to an easier slab finish.
6 bolts, 2-bolt anchor (50')
FA: Jason Baker, Luke Childers 2010

Point Break

The Tetanus Garden

 5min

 MOST OF THE DAY

 P.M. in SUMMER

6 Routes

≤5.8 5.9 5.10 5.11 5.12 5.13 5.14 proj

Crag Profile: This small cliff has a variety of fun, shaded climbs. So when High Wire is melting and you don't feel like the multi-pitchin' on the River Wall, head over here. For some moderates, climb *Shady Boy* (5.10c) or *Shady Girl* (5.10b), but if you're looking to push it a little more than try *Lockjaw* (5.12b), a test piece for the area. This wall is north-facing and is covered by trees, so it stays shaded all day and is a place to find cooler temps in the summer.

Approach: Park 6.0 miles up canyon as for New River and High Wire (next page). From the car, walk east for about 200 yards. There was no trail at the time of publication, so scramble up the hill on the south side of the road. However the best approach is to walk just east of the crag (back towards Golden) before hiking up the hill to avoid loose sections of dirt. The *Shady* routes are to the right on a slab while *Lockjaw* is about 60 yards to the left.

The Tetanus Garden Overview

Cobra

Lockjaw

Shady Affair

❶ Lockjaw 5.12b ★★★
Powerful and fun crimping tackles an overhanging headwall 60 yards left of *Shady Boy*. This seldom-climbed route is a hidden gem for the canyon. Start on the slab to the right, then climb up and left on okay rock (it's more solid than it looks) to get to the upper headwall. A brutal sequence on crimps leads to a good hold where you can scope out the final mantel move below the anchors.
9 bolts, 2-bolt anchor (60')
FA: Vaino Kodas 2003

❷ Cobra 5.12a ★★
Short, but fun. Locate the prominent, overhanging dihedral about 30 yards left of *Shady Boy*. Technical climbing up the thin crack and stemming leads to a powerful exit move to the upper section. From here, a moderate slab gets you to the top.
5 bolts, 2-bolt anchor (45')
FA: Kevin Capps 2013

❸ Shady Boy 5.10c ★★
A boulder problem at the start leads to fantastic 5.8 slab climbing to the top. Good stone and well protected. This is the leftmost bolted line for the *Shady* routes.
10 bolts, 2-bolt anchor (70')
FA: Richard Wright, Koko Kosila 2005

❹ Shady Affair 5.11b ★★★
Shady Affair is the bolted line to the left of the arête. Powerful climbing down low on sidepulls gives way to some technical slab moves above. After easing up with some semi-technical slab climbing, link up with *Shady Girl* on the top half of the route. *10 bolts, 2-bolt anchor (70')*
FA: Kevin Capps 2013

Shady Girl

5 **Shady Girl** 5.10b ★★

Climb the bolted line right of the arête. Technical movement tackles the arête and makes you think about your footwork. It's easier but more sustained than *Shady Boy*.
10 bolts, 2-bolt anchor (70')
FA: Richard Wright, Koko Kosila 2005

6 **Shady Baby** 5.9 PG13 ★

Climb the thin crack in the dihedral about five feet right of *Shady Girl*. Place small gear in the crack as you stem up the corner. Finish by busting out left and climbing the last three bolts of *Shady Girl*. Most will typically toprope this route due to the marginal gear. *3 bolts, rack to #1 Camlot, 2-bolt anchor (70')*
FA: Dave Rogers 2012

Evil Area

🚶 5min   ALL DAY   **3 Routes**

≤5.8 5.9 5.10 5.11 5.12 5.13 5.14 proj

Crag Profile: This climbing area holds a couple of good climbs including the test piece *Evil* (5.13b), but this area should be approached with great caution as these routes are located directly above the road, so anything you drop will go directly onto the road below.

Approach: Evil Area is situated just east of River Wall (p58) and about 100 feet up on the south side of the road. Park as for High Wire (p62), then hike west for about 100 yards along the road before seeing a small climber's trail on the south side of the road. Be very mindful not to drop rocks on cars when accessing this area.

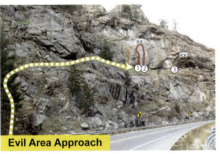

Evil Area Approach

1 **Not So Evil** 5.11b ★★

The leftmost bolted line on the wall has a challenging, hard to read sequence through the start. Gain a decent rest before tackling the techy slab and traversing out left at the fourth bolt. From here, continue up and right to the anchor. A variation exists by continuing straight up past the fourth bolt. *6 bolts, 2-bolt anchor (55')*

2 **Simpatico** 5.11b ★★

Start in the overhanging dihedral and power through it on decent holds. Easier climbing gains a rest below some thin moves and a difficult slab mantel. Some thin to medium gear can back up the fixed pin. Share anchors with *Not So Evil*. *5 bolts, 1 fixed pin, optional gear, 2-bolt anchor (55')*

3 **Evil** 5.13b ★★★

Just to be clear, climbing on this route is dangerous. The block at the base of the climb is loose and will slide down and fall into the road with the lightest touch. With that said, holy cow is this an awesome line! Steep gym-like climbing leads to an intriguing crux at the lip. It would be one of the best 5.13s in the canyon if not for the sketchy location.
9 bolts, 2-bolt anchor (60')
FA: Eric Johnson 1991

Evil Area

River Wall

5min

P.M. | MOST OF THE DAY

29 Routes
≤5.8 5.9 5.10 5.11 5.12 5.13 5.14 proj

Crag Profile: The River Wall has so much variety that it will keep you coming back for more once you get a taste. While High Wire gets blasted with direct sunlight all morning and most of the afternoon, River Wall stays in the shade until the summer evening hours. The wall is split up into a few different sectors with different styles of climbing in each of them. The lower section involves climbing single pitches to the ledge halfway up the wall and includes fun routes like *The Put In* (5.8+),

This is the parking area for every crag in this chapter except for Point Break.

Muddy Waters (5.10a), and *The River Mild* (5.10c). Most of theses routes are slabby to vertical, with thin cruxes and each of them can be used to access the ledge and upper pitches. The second half of the wall holds a handful of steep, hard routes, including the classic *Adventure Kayak Trundle* (5.12a). The upper routes are also separated by a block with a slot/squeeze chimney to the right of *Viagra Falls* called The Snead Slot. However you manage to squeeze through it, just know it's a little tougher on the way back. Passing the slot will allow you access to traverse to more belay anchors and more routes to the right of the upper wall like *Right to Life* (5.11d) and *Slacker* (5.12c). The wall is west-facing and only gets sun in summer evenings.

Approach: Drive 6.0 miles up the canyon and park at a long, narrow pullout on the north (right) side of the road. After parking, walk towards the tunnel. River Wall is on the south side of the road and before the bridge. The first route on the left that you will see is *The Put In*.

Note: The following routes are right off the highway. *The Put In* is the first route you will see and is only about 15 feet from the road.

1 The Put In 5.8+ ★★
The leftmost bolted line starts right off the road.
4 bolts, 2-bolt anchor (65')
FA: Alan Nelson, Richard Wright 1998

2 Overflow 5.11b ★★
Clip *The Put In*'s anchor, then continue up and left for some odd climbing out the corner.
4 bolts, 2-bolt anchor (85')
FA: Ken Trout, Kirk Miller

3 Original Route 5.9 PG13 ★
This route feels a bit historic for Clear Creek. Start just right of *The Put In* on a flake system. Slightly less than vertical climbing takes you past a couple of old, not to be trusted bolts, along with some limited protection and a fixed pin or two. Finish on *The Put In*. *2 bolts, 2 fixed pins, rack to #3 Camalot, 2-bolt anchor (70')*

4 Muddy Waters 5.10a ★★
A fun route on solid stone. Varied angles and slab lead to steeper rock guarding the chains.
6 bolts, 2-bolt anchor (80')
FA: Richard Wright, Alan Nelson 2000

5 Old Man River 5.10c ★★
Start from a small ledge before reaching the creek just downhill from *Muddy Waters*. Climb past the bushy ledges for the true start of the climbing. There are two different but equally challenging ways to negotiate this crux – a bolt to the left, or the bolt to the right; both meet up after the fifth bolt.
9 bolts, 2-bolt anchor (95')
FA: Alan Nelson 2000

6 Up a Creek 5.11c ★★
Belay down by the creek at the first belay anchor on the left. Scramble up the bushy ledges to get to a challenging pull past a bulge out to the right. Arrive at a good rest before the roof, then pull some funky moves to moderate slab climbing above.
10 bolts, 2-bolt anchor (105')
FA: Alan Nelson 2000

6a Float Trip 5.12a ★
This variation starts and finishes on *Up a Creek*, but cuts out left at the roof for a freakishly weird and hard mantel up and over onto the slab above. It can easily be toproped by climbing *Up a Creek*.
9 bolts, 2-bolt anchor (105')
FA: Alan Nelson 2000

7 Bottom Side Down 5.10d ★★
Start down by the creek below or at the first belay anchor on the left. Slab climbing up the right brings you to a crux pulling past the steep face before easing up on the upper slab. *12 bolts, 2-bolt anchor (105')*
FA: Alan Nelson, Richard Wright 1998

8 The River Mild 5.10c ★★★
Fun slab climbing with a small roof pull at the start leads to a steep face where the route continues along the bolt line up and left. Begin by using the second set of belay anchors from the left, or at the water's edge (the length is measured from the ledge below the anchors by the water).
11 bolts, 2-bolt anchor (110')
FA: Alan Nelson, Richard Wright 1998

Snead Slot

River Wall - left side

8a River Grill 5.10c ★★

A quick way to get to the upper right routes on the wall is to climb the first half of *The River Mild* to the second overlap then bust out right to finish on *Grilled Trout*.

12 bolts, slings, 2-bolt anchor (120')
FA: Alan Nelson 1998

9 Grilled Trout 5.10b ★★

A great line with some technical slab movement throughout. The route starts on the belay anchors that are third from the left.

10 bolts, 2-bolt anchor (95')
FA: Alan Nelson, Richard Wright 1998

10 Take Me to the River 5.11a ★★

This route features sustained climbing with a few thin and hard-to-read sequences that utilize your trusted footwork. Traverse out right to start this route on the belay anchors just left of *Flood Control*, or lower from *River Dance*'s belay anchor on the ledge. *11 bolts, 2-bolt anchor (95')*
FA: Alan Nelson, Richard Wright 1998

11 **Flood Control** 5.10b ★★ ☐☐
This is the rightmost route on this section of the wall and it starts from a bolted anchor to the right of *Take Me to the River*. Begin by traversing out right to the belay anchor, or lower in from River Dance's belay anchor. Mostly fun moderate climbing through sometimes heavy vegetation brings you to a challenging section near the top.
10 bolts, 2-bolt anchor (95')
FA: Alan Nelson, Richard Wright 1998

Note: The following routes start on the ledge. The easiest way to get to the ledge is via *The Put In* (5.8+). Traverse the ledge to the right for anchors to belay from.

12 **The River Wild** 5.12c ★★★ ☐☐
Just left of the giant boulder perched on the ledge are two fantastic 5.12s; this is the leftmost one. Climb up through a pumpy start to a quick but hard crux. *12 bolts, 2-bolt anchor (70')*
FA: Alan Nelson 1998

13 **Viagra Falls** 5.12c ★★ ☐☐
This is a fun route just right of *The River Wild*, which involves an interesting boulder problem between the third and fourth bolts that may leave you wondering what to do.
9 bolts, 2-bolt anchor (70')
FA: Alan Nelson 1998

14 **White Water** 5.12a ★★★ ☐☐
Sustained climbing on this rig makes you fight for it all the way 'til the end. Pull past the left side of the block to a crimpy section that leads to a roof. Pull a powerful roof crux to get to a quick rest before tackling the pumpy finish. *10 bolts, 2-bolt anchor (70')*
FA: Alan Nelson 1998

Note: The next few route are on the right side of the block and use The Snead Slot to get to them. There is a tight squeeze chimney on the inside of the block, be careful not to get stuck!

15 **Splash** 5.11c ★★ ☐☐
From the belay anchors on the right side of the block, climb up the block past a tough, thin sequence to get to the upper wall. From here, mostly moderate climbing with a couple of semi tough moves brings you to a finish in a short, right-facing corner.
9 bolts, 2-bolt anchor (75')
FA: Tod Anderson 1998

16 **Adventure Kayak Trundle** 5.12a ★★★★ ☐☐
One of the best routes at River Wall powers past a strenuous roof/mantel crux at the start to get established in the right-facing dihedral. Very enjoyable and exposed climbing takes you to the top with a bit of a pump before clipping the anchor. Closely bolted. *12 bolts, 2-bolt anchor (80')*
FA: Tod Anderson 1998

17 **River Dance** 5.12b ★★★ ☐☐
Excellent climbing with a pumpy finish begins at a bolted belay below a slab to the right of the preceding route. Hard climbing past the crux down low brings you to a rest before tackling the pumpy finish and shooting for the jug by the anchor.
12 bolts, 2-bolt anchor (85')
FA: Alan Nelson 1998

18 **River Jam** 5.11d ★★★ ☐☐
Climb the ramp up and right until you can go straight up to the roof. Pull a powerful sequence over the roof and follow the hand-sized (bolted) crack up and right to the chains. Great exposure. *12 bolts, 2-bolt anchor (100')*
FA: Alan Nelson 2000

19 **Pomona Panthers** 5.13b ★★★ ☐☐
Start on *River Jam*, and then continue up and to the left after the roof. Sustained 5.11 climbing leads to about a 15-foot V8 boulder problem. *12 bolts, 2-bolt anchor (95)*
FA: Jason Haas 07/14

Note: The next set of routes are even further to the right. Traverse over to different belay anchors along the wall to the right of *Adventure Kayak Trundle*.

20 **Slacker** 5.12c ★★★ ☐☐
Hard, cruxy climbing in a great position starts at a belay anchor around the corner to the right of *River Jam*'s belay anchor. Pull over the short face to get to a ramp and scramble straight up to the white face. Climb the seam up and left to get to one last hard sequence getting to the top. *12 bolts, 2-bolt anchor (100')*
FA: Alan Nelson 2001

21 **Human Rites** 5.10c ★ ☐☐
A large right-facing corner features some moderate climbing until you bust up and right past the short, overhanging wall.
4 bolts, 2-bolt anchor (40')
FA: Alan Nelson, Richard Wright 2001

22 **Nelsonator I** 5.12a ★★ ☐☐
Tackle a one-move-wonder past a sloper crux by the third bolt. Finish with a short layback corner and big holds on the second half.
5 bolts, 2-bolt anchor (35')
FA: Alan Nelson 2001

23 **Nelsonator II** 5.12a ★★★ ☐☐
Start on the hanging belay up and right of *Nelsonator I*. Fun and sustained moves on solid stone in the first half set you up for an easier yet pumpy finish.
5 bolts, 2-bolt anchor (35')
FA: Alan Nelson 2001

24 **Nelsonator III** 5.12b ★★ ☐☐
Powerful climbing with smeary feet brings you to a good hold about halfway up where you can cop a quick rest before busting to the anchor. It's a fun route despite the lichen, and it offers a solid pump for a short route.
6 bolts, 2-bolt anchor (35')
FA: Alan Nelson 2001

25 **Right to Life** 5.11d ★★ ☐☐
When climbing the seam, encounter a cruxy move on the face in the beginning. Finish in a left-facing dihedral. *4 bolts, 2-bolt anchor (30')*
FA: Alan Nelson 2001

26 **Right to Laugh** 5.9+ ★★ ☐☐
This is a fun and moderate extension or second pitch to *Right to Life*. Start up the mossy slab past the anchor and follow the prominent prow on the second half of the wall.
9 bolts, 2-bolt anchor (70')
FA: Alan Nelson, Richard Wright 2001

Note: The next three routes include some moderates with variations and a multi-pitch climb that begins by traversing the base of the wall past *Flood Control*, often wading through the creek, to get to a small beach past a metal spike where you can belay. Low water is necessary for doing these routes as all three share the same start.

27 **Water Sports** 5.11a ★ ☐☐
This is the first route you approach on the right side. Climb up the steep wall to an easier 5.9 finish. While you finish on *Right to Life*'s anchor, it's best to traverse right and lower or rappel off *River Walk*'s anchor.
12 bolts, 2-bolt anchor (115')
FA: Adam Huxley, Chuck Fitch 2013

**Clear Water Revival**
5.9 ★

After pulling the initial bulge, climb up and slightly left on the slab above. Rappel off of *River Walk*'s anchor to help your rope not land in the creek.
11 bolts, slings, 2-bolt anchor (115')
FA: Adam Huxley, Chuck Fitch 2013

29 River Walk 5.10c ★★
P1: 5.9 Climb past a small bulge, then head up to the right following a crack system. When the gear vanishes on the slab, a bolt protects a few moves before continuing up to the base of a dihedral with an anchor. *4 bolts, small to medium gear, 2-bolt anchor (115')*

P2: 5.10c Shoot up past the intimidating corner to an anchor on the slab above. With a few long slings, this can be combined with the first pitch. *4 bolts, 2-bolt anchor (40')*

P3: 5.7 Continue up the crack, passing a single bolt and finishing on a ledge by *Right to Laugh*. *1 bolt, small to medium gear (70')*
FA: Adam Huxley, Chuck Fitch 2012

River Wall - right side

High Wire

 10-15min

 A.M. P.M.

25 Routes

≤5.8 5.9 5.10 5.11 5.12 5.13 5.14 proj

Crag Profile: Quality stone, an easy approach, and plenty of classic moderates is how most describe High Wire. This wall is packed with excellent routes in the 5.8-5.10 range, including the multi-pitch classic *People's Choice* (5.10d), which climbs up a steep, exposed dihedral 200 feet above the base of the cliff. The only downside to this cliff is that it gets super hot in the summer morning/days and is often extremely crowded. However, it is a great wall to come to on a summer evening or a winter day with its southeastern position.

Approach: Located on the east side of Tunnel 2, park at a long, narrow pullout on the north (right) side of the road 6.0 miles up canyon. Do not park on the south side of the road; there has been a history of cars being smashed by loose blocks, and you may be ticketed. After parking, walk towards the tunnel, cross to the south side of the road and take the steep trail up a few feet of third class terrain before gaining a smoother approach trail that leads to the base of the cliff. The first climb encountered is *Nickels and Dimes*.

This is the parking area for every crag in this chapter except for Point Break.

❶ Pony Up 5.8 ★★★

This is the leftmost route on the wall. Power through the steep initial boulder problem to gain enjoyable face climbing on slightly less-than-vertical terrain.
7 bolts, 2-bolt anchor (75')
FA: Richard Wright 1997

❷ Poker Face 5.8+ ★★

This route has a challenging sequence to start the route and is hard for the grade, but eases up afterwards for some sustained 5.7 climbing on the slab.
8 bolts, 2-bolt anchor (75')
FA: Richard Wright 1997

❸ Stone Cold Moderate 5.7+ ★★★★

With an emphasis on the plus, this line has a bouldery start through the overhanging crack and into a beautiful right-facing corner and crack. Climb this thing with gear for a fun lead or clip bolts like everyone else.
7 bolts, 2-bolt anchor (80')
FA: Richard Wright 1997

❹ Fifth of July 5.9+ ★★★★

Power through the overhang at the start to gain the fantastic and sustained near-vertical slab above. Well bolted and a great lead!
10 bolts, 2-bolt anchor (90')
FA: Richard Wright 1997

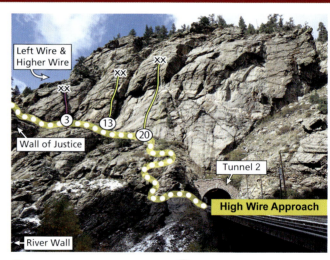

Left Wire & Higher Wire

Wall of Justice

Tunnel 2

High Wire Approach

River Wall

❺ Ace in the Hole 5.10a ★

Scramble up the gully while awkwardly clipping bolts above your head until you eventually have to commit to the face and crimp the rest of the way to the top. Careful not to fall back into the gully!
9 bolts, 2-bolt anchor (75')
FA: Richard Wright 1997

❻ Beginners on Crack 5.7 R ★

Start with the well protected, changing corners crack to the left of *Cracker Jack*, then continue up the runout prow to the anchor. Alternatively, climb the wide crack using a #4 Camalot just around to the right of the prow. **Rack to #2 or #4 Camalot, 2-bolt anchor (80')**
FA: Kevin Capps 2010

High Wire - *Stone Cold Moderate* Area

To Higher Wire
and Left Wire

To Wall
of Justice

High Wire - *Cracker Jack* Area

7 **Cracker Jack** 5.9- ★★
Climb the bolted crack to the right of
the break in the wall. After jamming
your way past the bulge, enjoy easy
slab climbing to the chains.
8 bolts, 2-bolt anchor (85')
FA: Alan Nelson 1998

8 **Bypass** 5.10c ★★
A fun and bouldery start up the
slightly overhanging face leads up
and right to join up with *Overpass* for
an easy finish.
7 bolts, 2-bolt anchor (85')
FA: Alan Nelson 1997

9 **Overpass** 5.11c ★★
An awkward mantel move gains a
nice rest where you can size up the
crux. Powerful climbing heads up
and right over the prow. This route is
a boulder problem with an extra 65
feet of 5.7 to finish.
8 bolts, 2-bolt anchor (85')
FA: Alan Nelson 1997

10 **Passing Lane** 5.9 PG13 ★
Begin in a shallow right-facing dihedral just right of *Overpass*. Some
moderate climbing brings you to a
cruxy traverse out left by bolt four;
you do not want to fall here. From
here, you have two more bolts protecting 45 feet of 5.6 climbing. This
would warrant an R rating if you are
not comfortable with easy, runout
slab climbing.
6 bolts, 2-bolt anchor (90')
FA: Alan Nelson 1998

High Wire - *People's Choice* Area

11 The Contrarian 5.9- ★
Clip the first bolt on *Passing Lane*, then continue up and right towards a crack that heads out a small, overhanging bulge. Use the first anchor on *Deuces Wild*. *1 bolt, rack to #3 Camalot, 2-bolt anchor (60')*
FA: Dougald MacDonald, Chris Blackmon, Robin McBeth 2007

12 Deuces Wild 5.10a ★★★
A long and fun pitch! Thin and crimpy moves get you started as you move through a white band of rock. Jug hauling brings you to a crack in a bulge past the first anchor, then fun climbing for another 75 feet gets you to the top of the wall. This route is best done as one long pitch, but descended with two rappels. If you do it as one rappel with two ropes, your ropes could get stuck.
First Anchor: 7 bolts (60');
Second Anchor: 18 bolts (135')
FA: Richard Wright 1997

13 Via Comatose Amigo 5.10b ★★
Start up the face to the left of the arête, just left of a big gully. Continuous climbing on blocky holds brings you to a corner system with some challenging moves, then an easier slab to the top. Be careful lowering with a 70-meter rope – there is just enough with stretch.
13 bolts, 2-bolt anchor (125')
FA: Richard Wright 1997

14 Jackpot 5.11d ★★
Easy slab climbing to the right of the gully leads to the base of the steep headwall. Give yourself a pep talk, then cruise straight up the intimidating wall doing your best not to get suckered into the crack. There are a few different ways to negotiate the crux to keep it at 5.11, but if you follow the bolt line closely, it is stiff for 11d.
14 bolts, slings, 2-bolt anchor (110')
FA: Richard Wright, Anna Brandenburg-Schroeder 2000

15 Road Rash Roof 5.12a ★★★
This is fantastically-exposed roof boulder problem! Romp up moderate climbing to a ledge rest below the ominous, horizontal roof. Clip a long sling, then pull on jugs to square up with a difficult mantel move to get onto the upper face.
11 bolts, slings, 2-bolt anchor (110')
FA: Alan Nelson 1997

16 Dead End Crack 5.8 ★
Climb the right of two cracks for the first half, then traverse about 10 feet left on a small ledge towards the top and finish in the wide, flaring crack. The last few moves are often covered in bird poo.
Rack to #2 Camalot, 2-bolt anchor (80')
FA: Kevin Capps 2010

17 The Savage 5.13a ★★★★
Classic! Climb *Road Warrior* to the roof, then pull a crux sequence that leads to a pumpy traverse out left. Finish on *Road Rash Roof*'s anchor.
10 bolts, 2 bolt anchor (95')
FA: Kevin Capps, Matt Lloyd 05/14

18 Road Warrior 5.12d ★★
Walk up the slab ledge to the first bolted anchor to belay. Mellow face climbing gains a rest before a juggy roof and lets you size up the technical sequences higher up. A final ballbuster sequence before clipping the anchor makes you work for it. A seldom climbed first pitch to this route has three bolts up a short slab with some 5.9+ climbing up to the ledge.
10 bolts, 2-bolt anchor (90' to Queen City Slab Ledge)
FA: Alan Nelson 1998

19 Road Kill 5.11d ★★★
This pumpfest has fantastic exposure on the steep upper wall. While this is a three-pitch route, climbers typically walk up the slab ledge to belay from the anchor that's furthest to the right in order to only climb the second pitch, which is amazing.
P1: 5.10a This move going up the bolted slab to the left of *People's Choice* gets you to the bolted belay anchor. This pitch is rarely climbed.
3 bolts, 2-bolt anchor (50')
P2: 5.11d The money pitch! Begin with some moderate climbing up featured rock, passing an anchor about 25 feet up. From here, figure out a tricky mantel before the large roof. Cop a quick rest, then take on the pumpy overhang, pulling on decent

Jamie Gatchalian sticks the dyno crux on *Head Up Dirty*, 5.12c, Right Wire, p76. 📷 Adam Bove

holds and enjoy every minute of it until pulling over to get to the chains. *10 bolts, 2-bolt anchor (85' to Queen City Slab Ledge)*
P3: 5.7 This moderate last pitch doesn't really add anything to the route but does give you a little more climbing. *4 bolts, 2-bolt anchor (40')*
FA: Alan Nelson 1997

20 People's Choice
5.10d ★★★★
A fantastic position in the slightly overhanging dihedral up high on the third pitch makes this a popular multi-pitch. You can combine the first two pitches, or climb this as one long pitch (watch for rope drag).
P1: 5.10b Vertical face climbing sets you up for a slabby crux before gaining the ledge. Technical footwork is a must. *6 bolts, 2-bolt anchor (50')*
P2: 5.6 Easy climbing on the ledgy slab. Belay below the breathtaking, overhanging dihedral. *6 bolts, 2-bolt anchor (50')*
P3: 5.10d Use your stemming technique to climb the overhanging dihedral. Pull on good holds before cruising up and left at the top of the corner. *8 bolts, 2-bolt anchor (70')*
Descent: Rappel - 170' to the ground, 120' to Queen City Slab Ledge
FA: Richard Wright, Anna Brandenburg-Schroeder 1997

21 Slot Machine 5.11c ★★
From the top of the second pitch of *People's Choice*, climb the steep, exposed face up and right. Pumpy climbing leads to a challenging mantel to get to the anchor.
8 bolts, 2-bolt anchor (70')
FA: Richard Wright 2000

Note: The next three routes start at an anchor to the right of the top of the second pitch on *People's Choice*.

22 Full House 5.12a ★
Climb up and left around the roof to meet up with *Slot Machine*. It's a bit contrived to reach the original grade of 12c but the route is still kind of a fun variation with some extra challenges available in the crux if you want. *8 bolts, 2-bolt anchor (70')*
FA: Richard Wright 2000

23 Bouncer 5.11d ★★
Start on *Wild Card*, then move up and left around the arête after the third bolt with some fun climbing that avoids the exposed feeling you get on *Wild Card*. Meets back up with *Wild Card* for the finish.
10 bolts, 2-bolt anchor (70')
FA: Richard Wright 2000

24 Wild Card 5.12a ★★★
The best route on this upper right section of the wall. Clip the first bolt with a sling, then power up the ominous face just right of the arête.
9 bolts, 2-bolt anchor (70')
FA: Richard Wright 2000

25 Nickels and Dimes
5.8+ ★★★
This is the first route you encounter when reaching the base of the cliff and features fantastic, near-vertical slab climbing. Climb the slab and ride the layback flake up higher. A thinner variation climbs out left on the face for an extra challenge.
7 bolts, 2-bolt anchor (55')
FA: Richard Wright 2000

Low Wire

 10-15min

 MOST OF THE DAY

 P.M. but all day in winter

8 Routes

≤5.8 5.9 5.10 5.11 5.12 5.13 5.14 proj

Crag Profile: These routes are situated on the lower portion of High Wire, closer to the creek. They provide some challenging and fun climbing in a good setting. *Land of the Lost* (5.11c) and *Fly Low* (5.12a) offer long and sustained climbing with multiple cruxes, while *Badgersaurus* (5.12a) and *Pound Town* (5.12b) climb more like boulder problems. It gets almost as much sun as High Wire does, but the crag is lower in the canyon so it remains more shaded.

Approach: The best way to get to Low Wire is to use the High Wire approach (p62), then take a left and hike downhill to the right at *Via Comatose Amigo* (p64). You should see the wall after about 100 feet of scrambling downhill to the right. The rightmost route and the first bolted line you will see is *Badgersaurus*. To access *Land of the Lost* and other routes that are on the lower tier, rappel or scramble down the slab to the left of *Vagini* using a two-bolt anchor. You can also lower down from the anchor of *Fly High* and then climb *Fly Low* to get out of there.

Note: There are three bolted lines on the main lower tier of the wall. *Land of the Lost* climbs straight up from the bottom of the slab, *Fly Low* scrambles up the slab before taking on the steep wall above, and *The Grizz* is to the left of both routes in the cave.

❶ The Grizz 5.13b ★★★★

Fight through thuggy climbing up the steepest part of the cave. Pull a hard boulder problem at the start to a nice rest at the base of the roof. Bouldery movement takes you through a heinous crux up and right before gaining the jugs at the lip. *6 bolts, 2-bolt anchor (50')*
FA: Kevin Capps 2013

❷ Land of the Lost
5.11c ★★

Interesting and varied climbing. Start at the bottom of the slab and climb straight up, pulling past a ball-busting mantel move over the first roof. Some tough face moves bring you to a second and slightly easier mantel over a bulge to gain easier terrain for a few bolts while moving up and right. Balance and crimp through the tricky slab moves that guard the anchor. *10 bolts, 2-bolt anchor (90')*
FA: Kevin Capps 2013

❷ₐ Lost Trad Variation
5.11b ★

After manteling the second roof, continue straight up instead of following the bolt line up and right. Thin to hand-sized gear is available as you climb the crack to the left of the slab. *6 bolts, rack to #1 Camalot, 2-bolt anchor (90')*

Low Wire Overview

❸ Fly Low 5.12a ★★★★

Excellent! Clip a sling on the first bolt of *Land of the Lost*, then climb up the slab to the right to get to the start of the route. Some 5.11- climbing brings you to a finger-shredding crimp crux that leads to a small shake before pulling a funky move with a lefthand sidepull undercling to get to the easier and fun climbing above. *10 bolts, 2-bolt anchor (100')*
FA: Kevin Capps 2013

Note: The next three routes are easily accessed on the upper tier.

4 Fly High 5.9 ★★
This fun moderate for the wall is a higher variation start to *Fly Low* that allows you to start the route while staying on the higher ledge. Start just left of *Vagini* and meet up with *Fly Low* at the fourth bolt.
7 bolts, 2-bolt anchor (45')
FA: Kevin Capps 2013

5 Vagini 5.10c ★★★
Climb up the crack in the slab to get to a juggy traverse out right under the roof. Pull a short-lived crux over the roof to easier climbing above.
7 bolts, 2-bolt anchor (65')
FA: Kevin Capps 2013

5a Vagini Direct 5.11d ★★★
Start up the slab and bust a long reach to a crimp rail over the roof, then mantel over to get to better holds. The powerful roof moves are easy for the grade if you're tall.
6 bolts, 2-bolt anchor (65')
FA: Kevin Capps 2013

6 Badgersaurus
5.12a ★★★★
Short and sweet! The rightmost bolted line climbs up the steep face. Begin on jugs, then pull a thin crux and crimp your way to the top.
5 bolts, 2-bolt anchor (40')
FA: Kevin Capps 2013

Note: The last two routes are found down to the right of *Land of the Lost* towards the creek. It is a short, overhanging wall with two bouldery routes.

7 Groove Town 5.12a ★★
Short, but fun. A powerful start brings you to good clipping holds for the second bolt. Pull a few tough moves in the groove to get to the easier climbing above. The start will feel hard for the grade if you're short, but easy if you're over 6 feet tall. It's the leftmost of the two routes down by the creek. *4 bolts, 2-bolt anchor (35')*
FA: Kevin Capps 2013

8 Pound Town 5.12b ★★
Stickclip the first bolt and make a committing move off large underclings to a seam and a good hold; join *Groove Town* at bolt three. There is also a fun variation that joins *Groove Town* by traversing left at the first bolt. *4 bolts, 2-bolt anchor (35')*
FA: Kevin Capps 2013

Low Wire Approach

Scott Clark on *Groove Town*, 5.12a, previous page. Kevin Capps

Wall of Justice

15min

A.M. PARTIAL   P.M.

16 Routes

≤5.8 5.9 5.10 5.11 5.12 5.13 5.14 proj

Crag Profile: If you're looking for some overhanging Clear Creek climbing, this is your wall! Starting high on a steep cliff, this wall offers great exposure with some classic overhanging climbs, including *The Great Escape* (5.12b). Always be careful here because of the walls position on the hillside. It is recommended to anchor in to the fixed lines when traversing, or belaying on a center route like *Miss Trial*. When the sun is high in the sky you may not be able to see when doing some of the lip encounter moves, but this crag is otherwise very sheltered from the sun with its massive overhangs.

This is the parking area for every crag in this chapter except for Point Break.

Approach: To get here, use the High Wire approach (p62) and walk past High Wire about 20 yards to the left of *Pony Up* (p62) to find a trail that leads downhill almost to the side of the cliff. The steep wall should come into your vision down and to the right. There is a fixed rope used by belayers and for getting to the different routes at the base of *Officer Friendly*.

1 Perjury 5.10d ★
This is the leftmost bolted route. Climb the moderate face to the left of the crack and bolt line to a big ledge before the overhanging final moves. A good warm up for the wall.
6 bolts, 2-bolt anchor (40')
FA: Alan Nelson 1999

2 Testify 5.12c ★★
Jam to the roof crux towards the top. This will feel hard for the grade if your jamming and finger lock techniques are a little rusty.
6 bolts, 2-bolt anchor (40')
FA: Alan Nelson

3 Finger Prince 5.13a ★★
This short, stout route shoots up the thin and powerful crack on the left side of the wall.
6 bolts, 2-bolt anchor (40')
FA: Alan Nelson

4 Justify 5.12b ★★
A hard start getting past the second bolt brings you to some good holds followed by a couple more strenuous moves to reach a ledge rest. Leaving the rest can be awkward, but bigger holds will reward you once you mantel over the roof.
7 bolts, 2-bolt anchor (40')
FA: Alan Nelson 1992

5 Judgment Day 5.11d ★★
This route has three distinct cruxes sandwiched between two rests. It climbs up and left of the small bulge above the third bolt.
5 bolts, 2-bolt anchor (40')
FA: Alan Nelson 1994

6 Hanging Judge 5.11b ★★★
Climb the first two bolts of *The Great Escape*, then head up and left on positive holds. Fun climbing!
5 bolts, 2-bolt anchor (45')
FA: Alan Nelson 1994

7 The Great Escape 5.12c ★★★★
A classic for the canyon! This is quintessential Clear Creek jug hauling on overhanging to horizontal rock. This route is full on after the third bolt, with a small crux leading to big plate jugs in the roof and a final redpoint crux pulling over the roof. Fixed chains in the roof make cleaning easy. *8 bolts, 2-bolt anchor (55')*
FA: Mark Rolofson, Alan Nelson 1994

8 Criminal Mischief 5.12a ★★
Thuggy jamming leads to a challenging mantel before the anchor.
6 bolts, 2-bolt anchor (50')
FA: Alan Nelson, Richard Wright 1992

9 Miss Trial 5.11d ★★
Do you undercling or crimp traverse? However you climb it, it's fun and eases off towards the end with big holds. *6 bolts, 2-bolt anchor (45')*
FA: Alan Nelson 1992

10 Slammer 5.12b ★★★★
Fun and sustained climbing with a little crux pulling onto the face leads to one last challenge below the anchor. Slings before the roof can help eliminate rope drag.
8 bolts, 2-bolt anchor (50')
FA: Alan Nelson, Dana Wright 1994

11 Child's Play project
A potential 5.14 project starts on *Speed Trap*, then busts out left via the steep roof. A few powerful and dynamic moves get you past the roof.
5 bolts, 2-bolt anchor (40')
Equipper: Luke Childers 2009

12 Speed Trap 5.12a ★★
A more challenging start to *Officer Friendly* adds a pump factor on the last hard moves. Share the last bolt with *Officer Friendly*.
6 bolts, 2-bolt anchor (40')
FA: Alan Nelson

fixed line

Wall of Justice

13 Officer Friendly

5.11c ★★★

This fun and popular overhanging jug haul with big moves is possible for short people too! This is the first super overhanging route you will see when approaching Wall of Justice. **6 bolts, 2-bolt anchor (40′)**
FA: Alan Nelson

14 L.A. Law 5.10b ★

Negotiate a funky mantel to get past the first bolt and enjoy easier climbing until pulling the bulge towards the top. **4 bolts, 2-bolt anchor (35′)**
FA: Alan Nelson

15 Lawsuit 5.10b ★

This is the rightmost bolted line. Moderate climbing brings you to a roof with a couple of reachy moves. **4 bolts, 2-bolt anchor (35′)**
FA: Alan Nelson

16 Countersuit 5.9 TR ★

This toprope climbs the face to the right of *Lawsuit*, utilizing that route's anchor. **(30′)**

Wall of Justice Right

Stella Noble, age 9, proves she's up for *The Great Escape*, 5.12b, Wall of Justice, p68. 📷 Walter Workman

Left Wire

 15min

 MOST OF THE DAY

 Late Afternoon

17 Routes

≤5.8 5.9 5.10 5.11 5.12 5.13 5.14 proj

Crag Profile: When you're looking to get away from the road noise or even the heavy crowds at High Wire, head south to Left Wire where you will oftentimes enjoy quiet seclusion and even a climb or two. Fun routes here include *Prevade* (5.10c), *Night Stick* (5.11b), and *Totality of Facts* (5.12a). This wall faces southeast and gets enjoyable winter sun.

Approach: Located on the east side of Tunnel 2 just south of High Wire, drive 6.0 miles up the canyon and park at a long, narrow pullout on the north (right) side of the road. Do not park on the south side of the road, there has been a history of cars being smashed by loose blocks, and you may also be ticketed. After parking, walk towards the tunnel, cross to the south side of the road and take the steep trail up a few feet of third class terrain before gaining a smoother approach trail that leads to the base of High Wire. Continue past *Pony Up* (p62) and take the higher trail south for about 100 yards before getting to the right side of Left Wire.

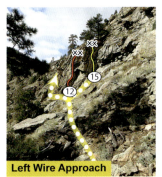

Left Wire Approach

Left Wire - left side

1 Ghetto Curb 5.13a
Start in a left-facing corner and crack that leads to an improbable (maybe impossible?) move out right through thin, crumbly pegmatite that guards a solid hold just right of the first bolt (stickclip it). From here, 5.12- climbing takes you up the seam to a crumbly finish. Not recommended.
6 bolts, 2-bolt anchor (40')
FA: Luke Childers 2000

2 Indifference 5.12d
Climb the bolt line to the left of the crack. Underclings by the second bolt start a difficult (but short) sequence to easier climbing past the fourth bolt on not-so-great rock quality. *5 bolts, 2-bolt anchor (35')*
FA: Luke Childers 2000

3 Jam it In 5.9+
Jam the offwidth and finish on *Indifference*'s anchors to the left. It's a bit crumbly and not worth the effort, but if you do, avoid continuing up the second half of the crack due to poor rock quality. *Rack to a couple #4 Camalots, 2-bolt anchor (35')*
FA: Kevin Capps 2012

4 Totality of Facts 5.12a ★★
Scramble up the slab and ledges to the base of a large, rounded roof. A short, but burly sequence brings you up and left for an easier and slightly runout finish.
5 bolts, 2-bolt anchor (50')
FA: Luke Childers 2000

5 Man on a Wire 5.9+ ★★
A crux sequence pulling past the second bolt leads to fun climbing with a layback flake and some good stemming up higher.
6 bolts, 2-bolt anchor (40')
FA: Kevin Capps 2013

6 Renounce Action 5.10d ★
Find some pegmatite face climbing just around the corner to the left of *Addicts* with a thin, technical crux down low. Holds have broken over the years making this rig harder than its original grade of 5.9+.
7 bolts, 2-bolt anchor (40')
FA: John Morgan 2000

7 Addicts 5.10a ★★
A fun mixed line. Balance your way up the moderate slab to a steep right-facing dihedral. Jam your way through this section and exit onto a slab and an easier finish. *5 bolts, 0.5 - #2, (2)#1 Camalots, 2-bolt anchor (60')*
FA: John Morgan 2000

Man on a Wire

8 No Fruit 5.10a ★★

Bust through a small roof at the start to gain the slab left of the corner. At the sixth bolt, step to the right to keep it 5.10a, or go left for a harder 10+ variation.
7 bolts, 2-bolt anchor (45')
FA: John Morgan 2000

9 Trad Intent 5.7 ★

Start on *Manifest* and then climb the dihedral crack to the left of *Manifest*. Finish at the anchors of *No Fruit* to the left or continue up and right to *Manifest*'s anchor.
Rack to #3 Camalot, 2-bolt anchor (50')
FA: Luke Childers 2000

10 Manifest 5.8 ★★

Begin just left of a cave-like roof on a right-facing flake system. Climb the flake and mantel onto a small bulge (place a medium-sized cam along the way). Continue up the thin slab to the top. *5 bolts, 0.75 Camalot, 2-bolt anchor (50')*   *FA: Luke Childers 2000*

11 Sho' Nuff 5.10a ★★

A long and fun moderate. Climb past the flake system to the right side of the arête above. A few steeper moves around the arête give way to a slab above. *9 bolts, 2-bolt anchor (65')*
FA: Luke Childers 2000

No Fruit

12 Night Stick 5.11b ★★★

A fantastic route with a technical finish. This is the first route you encounter when approaching Left Wire. Start in the large dihedral, and then climb higher around the arête until committing to the steep overhanging face out right.
7 bolts, 2-bolt anchor (60')
FA: Luke Childers 2000

13 Bewildered 5.10b PG13

Start in the wide corner, moving up and right of *Night Stick*. Power through the large roof and continue on easier climbing to the top. Poor rock quality. *Rack to #3 Camalot, belay from a large tree or move left to Night Stick's anchor. (60')*
FA: Luke Childers 2000

14 Awful Width 5.9+

Climb the burly offwidth crack to the left of *Prevade*. Fight your way through this one on toprope, or bring your big gear and wiggle your way to the top. You can climb to the anchors up to the right. *Rack #2 – #5 Camalot, 2-bolt anchor (60')*
FA: Leo Paik 2011

15 Prevade 5.10c ★★

The rightmost route is just uphill from *Night Stick*. Fun face climbing leads to a steep, juggy finish with a pump that will sneak up on you at the end as you pull one final hard move to the chains. *7 bolts, 2-bolt anchor (60')*
FA: Luke Childers 2000

Left Wire - right side

Note: These two short, bouldery routes lie above Left Wire. To access them, scramble up the gully to the left of *Ghetto Curb* for about 80 feet, then cut right and walk past a meadow to find this wall on your left, which was originally called the 90 Second Wall. These routes are dirty, don't see a lot of traffic, and are probably not worth the effort unless you're bored.

16 Calculation 5.13b ★   ☐☐
A few face moves get you to a defined, powerful, and slightly dynamic crux between bolts two and three. It feels more like a V8 boulder problem than a route and is a bit crumbly in spots. *3 bolts, 2-bolt anchor (30')*
FA: Luke Childers 2000

17 Formula 45 5.12d ★   ☐☐
The right line is comprised of hard climbing right off the ground with a couple of tough moves in the small corner. Reach a jug by the second bolt and size up the hard, cryptic sequence getting past bolt three.
3 bolts, 2-bolt anchor (30')
FA: Luke Childers 2000

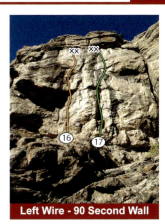

Left Wire - 90 Second Wall

Abbey Smith on *Twitch*, 5.12d, p78.
📷 Keith Ladzinski

Higher Wire

 15min A.M. P.M.

4 Routes

≤5.8 5.9 5.10 5.11 5.12 5.13 5.14 proj

Crag Profile: Nestled in above the *Stone Cold Moderate* area at High Wire (p62), Higher Wire is an okay little crag with one noteworthy climb. *Jack of Hearts* (5.11a) is a fun climb and probably worthy of the extra uphill effort, and *King of Spades* (5.11d) is not bad if you can ignore the crappy rock down low. This wall gets afternoon shade and has wonderful views of the canyon walls. It's a nice little hang out, it just doesn't have the greatest rock quality.

Approach: Located high up in the canyon on the east side of Tunnel 2, drive 6.0 miles up the canyon and park at a long, narrow pullout on the north (right) side of the road. After parking, walk towards the tunnel, cross to the south side of the road and take the steep trail up a few feet of third class terrain before gaining a smoother approach trail to the base of High Wire (p62). To get to Higher Wire, continue left, past High Wire to the left of *Pony Up* (p62) to a ridge with a large pine tree. There will be a faint trail on the right just past the tree that continues up and to the right to the base of the cliff.

Higher Wire Approach

1 Easy Pickens 5.10d
This is leftmost route on the wall. Moderate climbing on rotten rock brings you to a mildly entertaining sequence pulling over the final bulge towards the top.
12 bolts, 2-bolt anchor (90')
FA: Richard Wright 1999

2 King of Spades 5.11d ★
A small overhang at the start leads into some technical laybacking in a seam up and left. Once established in the dihedral, easier climbing takes you to the top. Crumbly rock down low, but kind of fun if you can ignore the rock quality.
8 bolts, 2-bolt anchor (50')
FA: Richard Wright 1999

3 Card Shark 5.12c
A bouldery start pulling through some flexible flakes and a mono leads to more reasonable climbing above for a few more bolts before easing off. Share the last three bolts with *Jack of Hearts*. It's hard for the grade, especially if any more holds break down low.
12 bolts, 2-bolt anchor (75')
FA: Richard Wright 1999

4 Jack of Hearts 5.11a ★★★
This is the best route on the wall! Fun and sustained climbing on decent stone brings you to a rest before tackling the final roof.
9 bolts, 2-bolt anchor (70')
FA: Richard Wright 1999

Higher Wire

Right Wire

10-15min   A.M.   P.M.   ≤5.8 5.9 5.10 5.11 5.12 5.13 5.14 proj   **11 Routes**

Crag Profile: Located on the north side of the road just downstream of Tunnel 2, this area was mostly undeveloped until just a few years ago. Lots of recent development has renewed the energy in this good year-round cliff. Due to its aspect, the wall receives morning sun and afternoon shade all year.

Approach: Located on the east side of Tunnel 2 on the north (right) side of the road, drive 6.0 miles up the canyon and park at a long, narrow pullout on the north side of the road. After parking, walk towards the tunnel; the approach trail will be on the north side of the road. Take the trail up the third class slabs (there is usually a fixed line in place), and then traverse the hillside to the left, towards the cliff.

Tunnel 2

High Wire Right Approach

1 Power Play 5.12b

Twenty-five feet of 5.5 scrambling gains a belay anchor above the roof (gear up to a #3 Camalot can protect this). From the anchor, cruise up the blank, slightly less than vertical slab with a bit of a runout between the first and second bolt (a fall from here would put you on your belayer). Sustained and technical climbing brings you up and right to the anchors on *Hip at the Lip*. The bolts on this route are a bit historic and are in need of replacement. *9 bolts, 2-bolt anchor (115' to the belay anchor, 130' to the base of Hip at the Lip)*
FA: Alan Nelson 1994

2 Hip at the Lip 5.12a ★★

Start in a seam below the roof with a super high first bolt. Pull a technical sequence in the seam to get to a powerful boulder problem getting past the roof, which then gives way to fun, sustained 5.11 climbing on the face above. It is mandatory to stickclip the first bolt, although really, this route could use another bolt below the roof for a lower first bolt. A 70-meter rope will just barely make it to the ground with stretch; be sure and knot your ends.
13 bolts, 2-bolt anchor (130')
FA: Alan Nelson 1994

High Wire Right Overview

3 Ghetto Activity 5.10b ★

This wandering route is the warm up of the cliff, although the crux is leaving the ground. This route takes an odd path on the wall so pay attention and use slings to ease the rope drag.
8 bolts, slings, 2-bolt anchor (40')
FA: Jose Rodriguez 2011

4 Head Up Dirty 5.12c ★★★

Fun, overhanging face climbing leads to a wild one move wonder of a roof; make sure to have your dyno skills sharpened! If you're tall, this route will feel easier.
9 bolts, 2-bolt anchor (40')
FA: Matt Lloyd 2011

5 Idiot Roof 5.11b

Climb the right-facing dihedral just left of the *Machine Gun Funk* start to the much larger left-facing corner, clipping the first few bolts on that route. Climb up through dirty, steep rock, but don't get suckered into climbing into the roof (ignore the bolt which belongs to another unfinished climb). Continue straight up higher than you think you should and eventually reach the anchor of *Machine Gun Funk*. **Standard rack (60')**
FA: Kurt Smith 1990

6 Everyday Struggle
5.10c ★

A second pitch can be added to *Idiot Roof* or *Machine Gun Funk*. Climb up and right on fun, engaging terrain. Rap to the ground with a 70-meter rope from the anchors.
7 bolts, 2-bolt anchor (50')
FA: Matt Lloyd 2012

7 Machine Gun Funk
5.13a ★★★★

This is maybe one of the cooler routes you will do in Clear Creek. Climb the juggy 5.11 overhang through some small, stepped roofs to the base of the giant roof. (stopping here is a great climb by itself). Make sure to use some long draws at the base of the roof and bust out the bouldery crux, using heel hooks and other trickery. Once you gain the lip, climb the easy, runout finish to anchors and the start of *Everyday Struggle*. **11 bolts, 2-bolt anchors (75')**
FA: Matt Lloyd 2012

8 Indirect Savant 5.12c ★★

A difficult start on the vertical slab guards the beginning of this better-than-expected route. The two routes to the right share this anchor.
7 bolts, 2-bolt anchor (50')
FA: Kurt Smith 1990

9 Idiot Savant 5.11d ★★

A very enjoyable climb with fun, varied climbing busts out the roof on good holds and works up and right to the chains. *6 bolts, 2-bolt anchor (50')*
FA: Kurt Smith 1990

10 Notorious 5.12d ★

A bit of a squeeze job, this route is rather odd but surprisingly fun. Climb the hard, reachy start just three feet right of *Idiot Savant*. Begin with a powerful mantel and finish with a sweet throw. Share anchors with *Idiot Savant*. *6 bolts, 2-bolt anchor (50')*
FA: Matt Lloyd 2013

11 Life After Death 5.13c ★★

This route can be summed up as 50 feet of so/so, easy climbing on poor rock to a wonderfully challenging, technical eight-move boulder problem just below the roof. First bolted years ago, this project was abandoned until only recently. It's good, but not great.
12 bolts, 2-bolt anchor (80')
FA: Matt Lloyd 2013

Matt Lloyd believes in
Life After Death, 5.13c 📷 Keith North

Twitch Rock

5-10min P.M. A.M.

6 Routes

≤5.8 5.9 5.10 5.11 5.12 5.13 5.14 proj

Crag Profile: The reason you come to Twitch Rock is for the beast itself, *Twitch* (5.12d). There is now a nice little warm up here so this wall can be a one-stop shop. With morning shade, it makes for sending temps late into the summer months.

Approach: Located on the east side of Tunnel 2 on the north side of the road, drive 6.0 miles up the canyon and park at a long, narrow pullout on the north (right) side of the road. After parking, walk towards the tunnel; the approach trail will be on the north side of the road. Take this trail east/downhill for a few hundred feet until taking a short trail uphill to reach the base of the cliff that is slightly hidden by a tree.

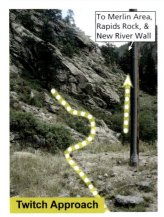

To Merlin Area, Rapids Rock, & New River Wall

Twitch Approach

1 Stone Cold KiLLaz
5.12b ★★
This is a fun new addition to the Twitch area. It climbs through a bouldery slab mantel at about mid-height that leads to a roof pull and jams through the parallel crack system at the top. Do not belay from directly below the route as there are still a few suspect blocks in the initial roof pull. *8 bolts, 2-bolt anchor (65')*
FA: Kevin and Laura Capps, Laura Wilson 05/14

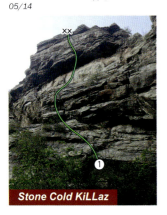

Stone Cold KiLLaz

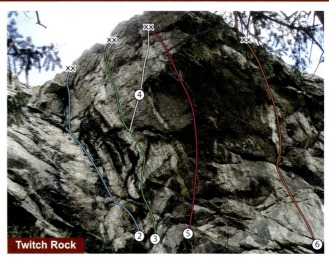

Twitch Rock

2 G'Owen Rogue 5.9+ ★★
This interesting warm up pitch is harder than it looks. Stem up the corner that goes up and left of *Twitch* – it's a bit awkward clipping the anchors. *5 bolts, 2-bolt anchor (50')*
FA: Jason Baker, Luke Childers 2010

3 Twitch 5.12d ★★★★
One of the best 5.12ds in the canyon! Powerful climbing leads to some thin holds and a deadpoint move that takes you through the crux sequence. *5 bolts, 2-bolt anchor (45')*
FA: Pete Zoller 1991

4 Twitch Variation project
A project (5.13+?) starts on *Twitch* and traverses right after the third bolt via an improbable sequence leading to the prow.
5 bolts, 2-bolt anchor (40')

5 Prowler 5.14a ★★★
Power your way up the steepest part of the wall on the prow. This was a project for many years before Mark was introduced to it.
6 bolts, 2-bolt anchor (40')
FA: Mark Anderson 2014
Equipper: Jason Baker 2010

6 Choss Roof 5.11d
Find the rightmost route on the wall. A high first bolt leads to steep climbing on death blocks to get to the top. Not recommended.
4 bolts, 2-bolt anchor (45')

Juan Rodriguez on *Machine Gun Funk 5.13a*, High Wire Right, p76. 📷 Keith North

Merlin Area

 10-15min

 A.M.

 P.M.

2 Routes

≤5.8	5.9	5.10	5.11	5.12	5.13	5.14	proj

Crag Profile: This little wall is nestled down by the creek just west of New River Wall. The route *Merlin* (5.11d) is commonly used as a warm up for those going to try the classic *Sonic Youth* (p83), or something harder. However, this wall now has a bouldery test piece of its own, *Dragonslayer* (5.12d), which is worth the effort.

Approach: Approach: Drive 6.0 miles up the canyon and park on the north (right) side of the road. The first wall on the north side of the creek you will see is New River Wall (p82); the next wall west is Merlin Area. After parking, walk towards the tunnel; the approach trail will be on the north side of the road. Take the trail east/downstream past Twitch Rock (p78) and take a trail down a gully to gain the base of the wall.

1 Merlin 5.11d ★★
Climb the crack on the left side of the wall. Big holds lead to a tricky, insecure crux in the crack halfway up.
4 bolts, 2-bolt anchor (45')
FA: Alan Nelson, Richard Wright 1993

2 Dragonslayer 5.12d ★★
A hard, thin boulder problem near the ground leads to much easier climbing above. Wait for cold temps for this one as it's kind of a one-move wonder that is hard for the grade.
4 bolts, 2-bolt anchor (40')
FA: Jason Baker 2008

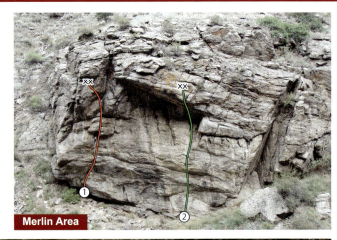

Merlin Area

Bethany Lukens on *The Eddy*, p81, Rapids Rock. Matt Lloyd

Rapids Rock

 5-10min

 A.M.   P.M.

3 Routes

≤5.8 5.9 5.10 5.11 5.12 5.13 5.14 proj

Crag Profile: This wall offers a fun little adventure by the creek if you're looking for something new. On the left side of the wall, there's a 5.9 that is pretty fun for someone looking for a moderate. The two routes to the right offer plenty of challenge with not only the climbing itself, but also rope maintenance and accessibility.

Approach: Drive 6.0 miles up the canyon and park on the north (right) side of the road. The first wall on the north side of the creek you will see is New River Wall (next page). The next wall west is Merlin Area (previous page) and then you will see Rapids Rock. After parking, walk towards the tunnel; the approach trail will be on the north side of the road. Take the trail east/downstream past Twitch Rock (p78) and you will find anchor bolts on the top of a creek side cliff. It is best to rappel or lower to *The Eddy*. For the other two routes, hike around the east side of the cliff to access the fixed line.

1 The Eddy 5.9 ★★

A fun but seldom climbed route. From the top anchors, you can rappel or lower to the anchor at the base of the route on the far left side of the wall. Easy climbing up the slab brings you to a steep section with a few fun moves towards the top of the wall.
4 bolts, 2-bolt anchor (40')

Note: The next two routes are best approached via a fixed line at the lower righthand side of the wall. *B.F.F.F.* starts on the far left side of the fixed line and Fleshwound is to the right.

2 B.F.F.F. 5.12c ★★★

Excellent climbing on good stone. Two stout, overhanging boulder problems are separated by a good rest.
7 bolts, 2-bolt anchor (45')
FA: Jason Baker 2008

3 Fleshwound 5.11d ★

Climb up the featured, overhanging wall on the right side of the fixed line using a variety of underclings, jugs, and crimps. A low crux gives way to some fun climbing and one more tough sequence before going over to the slab at the top.
6 bolts, 2-bolt anchor (45')
FA: Jason Baker 2008

Rapids Rock

New River Wall

 10-15min

 A.M.   P.M.

9 Routes

≤5.8 5.9 5.10 5.11 5.12 5.13 5.14 proj

Crag Profile: You like steep hard sport climbing? Well this is the spot for you! This cliff hosts the ultra-classic *Sonic Youth* (5.13a) and *Public Enemy* (5.13c), as well as a menagerie of link ups to keep you busy all year long. As a bit of a side note, this wall hosts many, many link ups, the best and least contrived link ups are listed, but many more can be found.

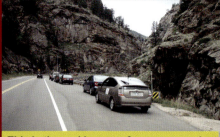

This is the parking area for every crag in this chapter except for Point Break.

Approach: Drive 6.0 miles up the canyon and park on the north (right) side of the road. Look across the creek to find the ominous looking New River Wall. After parking, walk towards the tunnel; the approach trail will be on the north side of the road. Take the trail east/downstream past Twitch Rock (p78) and take a trail down a gully, passing by the base of Merlin Area (p80) to gain a trail towards the creek. Continue for another couple hundred feet to find yourself uphill to the left of the wall where there is a fixed rope in place to get to the base of the cliff. During low water, you can approach it from lower down for an easier hike, or even wade across the creek.

❶ Beta Test 5.11c ★
Climb up the steep, vertical face on the left side of the wall. It has a challenging crux and is a bit runout at times. *4 bolts, 2-bolt anchor (60')*
FA: Alan Nelson 1990

❶a Master Beta 5.12a ★
A hard extension to *Beta Test* climbs through the roof and mantels over onto the slab above. *7 bolts, 2-bolt anchor (75')*
FA: Alan Nelson 1994

❷ Fountain of Youth 5.13d ★★★
Start on *Sonic Youth*, and then pull out left onto the blunt arête. The line is magnificent and the climbing is classic. *9 bolts, 2-bolt anchor (70')*
FA: Daniel Woods 2006

New River Wall

❸ Sonic Youth 5.13a ★★★★ 　☐☐

Classic! An overhanging and thuggy start gets you established in the overhanging dihedral. With some stemming, cop a quick rest, then take on the technical and powerful finish through the small roof. This used to be soft for the grade, and then a hold broke in the crux, making it the benchmark for 13a in the canyon. *9 bolts, 3-bolt anchor (70')*
FA: Kurt Smith, Mike Pont 1990

❹ Sweet Inspirations

5.13c ★★★ 　　　　☐☐

Climb *Sonic Youth* to the rest below the roof (just before the final crux). Shake out then bust right to the arête and around the corner to a fantastic bouldery crux. Finish up the heart-breaker enduro culmination of *Public Enemy/Love Your Enemies*. This is perhaps the best of the links ups. *12 bolts (70')*

❺ Positive Vibrations

5.14b ★★★ 　　　　☐☐

A hardman's link-up starts on *Sonic Youth*, then busts up and right through the roof to gain a decent hold. From here, climb through another hard crux and finish on *Public Enemy*. *10 bolts (70')*
FA: Brian Kimball 2011

❻ Kinky Reggae 5.14a ★★★ 　☐☐

Climb up as for *Public Enemy*, but instead of busting into the pocket crux, climb straight left for 20 feet on slopey angled jugs. Get a good jug and shake out to get ready for a crazy set of crosses from dilled pocket to drilled pocket then into a small crimp at the base of the roof on the arête. From here climb left and finish through the crux of *Sonic Youth* and its anchors, or for a bump in grade try and climb back right to the finish of *Public Enemy*. While it's a link-up, it's still fun as hell.
9 bolts, 2-bolt anchors. (80')
FA: Brian Kimball

❼ Public Enemy 5.13c ★★★★ ☐☐

If you're looking for one of the best 5.13s in the canyon, this is it. This route has an interesting background – it was drilled and manufactured, and even hosted some bolt-on holds in the '90s. After the initial controversy, the route was forgotten about until Brian Kimball came along and cleaned it up, filled in some of the drilled pockets (one still remains, but the route can be climbed without it, although it's much harder), and hung fixed draws. Locate this route by climbing up the slab and quickly entering the steep roof below *Love Your Enemies*. Climb up the crimpy start until you get to the large throw to a drilled three-finger pocket. Campus and crank to the chains. *8 bolts (70')*
FA in current form: Brian Kimball 2011

❽ Love Your Enemies

5.12a ★★★ 　　　　☐☐

The warm up for the cliff climbs the slab on the right side of the wall. From the third bolt, grab the awesome jugs on the steep wall to your left and begin climbing up and left over spectacular stone to a boulder problem going to the finishing jug below the large roof. *7 bolts (70')*
FA: Brian Kimball 2011

❾ Enjoy Your Youth

5.13c ★★ 　　　　　☐☐

Climb *Love Your Enemies* to the horizontal seam and then traverse all the way left to finish on *Sonic Youth*. Being taller helps on the extremely boulder crux due to a good low foothold. *12 bolts, 2-bolt anchor (80')*
FA: Brian Kimball 2011

Matt Lloyd finds *Sweet Inspirations*, 5.13c, at the New River Wall.
📷 Celin Serbo

Highlander

 20min

 ALL DAY

 ≤5.8 5.9 5.10 5.11 5.12 5.13 5.14 proj

34 Routes

Crag Profile: Situated high in the canyon north of Tunnel 2, Highlander is a great place to come for some sun and exposure. This wall has a wide variety of classic climbs to keep all skill levels satisfied, even in the winter. *Get a Job* (5.11b), *Blue Sky Mining* (5.11d), and *Peer Review* (5.12b) are all worthy of the hike uphill. With so many tall, classic routes up at Highlander, it is a destination for the winter months. The wall faces south and gets warm temperatures all winter long.

This is the parking area for every crag in this chapter except for Point Break.

Approach: Situated high on the hillside just east of Tunnel 2, drive 6.0 miles up the canyon and park at a long, narrow pullout on the north (right) side of the road. After parking, walk towards the tunnel to find the approach trail on the north side of the road. Take this trail back east, going downhill past Twitch Rock (p78). The easiest path up the slabs is usually marked by a cairn, which will take you up and eventually move left towards the cliff.

Highlander Approach

1 Tarzan 5.12c ★
The leftmost route on the wall features painful and unpleasant hand jams out the roof.
7 bolts, 2-bolt anchor (50')
FA: Alan Nelson 1996

2 Leap of Faith 5.12d ★★
One of the better routes on this side of the wall tackles hard climbing up higher, which gets harder and harder until you clip the anchor. It climbs longer than it looks.
8 bolts, 2-bolt anchor (50')
FA: Alan Nelson 1996

3 Microchip 5.13a ★★
This height-dependent route has one wild move... with a microchip. Climb the easier terrain to a long, hard reach to a tiny crimp and finish out the roof. *7 bolts, 2-bolt anchor (50')*
FA: Derek Peavey 2013;
Equipped by Alan Nelson

4 Red Tag Hag 5.13a ★
A crux traverse out left awaits you once you pull onto the upper headwall and bouldery climbing with a hard clip gets you to the anchor. This was once 5.12d, but then a hold broke and it doesn't get climbed much anymore.
8 bolts, 2-bolt anchor (50')
FA: Derek Peavey 2011 (before hold broke)

5 Wind Machine 5.11d ★★
The easy slab climbing brings you to steep and juggy climbing. This fun but short route has a crux going to the anchor. *6 bolts, 2-bolt anchor (50')*
FA: Alan Nelson 1996

6 Highlander 5.10d ★
A hard pull to get past the roof by the first bolt brings you to easier terrain until the upper wall. Clip a high fourth bolt off the ledge, and then initiate a crunchy layback on good holds leading up to the overhanging wall above. *5 bolts, 2-bolt anchor (50')*
FA: Alan Nelson 1995

7 Stiff Upper Lip 5.12a ★★
This route is characterized by thuggy and gymnastic roof climbing on positive holds and jugs. Pull past the first roof and mantel over for a decent rest before conquering the powerful crux moves going to the anchor. It would have three stars if the rock quality were a bit better.
8 bolts, slings, 2-bolt anchor (65')
FA: Alan Nelson 1996

8 Get a Life 5.7 ★
P1: 5.7 Start up the broken dihedral on easy terrain and climb through a corner to get to a belay anchor. *Rack to #2 Camalot, 2-bolt anchor (70')*
P2: 5.7 Climb up and to the left past some ledges and continue up the corner above. *Rack to #2 Camalot, 2-bolt anchor (70')*
FA: Alan Nelson 1997

9 Get Insurance 5.10a ★
Climb the first pitch of *Get a Life* to the belay anchor. From here, continue up and right along the crack and corner system. *Rack to #2 Camalot, 2-bolt anchor (140')*
FA: Alan Nelson 1997

10 Get a Job 5.11b ★★
A long and fun route climbs the face to the left of *Job Review* and pulls around a roof to get to a thin and technical sequence above.
13 bolts, 2-bolt anchor (135')
FA: Alan Nelson 1997

Highlander - left side overview

11 **Job Review** 5.11a ★★
This is the first route to the left of the *Peer Pressure* ledge. A challenging pull around a roof about a third of the way up will test your abilities. A few more tough moves moving through the face up higher bring you to the top of the wall.
13 bolts, 2-bolt anchor (135')
FA: R. Wright, Thomas McFarlane 1995

12 **Peer Review** 5.12b ★★★★
One of the best 12bs in the canyon! Sustained climbing up the crack on the first half brings you up and right to a decent rest before pulling some thin and techy moves in the seam.
9 bolts, 2-bolt anchor (75')
FA: Alan Nelson, Richard Wright 1997

13 **Peer Pressure** 5.12a ★★★
Climb the crack on *Peer Review* and then bust left around the corner to a shallow right-facing dihedral with some smeary feet and technical movement. Sustained climbing brings you up and left to a small roof before continuing up to the anchor.
13 bolts, 2-bolt anchor (100')
FA: Richard Wright, Alan Nelson 1995

Highlander - left side

Highlander - mid-left overview

14 Peer 42 5.13a ★★★★

This is a fantastic extension to *Peer Review*. After clipping the anchors, cop a quick rest before heading up and left through a bouldery crux slapping up the arête with great position on the upper roofs. Bring slings to reduce drag.
16 bolts, slings, 2-bolt anchor (100')
FA: Mark Felty, Tod Anderson 2002

14a Peer Project

From the *Peer Review* anchor, continue up and right of the anchor. Finish on *Peer 42*. This will probably go around 5.13.

15 Gear Head 5.10a ★

Climb the crack in the dihedral to the right of *Peer Review*. A bolt protects the climbing towards the top. Share anchors with *Air Head*.
1 bolt, rack to #1 Camalot (75')
FA: Alan Nelson 1996

16 Air Head 5.9 ★★

Climb the steep and juggy face up the right side of the arête. Belay from the ledge on the right side.
7 bolts, 2-bolt anchor (75')
FA: Alan Nelson 1995

17 Herb-a-Med-a-Veg-a-Matic 5.11c ★★★

Hard and technical movement in the large right-facing dihedral on the top half of this route makes you use all of your stemming trickery to send this one. It's a little runout between bolts two and three.
10 bolts, 2-bolt anchor (103')
FA: Alan Nelson 1998

18 Neo-Quasi Bugaloo 5.10b ★★★

Low-angled terrain brings you to a thin and technical sequence before a short, right-facing corner bulge. Once you pull over the bulge, only a few more tricky face moves separate you from the anchor.
12 bolts, 2-bolt anchor (105')
FA: Alan Nelson, Richard Wright 1995

19 Learning to Crawl 5.10a ★★

Sustained moderate climbing with some tricky sequences brings you past a short left-facing dihedral. Finish on easier slab climbing above.
11 bolts, 2-bolt anchor (95')
FA: Alan Nelson, Richard Wright 1995

20 Blue Sky Mining 5.11d ★★★

Hard face moves bring you past the initial crux to a slab above that lets you cop a quick rest before entering the harder moves through the small roof. Long moves get you past the first bulge, and then a hard mantel deposits you onto easier climbing above. *11 bolts, 2-bolt anchor (90')*
FA: Alan Nelson 1995

21 Burning Chrome 5.11c ★★

A few tough moves on the first half lead to a ledge where you can scope out the upper headwall. Crimp straight up and a little to the left for a fun finish; don't get suckered out to the right. *9 bolts, 2-bolt anchor (80')*
FA: Alan Nelson 1996

22 Job Security 5.11c ★★

This fun long route has an intermediate anchor if you want to break it up into two pitches. Stem through a right-facing dihedral to gain some technical movement on the steep upper wall and a final hard sequence pulling over the overhang at the top. *First Anchor: 5.11a, 5 bolts (55'); Second Anchor: 13 bolts, slings (100')*
FA: Richard Wright 1995

Kevin Meurer enjoys a little *Peer Review*, 5.12b, p85. Kevin Capps

Highlander - *Peer Review* area

23 Not One of Us
5.12a ★★★★

An excellent and tall sport route finishes on a steep, exposed headwall. It can be done as one long pitch with slings but is better split up into three short pitches due to rope drag.

P1: 5.11b This tricky little pitch requires some technique to get to the belay that is shared with *Resume*.
6 bolts, 2-bolt anchor (50')

P2: 5.11d Continue up to the steep face on the right side of the arête via excellent and sustained movement.
7 bolts, 3-bolt anchor (55')

P3: 5.12a Start from the three-bolt anchor or move up to the belay bolt on the ledge. A hard move at the start leads to the base of the roof and the steep headwall above. Fight the pump and enjoy the exposure.
7 bolts, 2-bolt anchor (60')
FA: Richard Wright, Alan Nelson 1996

24 Resume 5.9 ★

A great warm up for the wall, which is fun and sustained for a 5.9.
5 bolts, 2-bolt anchor (50')
FA: Richard Wright 1995

Highlander - *middle overview*

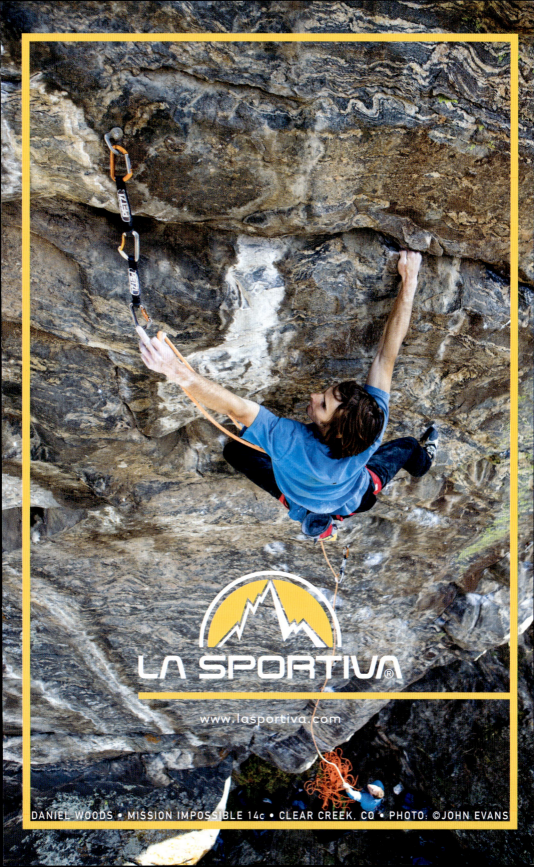

25 The Outsider 5.11d ★★
A hard boulder problem moving over the roof to the right out of the dihedral towards the top. Shares anchors with *Smack that Bitch Up.*
10 bolts, 2-bolt anchor (100')
FA: Richard Wright 1997

26 Smack that Bitch Up 5.11b ★★★
This is the rightmost route on the wall before going around the corner. After clipping a runout second bolt, arrive at a glorious finger crack. Finger lock to the base of a roof and pull a few tough moves to get to better holds.
12 bolts, 2-bolt anchor (100')
FA: Tod Anderson 1997

27 Big Man on Campus 5.12a ★★
This is the first route around the corner to the right of *Smack that Bitch Up.* Multiple thin cruxes on the first half bring you to the upper headwall, which has hard moves going to the anchor up and right.
12 bolts, 2-bolt anchor (100')
FA: Tod Anderson 1997

Note: To get to the next four routes, scramble up the slab to the right of *Big Man on Campus* to get to a nice ledge. The first route you'll see is the trad line *Dirty Slut Crack*.

28 Dirty Slut Crack 5.11b ★
Desperate jamming makes this a fun route if you don't mind choss. Start in a short chimney that brings you to a break before climbing up the flaring finger-to-hand-sized crack on the steep face. When the crack ends, trend up and right towards the *Drop Zone* anchor. All of the gear placements are good, but there is some questionable rock on this route.
Rack doubles to #1, (1) #2 - #3 Camalot, 2-bolt anchor (75')
FA: Kevin Capps 2013

29 Drop Zone 5.10d ★★
The leftmost bolted line on the wall is better than it looks. Easier terrain brings you to some challenging movement in the right-facing corner.
8 bolts, 2-bolt anchor (75')
FA: Alan Nelson 1996

30 The White Whale 5.12d ★★★★
Excellent climbing, with a crux roof sequence at the start, brings you into the steep upper headwall. Traverse out right below the roof for a nice finish. *7 bolts, 2 bolt anchor (70')*
FA: Kevin Capps 2013

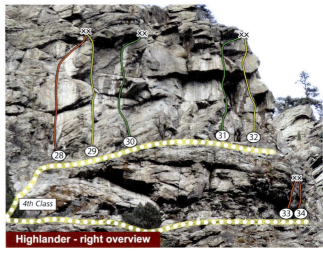

Highlander - right overview

31 Dirt Me 5.12a
A not-so-great route features moderate climbing on crumbly rock. Bust out the roof via a thin hand crack, after which awkward movement brings you up to the right and finishes at *Lord of the Rings'* anchor.
9 bolts, 2-bolt anchor (75')
FA: Alan Nelson 1996

32 Lord of the Rings 5.10b ★★
The rightmost bolted line on the wall features a crux sequence pulling over the short roof.
9 bolts, 2-bolt anchor (75')
FA: Alan Nelson 1996

Amie Bergeson on *Neo-Quasi Bugaloo,* 5.10b, p86. Kevin Capps

Note: The next two are both short, boulder problem-style routes that are located just below *Lord of the Rings.* They are reached by walking around the corner past *Big Man on Campus* and continuing over to the right (instead of scrambling up the slab).

33 Wheezer 5.11d ★
The left of the two routes has fun moves on jugs. Some heel hooking leads to a tougher sequence going to the anchor shared with *Geezer.*
3 bolts, 2-bolt anchor (25')
FA: Alan Nelson 1996

34 Geezer 5.11b ★
Short, but fun bouldering on overhanging rock. Big moves are the challenge on this one – no pump factor or no beta required.
3 bolts, 2-bolt anchor (25')
FA: Alan Nelson 1996

4

TUNNEL TWO WEST

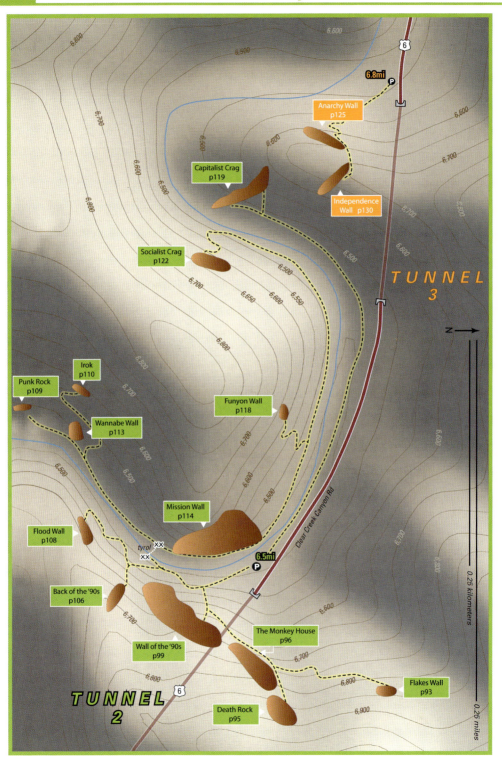

Flakes Wall

20min   P.M.   ≤5.8 5.9 5.10 5.11 5.12 5.13 5.14 proj   **2 Routes**

Crag Profile: Those that venture a little further into the forest will be rewarded with this cool wall. The seclusion is a nice change of pace from standing around at the base of *Reefer Madness* at Wall of the '90s (p99). The rock at this wall is interesting as there are quite a lot of flakes that cover the bullet hard stone. Flexible Flakes is a very intimidating line, and is worthy of the hike up the hill. The is west facing and is sheltered by trees, but receives afternoon sun.

Approach: Use the same approach as for Monkey House (p96) by parking on the west side of Tunnel 2 after driving 6.5 miles up the canyon. Walk past Monkey House and continue uphill to the left for a few hundred feet on a faint trail until finding the wall.

1 Head & Shoulders
5.10b ★★
A bouldery start begins on the left side of the gully and climbs up the slabby face, following a thin seam. You may use the cheater tree to stem off of to downgrade the route to 5.9 and also make the first clip a bit easier. **6 bolts, 2-bolt anchor (70')**
FA: Kevin Capps 2014

2 Flexible Flakes 5.13c ★★
This vertical test piece climbs up the gently overhanging, blank face. As the name suggests, there are some small flakes and crimps that are a bit flexible, but this is still a very fun route and worthy of the effort.
8 bolts, 2-bolt anchor (65')
FA: Kevin Capps 2014

Flakes Wall

STEEL IS REAL

ClimbTech PermaDraws are made with steel carabiners and galvanized aircraft cable for maximum strength & durability.

Clip with Confidence.

www.ClimbTechGear.com

Death Rock

 15min MOST OF THE DAY P.M.

3 Routes

≤5.8 5.9 5.10 5.11 5.12 5.13 5.14 proj

Crag Profile: Death Rock is up and left of Monkey House and holds a few fun routes, including two test pieces: *The Sprawl* (5.12b), and *Homeboy Bananza* (5.12d). Since it's so close to the other walls, head up here for a route or two in the summer for some shade.

Approach: Drive 6.5 miles up canyon and park on the west side of Tunnel 2 on the south (left) side of the road. Use the same approach trail as for Wall of the '90s (p99) then continue uphill to the left, passing the Monkey House (p96) to find Death Rock.

1 Homeboy Bonanza
5.12d ★
Start on the steep face to the left of *The Sprawl*. Sustained face climbing brings you to hard, bouldery moves through a few pockets on the overhanging prow.
9 bolts, 2-bolt anchor (75')
FA: Pete Zoller 1991

2 The Sprawl 5.12b ★★★
A very fine route with steep climbing up a beautiful sustained wall delivers you to a ledge where you can get it all back, and then it's in your face until the chains.
7 bolts, 2-bolt anchor (60')
FA: Pete Zoller, Curt Fry, K. Katon 1991

3 Monkey Shine 5.9+ ★
This route is dirty and it wanders but at least it's long. With that said, it's a decent warm up for the harder routes above.
11 bolts, 2-bolt anchor (95')
FA: Richard Wright 1999

The Sprawl

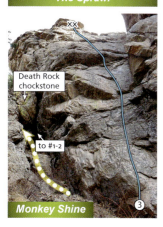
Death Rock chockstone
to #1-2
Monkey Shine

Matt Lloyd embraces *The Sprawl*, 5.12b. Colin Coulson

The Monkey House

10-15min | MOST OF THE DAY | P.M. | **12 Routes**

≤5.8 5.9 5.10 5.11 5.12 5.13 5.14 proj

Crag Profile: The Monkey House is a great alternative to Wall of the '90s if that crag is too busy. It offers classic face climbing on *Convicted Felon* (5.12b) to overhanging thug fests like *Monkey See, Monkey Do* (5.12b). Sitting high in the canyon just uphill and left of Wall of the '90s, some routes on this wall can see sun in the afternoons and routes like *Monkey See, Monkey Do* are sheltered from the sun on a summer day.

Approach: To get here, park on the west side of Tunnel 2 on the south side of the road. Use the same approach trail as Wall of the '90s (p99), but then continue uphill to the left for a few hundred feet to the short overhanging face of *The New Pollution*. Continue uphill for routes like *Convicted Felon* and *Schwing Salute*.

Felicity Muth on *Face Full of Bush*, 5.10d. Matt Lloyd

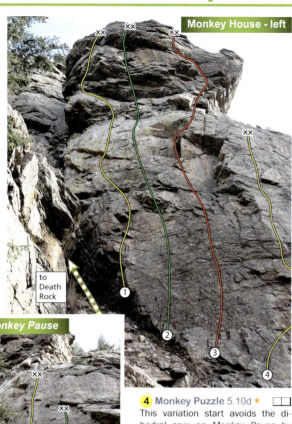

Monkey House - left

to Death Rock

Monkey Pause

1 Face Full of Bush
5.10d ★★★
The leftmost route has fun climbing up and left to jugs in the roof and a crux that guards the chains. *11 bolts, long slings, 2-bolt anchor (100')*
FA: Greg Purnell 1999

2 Monkey Bars 5.12a ★★
Moderate climbing gains a ledge where you can size up the hard bit. A reachy crux right off the ledge leads to fantastic 5.11 jug hauling. *14 bolts, long slings, 2-bolt anchor (95')*
FA: Richard Wright, Nevada Montagu 1999

3 Monkey Business
5.11d ★★
A short slab leads to more moderate climbing to gain the ledge. From here, pumpy, juggy, and well-protected climbing leads to the top. *13 bolts, long slings, 2-bolt anchor (100')*
FA: Richard Wright 1999

4 Monkey Puzzle 5.10d ★
This variation start avoids the dihedral crux on *Monkey Pause* by traversing in from the left for a few quick 5.10 sequences. Bring slings for the first two bolts to reduce rope drag. *5 bolts, 2-bolt anchor (65')*
FA: Alan Nelson, Ken Trout 1991

5 Monkey Pause 5.11d ★★
Start in a short corner, pull a stemming crux, and then exit out onto the face. After establishing yourself, enjoy easier climbing to the top. It's a little runout between bolts two and three. *6 bolts, 2-bolt anchor (65')*
FA: Alan Nelson, Ken Trout 1991

6 Monkey See, Monkey Do
5.12b ★★
A techy and powerful start leads to some decent rests before tackling the thuggy roof moves.
6 bolts, 2-bolt anchor (50')
FA: Alan Nelson, Ken Trout 1991

7 Schwing Salute 5.11c ★★★
Quartz climbing gets you to the fun and technical face, which doesn't let up until the anchor.
6 bolts, 2-bolt anchor (60')
FA: Alan Nelson, Ken Trout 1992

8 Convicted Felon
5.12b ★★★★
Crimpy, sustained, and classic! Steep climbing up and left leads to a super thin sequence near the last couple of bolts. *8 bolts, 2-bolt anchor (75')*

9 Soap on a Rope
5.12c ★★★
An extraordinary variation that's just a little harder and crimpier than its counterpart. Start and finish on *Convicted Felon*, but veer up and right after the fourth bolt for some cryptic crimping. *8 bolts, 2-bolt anchor (75')*
FA: Dave Montgomery 2014

10 Punishment for Shoplifting
5.10d ★★
Stiff moves getting past the first few bolts gains an enjoyable crack system. *7 bolts, 2-bolt anchor (70')*
FA: Ken Trout 1992

11 Psycho Hose Beast
5.11a ★★
This seldom-travelled route is often wet and dirty, but is actually pretty fun if you catch it dry and clean. Easy climbing past a high first bolt leads to a crux sequence through the upper section with some long and powerful moves going over the bulge.
10 bolts, 2-bolt anchor (80')
FA: Ken Trout 1992

Monkey House - right

Abbey Smith had the *Reefer Madness*, 5.11a, p102 long before Colorado's new law. Keith Ladzinski

⑫ The New Pollution
5.12c ★★
Powerful moves through the over-hanging face lead to a pumpy finish. Locate this route about 50 yards up-hill to the left of *Alone Time with My Banana* (at Wall of the '90s, p???). You can belay from the ground or the ledge. **4 bolts, 2-bolt anchor (40')**
FA: Greg Purnell 1999

Wall of the '90s

 10-15min   A.M.   P.M.

32 Routes
≤5.8 5.9 5.10 5.11 5.12 5.13 5.14 proj

Crag Profile: This fantastic and popular wall has just about every type of climbing Clear Creek Canyon can offer. From crimpy face climbing to slopers, overhanging jug hauls with beautiful features to even a few classic crack climbs like *Roadrunner* (5.11a) and *.30-06* (5.12a). This west-facing wall can be easily seen on the west side of Tunnel 2 by looking up and spotting the chalked up holds on *Ten Digit Dialing* (5.12c) and *Reefer Madness* (5.11a). Both classic climbs almost always have someone climbing them. The wall gets shade all morning while most of it gets sun in the afternoon.

Approach: Park on the west side of Tunnel 2 on the south (left) side of the road 6.5 miles up the canyon. The well-established trail exits the parking lot to the east and goes directly towards the main wall.

❶ Alone Time with My Banana 5.6 PG13 ★★
The leftmost route on the wall before hiking uphill to the Monkey House starts 30 feet left of *Leftover Stuff*. Fun climbing through featured rock leads to a steep section around the last bolt. It's a little run out but you will find a bolt where you need one. **6 bolts, 2-bolt anchor (85')**
FA: Mike Cichon 2005

❷ Leftover Stuff 5.10c ★★★
Climb the runout slab to more verti-cal climbing before encountering a thin, balancy sequence towards the top. A 70-meter rope is required, es-pecially if your belayer doesn't want to scramble up the ledges while low-ering. **10 bolts, 2-bolt anchor (110')**
FA: Thor Kieser 2005

❸ Hot Stuff 5.10c ★★★★
The vertical face climbing offers a little bit more of a pump than its neighbor to the left. A 70-meter rope is recommended.
First Anchor: 11 bolts (110');
Second Anchor: 15 bolts (135')
FA: Richard Wright, Alan Nelson 1996

Monkey House — to Death Rock — Wall of the '90s — Back of the '90s — Flood Wall — Tunnel Two (west side) — to tyrol →

The parking area for all of the crags in this chapter

Sarah Watson on *Black and Tan*, 5.13b, p102. Keith Ladzinski

4 **Pretty Woman** 5.10a ★★★ ☐☐
Moderate climbing to a small and juggy roof makes this one of the best routes on this side of the wall.
13 bolts, 2-bolt anchor (90')
FA: Ryan and C. Laird 2008

5 **Hey Good Lookin'** 5.11d ★★★ ☐☐
Climb the slab up and right until reaching a good stance below the steep roof. A tensiony sequence traversing left out the roof leads to a glory jug and more vertical climbing above. *First Anchor: 10 bolts (95');*
Second Anchor: 15 bolts (140')
FA: Alan Nelson 1994

6 **Vixen** 5.10d ★★ ☐☐
A challenging sequence over the bulge after the third bolt leads to fun and easier climbing on great stone.
10 bolts, 2-bolt anchor (70')
FA: Richard Wright 1998

7 **Vixen Extension** project ☐☐
Bust out the large, horizontal roof above *Vixen's* anchor. Underclings and awkward holds lead to a tough sequence moving past the lip. The holds could use a cleaning but will yield a 5.13+ route. Bring long slings to reduce rope drag.
17 bolts, 2-bolt anchor (102')

8 **Y2K** 5.12c ★★★★ ☐☐
Locate the giant, awe-inspiring roof and clip long draws on one of the best routes of its grade in the canyon. Climb some techy and sometimes reachy vert to the all-out hero roof climbing, while enjoying a hard crux high on the route.
18 bolts, 2-bolt anchor (104')
FA: Richard Wright, Tod Anderson 1998

9 **Goin' the Distance** 5.12d ★ ☐☐
Begin 20 feet right of *Y2K* and climb up an easy ramp to the first bolt and immediately into fun 5.11 climbing. Superb roof climbing with a fierce mantel crux will lead you into the last two bolts of *Y2K* and shared anchors. *17 bolts, 2-bolt anchors (104')*
FA: Richard Wright, Rich Magill, P. Murwick 2001

First Set of Anchors: 5.11c ☐☐
Stop at the first set of anchors below the roof.

10 **Sweet Thing** 5.12c ★★ ☐☐
Start on the belay block about 20 feet under the first bolt. Climb easy 5.9 face climbing to a ledge rest where you can scope out the crux. From here, it's just a short boulder problem separating you from easier climbing and the anchor. A 60m rope will just barely make it; knot the end.
13 bolts, slings, 2-bolt anchor (105')
FA: Richard Wright 1998

11 **Recovery** 5.10c ★★ ☐☐
Vertical face climbing leads to a left-facing dihedral and a challenging exit move pulling out of the corner.
10 bolts, 2-bolt anchor (85')
FA: Richard Wright 1998

12 **Foxy** 5.11a ★★ ☐☐
Move 10 feet right of *Recovery* to an optional belay bolt. A fun and cruxy traverse about a third of the way up takes you to a roof and a super awkward sequence pulling over where part of you wants to stay wedged into the flake and the other part wants to get out of it.
8 bolts, 2-bolt anchor (80')
FA: Richard Wright 1998

13 **Little Kitten** 5.10b ★★ ☐☐
Climb the crack system through the interesting changing corners dihedral. You never really have to crack climb, but you have the option at times. *6 bolts, 2-bolt anchor (60')*
FA: Richard Wright 1998

14 **Slender Babe** 5.12c ★ ☐☐
Thin, technical, and often crumbly face climbing starts at a belay anchor up and left on the ledge above *Little Kitten's* anchor. Combining both pitches can create some serious rope drag through the last few moves, even with long slings.
7 bolts, 2-bolt anchor (110' to ground)
FA: Richard Wright 1998

Wall of the '90s - left side

15 Curvaceous 5.11b ★★★★ ☐☐
This is like *Wet Dream*'s easy sister that's defined by fun climbing, and a lot of it! Some long slings before the roofs can help eliminate rope drag. *15 draws, 2-bolt anchor (105')*
FA: Richard Wright 1998

16 Wet Dream 5.12a ★★★★ ☐☐
Worthy of the name. Big moves on overhanging jugs, vertical face climbing, technical slab climbing, and cruxy crimp moves all packed into one mega route. A 60-meter rope will just barely make it to the ground, so knot the end. *16 draws, slings to reduce rope drag, 2-bolt anchor (105')*
FA: Mark Rolofson, Richard Wright, Alan Nelson 1998

17 Centerfold 5.10c ★★ ☐☐
This is the bolted crack in the corner to the right of *Wet Dream* which can easily be done as one pitch.
P1: 5.10a Excellent and juggy climbing leads to a wide crack with some optional face holds that allow for some stemming if your offwidth technique is a little rusty. It's a great warm-up for the wall. *7 bolts, 2-bolt anchor (55')*
P2: 5.10c From the anchors, veer 15 feet right on the ledge for a bolt. Climb up and left on good holds until reaching another offwidth crux. Unclipping the first bolt of the second pitch from above helps eliminate drag if linking the two pitches. Also, if toproping this pitch, bring slings for the anchor so your rope doesn't rub against an edge. *8 bolts, 2-bolt anchor (50')*
FA: Lawrence Hamilton (without bolts)
Bolted: Richard Wright 1998

18 Ten Digit Dialing
5.12c ★★★★ ☐☐
Classic for the canyon! An interesting story about this route, it was originally called *Floater* due to the first ascensionist seeing a dead body floating down Clear Creek one day. This route was 13a, then 12d and now is a canyon standard at 12c. As good as it gets in CCC? Maybe.
7 bolts, 2-bolt anchor (60')
FA: Alan Nelson 1998

19 Reefer Madness
5.11a ★★★★ ☐☐
A must do for the canyon! Tackle crimpy face climbing to a horizontal break and rest halfway up, and then climb the slightly overhanging seam to the ledge.
7 bolts, 2-bolt anchor (60')
FA: Alan Nelson 1998

20 Porn Queen 5.11c ★★ ☐☐
A fun extension to *Reefer Madness* continues above the anchor through steep bulges. Clip a long sling on the anchor and try not to get pumped.
14 bolts, slings, 2-bolt anchor (105')
FA: Richard Wright, Alan Nelson, Mark Rolofson 1998

21 Stone Free 5.11b PG13 ★ ☐☐
Balance your way to a dangerously high first bolt on the line to the right of *Reefer Madness* before pulling a thin and crimpy sequence about halfway up. Continue up and right to a left-facing dihedral crack, or to avoid the bird poo-filled crack, continue up and left to join up with *Reefer Madness* for a fun finish.
7 bolts, 2-bolt anchor (60')
FA: Kurt Smith, Alan Nelson 1990

22 Casual Stone 5.11c R ★ ☐☐
Cruise up *Stone Free*, and then head up and right past some overhanging bulges and a tough mantel move with some sizable runouts up high. Some small cams can protect the runouts.
12-bolts, slings, 2-bolt anchor (105')
FA: Richard Wright, Alan Nelson 1998

23 Casual Gods 5.11d R ☐☐
This is a dangerous trad lead that climbs the thin crack to the left of *Double Stout*, then continues up and left out the roof and eventually meeting up with *Casual Stone*. Bird poo everywhere!
P1: 5.11d Be creative with your thin gear placements on the first pitch in the crack. Belay at the anchor below the roof to the right. *Thin and tricky gear, 2-bolt anchor (70')*
P2: 5.11c Climb up and left out the roof following a hand-sized crack to eventually meet up with *Casual Stone. Rack to #3 Camalot, 2-bolt anchor (70')*
FA: Alan Nelson, P. Steres 1990

24 Double Stout 5.13b ★★★★ ☐☐
Technical and sustained face climbing starts with the first few bolts of *Black and Tan*, then busts up and left on the vertical face. Temperature dependent holds.
9 bolts, 2-bolt anchor (70')
FA: Darren Mabe 2009

25 Double Stout Extension ☐☐
project ★★★★
This superb open project extends out the roof past the first anchor. It is amazing that no one has sent this yet as it's truly a proud line. Amazing, hard crux moves out the roof (5.13+?) lead to some 5.12 climbing on the upper headwall. *17 bolts (in all), slings, 2-bolt anchor (115')*
Equipper: Darren Mabe 2009

26 Black and Tan 5.13b ★★★ ☐☐
Fantastic! Technical footwork and crimping on what feels like a vertical slab. Two distinct cruxes with cryptic beta challenge you all the way to the anchors. It's the first bolted line to the left of *.30-06*. A hold broke in the crux, bumping it up to 13b.
10 bolts, 2-bolt anchor (70')
FA: Gregg Purnell 2001

27 .30-06 5.12a ★★★ ☐☐
Climb the moderate, varying width crack for 50 feet to the base of the roof and traverse left. Back up the fixed pin and bust through the bouldery overhanging dihedral, stemming and liebacking into a perfect thin hands crack above. The bird droppings can be a nuisance. Truly, a trad test piece for CCC. *Rack to #3, doubles to .75 Camalot, 2-bolt anchor (115')* FA: L. Hamilton, S. Weaver; FFA: Jeff Achey, Kent Lugbill

28 Wild Horses 5.13a ★★ ☐☐
Start up the same moderate crack as for *.30-06* but upon reaching the mega horizontal roof don't traverse, instead avoid the bird shit and clip a bolt and do the wild and dynamic crux through the roof. It's not over once you reach the lip, some delicate and balancy moves await you as well as a bolt (clip the new and shiny not the old and busted). Then traverse right into the last bit of *Roadrunner*. A good challenge although the route can be a bit dirty. Part of the CCC trad trifecta. *Bring a single set of cams and lots of long slings, 3 bolts and a pin, 2-bolt anchor (110')*
FA: Darren Mabe 2008

29 American Mustang
5.14a ★★ ☐☐
Techinical slab climbing between two cracks brings you to the Wild Horses roof moves before pulling a thin face crux on the upper headwall. Bring slings to reduce rope drag.
12 bolts, 2-bolt anchor (115')
FA: Mark Anderson 03/14

30 Roadrunner 5.11a ★★★

This is a moderate that looks way more intimidating than it is. Climb up the right of the two main cracks below the giant roof. Gain a good ledge (where you could make a belay to reduce rope drag) and bust out the large roof to a single bolt (clip this to avoid getting your rope stuck in the crack) and up the varying size crack to the anchors above. Climbing this route without significant rope drag requires some effort but can be done with long slings and strategic placement of cams. A 70m rope is necessary for a lower all the way down although a 60 and some down climbing can get the job done.

1 bolt, rack doubles from 0.3 - #3 Camalots, slings, 2-bolth anchor (105')

31 Mission Impossible
5.14c ★★★★

This classic is one of the hardest routes on the Front Range. Two heinously thin cruxes on gently overhanging and beautiful stone are separated by a rest at half-height. Great vision by Jay Samuelson for bolting this rig, and inspiring determination by Daniel Woods for unlocking the moves. *9 bolts, 2-bolt anchor (80')*
FA: Daniel Woods 2012;
Equipper: Jay Samuelson

31a Mission Overdrive
5.14b ★★★★

A link-up climbs through the first crux of *Mission Impossible* to bolt five, then traverses right to *Interstellar Overdrive* and into the finger shredding crimp crux of that route. Put a sling on the sixth bolt.
10 bolts, 2-bolt anchor (80')
FA: Jonathan Siegrist 2012

32 Interstellar Overdrive
5.13d ★★★★

Fantastic movement follows the left-leaning crack to a desperate crux on razor blade crimpers (supported with a little glue) that guards the chains. It hasn't seen many ascents, perhaps because it's hard for the grade. It's also the rightmost bolted line on the wall.
9 bolts, 2-bolt anchor (70')
FA: Tommy Caldwell 1996;
Equipper: Kurt Smith 1991

Vanessa Compton on *Ten Digit Dialing*, 5.12c, p102. ◉ Keith Ladzinski

Back of the '90s

 10-15min

 A.M.

 P.M.

3 Routes

≤5.8   5.9   5.10   5.11   5.12   5.13   5.14   *proj*

Crag Profile: Want to get away from the crowds and find some long moderates in the shade? This is your wall. Good routes and a nice belay spot make for a nice day; it's a very worthwhile spot that is under visited. This wall faces west and receives plenty of morning shade.

Approach: Park on the west side of Tunnel 2 on the south (left) side of the road 6.5 miles up the canyon. From here, do not walk up towards Wall of the '90s. Instead, stay on the level trail before taking a loose trail down to the creek. Continue downstream before locating the crag uphill just past Wall of the '90s, but a little behind it to the right. Take the faint trail up to the cliff. An alternative approach is to hike up to Wall of the '90s, walk to the right of *Interstellar Overdrive* (previous page), and hike straight across a gully to the wall.

1 Priapos 5.10d ★

Locate the large pine tree on the right side of the gully. After the fourth bolt, head straight up on crispy edges. This route would benefit from more traffic. While not as good as it's neighbor, it is more direct.
10 bolts, 2-bolt anchor (105')
FA: Darren Mabe 2004

2 Aphrodite 5.10d ★★★

Clip the first four bolts of *Priapos* before busting out right on fun and varied terrain. This route wanders a bit and thus some long draws would be nice. ***12 bolts, 2-bolt anchor (105')***
FA: Darren Mabe 2004

3 Mission Vision 5.10b ★

This fun climb is still a bit dirty. Enjoy a wide array of climbing as you find your way through some steep bulges to a ledge at the top. There are optional anchors just before the top if you don't have a 70-meter rope.
12 bolts, 2-bolt anchor (110')
FA: Darren Mabe, John Choboian, Matt Juth 2004

The trail from the parking area

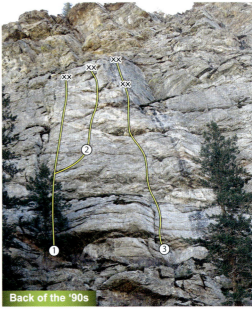

Back of the '90s

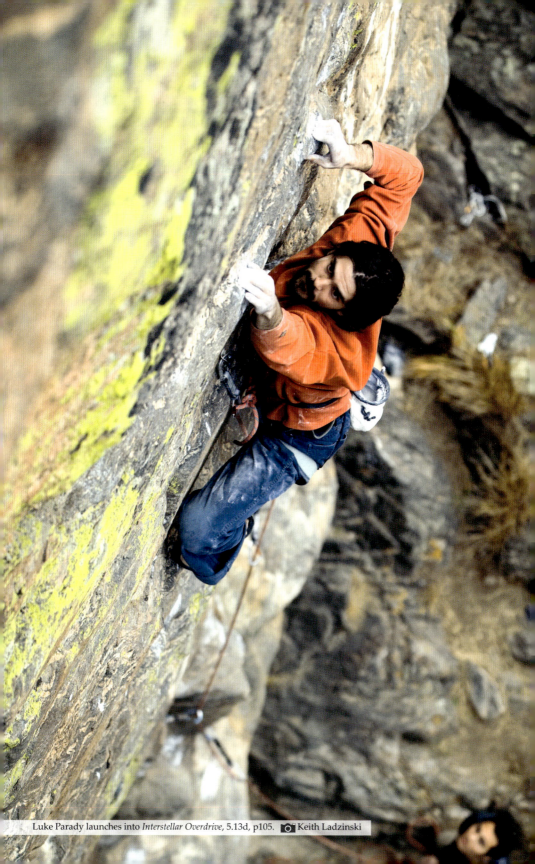

Luke Parady launches into *Interstellar Overdrive*, 5.13d, p105. Keith Ladzinski

Flood Wall

15min
          A.M.   P.M.

6 Routes

≤5.8 5.9 5.10 5.11 5.12 5.13 5.14 proj

Crag Profile: This newly developed wall is reminiscent of Anarchy Wall (p125). It is packed with excellent routes with sustained movement and sloper cruxes. Since this is a relatively new area, some of the holds are still a bit dirty, but for the most part it's a great crag. This wall gets morning shade and afternoon sun.

Approach: To get to Flood Wall, use the same approach for Wall of the '90s (p99). From the parking area, hike down to the creek and continue downstream for about 50 yards until finding a faint uphill trail that trends up and to the right. Hike uphill for a few hundred feet until seeing the crag up to your left and continuing on the trail to the base of the cliff.

Flood Wall

Flood Wall approach

① Crest 5.12d ★★★
Head up and right, traverse the lip of the roof left, then head straight up. Hold on tight and you'll be rewarded with an easier finish.
9 bolts, 2-bolt anchor (60')
FA: Madeleine Sorkin, Josh Gross 2013

② Deluge 5.11c ★
Climb up and right on dirty rock before jamming up the vertical crack (0.5 to #1 Camalot). *9 bolts, optional gear, 2-bolt anchor (60')*
FA: Josh Gross, Will Mayo 2013

③ Act of God 5.12c ★★★★
A great route that is cruxy, technical, slopey and very reminiscent to the climbing on Anarchy Wall! A tensiony start brings you to a nice rest before taking on the sustained climbing on the upper section, with difficulty that builds as you get closer to the anchor. *8 bolts, 2-bolt anchor (60')*
FA: Josh Gross 2013

④ Higher Ground 5.11b ★
Begin on the following route, and then bust up and left, following the broken seam with a tough sequence pulling over towards the top.
8 bolts, 2-bolt anchor (55')
FA: Josh Gross, Bart Paull 2013

⑤ Detour 5.11c ★★★
Excellent climbing! After pulling a short lived crux at the start, you arrive at a ledge. Finish by climbing on wonderful edges and slot-jugs on the steep upper wall.
7 bolts, 2-bolt anchor (45')
FA: Josh Gross, Bart Paull 2013

5a Displaced 5.10c ★★
A link-up climbs through the opening boulder problem on *Recovery Efforts* to the ledge and then finishes on the *Detour* arete.
6 bolts, 2-bolt anchor (45')
FA: Madoline and Josh Gross 2013

⑥ Recovery Act 5.10a ★★
A decent warm up for the wall. A challenging opening sequence leads to a nice ledge rest, then continue on sustained moderate climbing to the top. *7 bolts, 2-bolt anchor (55')*
FA: Madoline and Josh Gross 2013

Flood Wall

Punk Rock

 15min

 A.M.

 P.M.

3 Routes

≤5.8 5.9 5.10 5.11 5.12 5.13 5.14 proj

Crag Profile: For a nice break from the ordinary with two worthwhile routes, head downstream to Punk Rock. You can warm up on Wannabe Wall (p113) on your way here, then hop on *Sex Pistols* (5.12a) or *Johnny Rotten* (5.11a) for a solid pump on a long route. This is a nice hang out for afternoon shade in the summer time.

Approach: Drive just past Tunnel 2, going 6.5 miles up canyon, and park immediately on the left in a large pullout as for Wall of the '90s. Walk along the river, going past the Wall of the '90s left-hand turnoff. Head down a scree slope to the river, and spot a steel cable going across the river. The steel tyrol will trash a carabiner, so either bring a junk biner, steel carabiner, or better yet, a pulley. Once across the river, walk south/downstream on an easy trail until coming into clear view of the wall and taking a couple switchbacks to get to the base.

Irok

Punk Rock

Wannabe Wall

tyrol

xx

xx

Mission Wall

The tyrol approach

1 **Never Mind the Bollocks** 5.12a ★
Enjoyable climbing down low leads to a loose, sketchy pegmatite band.
10 bolts, 2-bolt anchor (75')
FA: Keith Ainsworth 2002

2 **Sex Pistols** 5.12a ★★
Probably the best route on the wall takes the most obvious line on the right side, climbing up the overhangs and wandering around a bit towards the end. The route will probably clean up with more ascents as it features enjoyable climbing but on less than enjoyable rock. *14 bolts, (bring some longs draws to extend in the roof), 2-bolt anchors (80')*
FA: Keith Ainsworth 2002

3 **Johnny Rotten** 5.11a ★★
Climb the steep, fractured beginning to a fun roof, gaining the excellent and technical face above. After climbing the face, ascend up and to the right to the anchors on the arête.
11 bolts, 2-bolt anchor (90')
FA: Kirk Miller, Keith Ainsworth 2002

Punk Rock

Irok

 20min

 A.M.   P.M.

8 Routes

≤5.8 5.9 5.10 5.11 5.12 5.13 5.14 proj

Crag Profile: Irok is the solid-looking piece of rock uphill on the west side of the creek behind Wannabe Wall. The route names reference the Iraq War like *Kick Their Ass* and *Take Their Gas*. The routes on the upper right side of the wall have a two-bolt belay anchor. The left side of the wall holds a few fun and hard 5.12s that start with some steep climbing for the first part and ease up to a slab finish. The crag is a worthy venture for people looking for a secluded wall. It also gets sun during the first part of the day.

Approach: Drive just past Tunnel 2, going 6.5 miles up canyon, and park immediately on the left in a large pullout as for Wall of the '90s. Walk along the river, going past the Wall of the '90s left-hand turnoff. Head down a scree slope to the river, and spot a steel cable going across the river. The steel tyrol will trash a carabiner, so either bring a junk biner, steel carabiner, or better yet, a pulley. Once across the river, walk south/downstream past Wannabe Wall (p113) to find a faint uphill trail that switchbacks up to the wall.

❶ Kick Their Ass 5.12a ★
The leftmost route on the wall starts off easy, but leads to a very crimpy boulder problem.
7 bolts, 2-bolt anchor (50')
FA: Mark Felty, Tod Anderson 2003

❷ Take Their Gas 5.12c ★★
Powerful climbing down low is matched with great technical climbing above. *8 bolts, 2-bolt anchor (50')*
FA: Mark Felty, Tod Anderson 2003

❸ Bunker Buster 5.12b ★★★
This is a very good climb despite the suspect flakes on the lower section. Make long pulls on incut edges to a slopey, technical mantel. After the initial climbing the route eases to moderate 5.10.
13 bolts, 2-bolt anchor (95')
FA: Mark Felty, Tod Anderson 2003

❹ Shock & Awe 5.12b ★★★
Fantastic movement on solid stone! Pull over the initial roof to get past bolt three to start the hard climbing with long moves to slopers. A final hard mantel to get onto the slab above will try and spit you off right before you send.
9 bolts, 2-bolt anchor (60')
FA: Mark Felty, Tod Anderson 2003

Irok

5 Towelhead 5.11a ☐☐
Scramble up the ramp to get to the first bolt. Climb past the rotten band of rock that surrounds the first bolt, then pull a quick crux over the bulge to get to the more moderate slab above. *7 bolts, 2-bolt anchor (60')*
FA: Gern Blisten, Tod Anderson 2006

6 M1A1 5.10d ★★ ☐☐
The warm up of the wall starts just left of the two belay bolts located up the ramp to the right. Climb up and right until you reach the final roof. Resist the urge to go right and stay left around the final bolt for an easier-than-it-looks ending.
10 bolts, 2-bolt anchors (70')
FA: Gern Blisten, Tod Anderson 2006

7 MOAB 5.11b ★ ☐☐
Climb straight up a curvy crack before stepping out left onto some technical face moves that bring you to the base of the roof. Some fun moves on big holds bring you up and right past the roof. A few suspect blocks exist at the start of the roof.
9 bolts, 2-bolt anchor (75')
FA: Gern Blisten, Tod Anderson 2006

8 Bagmom 5.10a ★★ ☐☐
From the bolted belay, scramble up and right to a high first bolt. Balance and crimp your way through some thin face moves to a midpoint rest before pulling around some bad rock and onto the fun headwall finish above. *6 bolts, 2-bolt anchor (75')*
FA: Gern Blisten, Tod Anderson 2006

Whenever Kevin Capps guides a client, they are in *Shock and Awe*, 5.12b, at his abilities and professionalism. 📷 Laura Capps

Jose Rodriguez asks, how do you write a nonpreverted caption for *Wet Dream*, 5.12a, p102. Scott Clark

Wannabe Wall

15min   A.M.   MOST OF THE DAY   **4 Routes**

≤5.8 5.9 5.10 5.11 5.12 5.13 5.14 *proj*

Crag Profile: Whether you're warming up for Irok or Punk Rock, crushing some fun moderates, or just escaping the crowds, Wannabe Wall is an often shaded little crag with some off the beaten path fun. This wall faces east.

Approach: Drive just past Tunnel 2, going 6.5 miles up canyon, and park immediately on the left in a large pullout as for Wall of the '90s. Walk along the river, going past the Wall of the '90s left-hand turnoff. Head down a scree slope to the river, and spot a steel cable going across the river. The steel tyrol will trash a carabiner, so either bring a junk biner, steel carabiner, or better yet, a pulley. Once across the river, turn left and head downstream about 100 yards before approaching a small creek side block with a few bolted lines on it.

1 Wannabe Left 5.10a
A good warm up shares anchors with *Wannabe Right*.
5 bolts, 2-bolt anchor (40')
FA: Keith Ainsworth 2000

2 Wannabe Right 5.10c ★★
A hard techy start leads to easier climbing above.
5 bolts, 2-bolt anchor (40')
FA: Keith Ainsworth 2000

3 Wannabe Protected 5.8
Start in the chimney to the left of *Wannabe Bolter*, and then commit to the face higher up.
Rack to #4 Camalot, 2-bolt anchor (40')

4 Wannabe Bolter 5.8+ ★
This fun little climb makes for a great first lead. Enjoy some thin moves that are a touch on the reachy side.
4 bolts, 2-bolt anchor (40')
FA: Mike Slavens 2009

Wannabe Wall

Mission Wall

 10min

 A.M.

 P.M.

16 Routes

≤5.8 5.9 5.10 5.11 5.12 5.13 5.14 proj

Crag Profile: The brooding north and east-facing Mission Wall watches over the Wall of the '90s, though few venture over to it. The cliff is one of the tallest in Clear Creek, as well as houses a cluster of projects. While the rock is not the highest quality, *Ride the Snake* into *Nice Ride* is a classic, multi-pitch 5.10a moderate.

Flood Wall

Mission Wall

tyrol

Mission Wall approach

Approach: Drive just past Tunnel 2 (6.5 miles up canyon) and park immediately on the left in a large pullout as for Wall of the '90s. Walk along the river, going past the Wall of the '90s left-hand turnoff. Head down a scree slope to the river, and spot a steel cable going across the river. The steel tyrol will trash a carabiner, so either bring a junk biner, steel carabiner, or better yet, a pulley. Once across the river, turn right and walk back towards the highway to the base of the climbs.

Descents from Surrette Ledge: It is possible to walk off to the left from the summit, although the best method is to rappel. To rap from Surette Ledge, you can rap a number of routes, but the easiest and most efficient way is to rap *Rocketman* with two 60-meter ropes.

Rocketman Rappel: An easy to access top anchor lets you rap about 60 feet down to an anchor. Then, an airy 200-foot double rope rappel brings you to the ground. You could swing in and clip a few directionals, if you only have one rope, to access intermediate anchors.

Gniess Route Rappel: This involves a little bit more of a commitment to get to the top anchor and does not have as good of anchor systems, but it is a good option if you only have a 70-meter rope.

Wild Child Rappel: If you only have one 60-meter rope, you can rappel *Wild Child*, stopping at every anchor. It helps to have climbed the route to find the anchors, otherwise just follow the bolt line on your way down. You may have to clip a directional at times.

① **Garrett's Revenge** 5.11d ★★★★

This great route contains one of the longest pitches in the canyon.
P1/P2: 5.9 Climb *Ride the Snake* to the top of the second pitch. From here, traverse down and left past a couple of bolts to get to an anchor at the base of the third pitch on a slab.
P3: 5.11d Continue up on moderate terrain to a hard pull over the roof (the left of the two bolted lines). After pulling the crux, some face climbing brings you to an anchor at the base of a right-facing corner. *16 bolts, 2-bolt anchor (150')*
P4: 5.10b From the belay, follow the bolts up and left, going around an arête and a large, right-facing corner to a belay on Surette Ledge. *4 bolts, 2-bolt anchor (45')*

Descent: Traverse right on Surette Ledge, and choose a rap route.
FA: Darren Mabe, Casey Bernal 2002

② **Billy the Kid** 5.12b ★★

Start on *Garrett's Revenge*'s third pitch, then bust up and right at the roof, pulling on a crimp rail to get to some large pockets and easier climbing. Reach an anchor, belay, and finish on *Garrett's Revenge*. *15 bolts, slings, 2-bolt anchor (150')*
FA: Darren Mabe 2003

③ **Ride the Snake** 5.10a ★★★

This is the leftmost route starting from the ground and should be done in combination with *Nice Ride* (described as P3/P4).
P1: 5.8+ Get onto a pedestal and follow the bolts up to a roof. Muscle over it and angle left to an anchor, or continue with pitch two. *8 bolts (60')*
P2: 5.9 Move a bit left and then continue up steep terrain to an anchor at a small ledge. *6 bolts (55')*
Note: *The next two pitches are the logical extension to the route but are*

known as Nice Ride.
P3: 5.9 Head up a groove/left-facing corner. After the second bolt, cut hard left under the roof and find a bolt just beyond it. A 0.5 Camalot can be placed on this traverse but is not critical. Head up to Ashtray Ledge to belay. *3 bolts, 0.5 Camalot (40')*
P4: 5.10a Head up a left-facing corner to a big, intimidating roof with a hand crack splitting it. Angle right along the juggy hand traverse to a big mantel move. Continue past the true crux and run up to Surette Ledge to belay. *7 bolts, rack to #3 Camalot (100')*
FA: P1/P2 - Darren Mabe, Casey Bernal 03/04; P3/P4 - Mabe, Bernal 12/02 (aka Gneiss Roof)

P4 Variation: 5.11a ★★

Climb up to the big roof and tackle the hand crack head on as it tapers to fingers. Angle back right back into the normal line.

Surrette Ledge

Mission Wall

4 Gneiss Route 5.12a ★★ ☐☐

P1: 5.11b A technical first pitch with multiple 5.11 cruxes and sustained climbing guards the anchor. Move over to the top anchors on *Billy* to start the next pitch. *12 bolts, 2-bolt anchor (120')*

P2: 5.12a Continue up and slightly left before taking the bolt line to the right, which heads up and over the black roof. You may combine this with the next pitch. *9 bolts, 2-bolt anchor (70')*

P3: 5.8 A short, moderate slab pitch brings you to the ledge. *5 bolts, 2-bolt anchor (50')*

Descent: Two raps with a 70-meter rope will get you to the ground and the base of *Billy*.

FA: Greg Purnell 2000

5 Billy 5.11b ★★★ ☐☐

A long, sustained pitch with pumpy climbing culminates into a final crux roof pull before getting to the anchors. Use slings to reduce drag.

15 bolts, slings, 2-bolt anchor (115')
FA: Rob Pizem 2000

7 Wild Child 5.11b ★★★

This great route features fun climbing getting up to the crux pitch on the upper headwall.

P1: 5.9+ This nice and easy first pitch gets you warmed up for the rest of the route. Start to the left of *Eye of the Beholder*, which is directly left of *Challenger*. *6 bolts, 2-bolt anchor (75')*

P2: 5.11a Climb up and slightly right over a series of juggy roofs and ledges to an anchor tucked in beneath an A-shaped roof. *10 bolts, 2-bolt anchor (70')*

P3: 5.10b Pull up and left past the small roof to more moderate climbing until reaching Surette Ledge. *10 bolts, 2-bolt anchor (80')*

P4: 5.11b Traverse 20 feet right on the ledge, then ascend the face angling up and to the right on up the upper headwall. This is the most technical pitch on the route and has great exposure! *9 bolts, 2-bolt anchor (80')*

Descent: Rapell the route.
FA: Thor Kieser 2002

As a parent, Jason Haas now fears his own *Wild Child*, 5.11b (P4). 📷 Dan Gambino

6 Rocketman 5.12c ★★★ ☐☐

P1: 5.11b Climb the first pitch of *Billy* for a long warm up. *15 bolts, slings, 2-bolt anchor (115')*

P2: 5.12a Continue up and left for a short pitch to get ready for the crux. *3 bolts, 2-bolt anchor (40')*

P3: 5.12c The money pitch! Bust out the exposed, crux roof above for a fun but challenging sequence at the steepest part of the roof. Belay at the top of the roof. *8 bolts, 2-bolt anchor (70')*

P4: 5.7 Enjoy an easy finish to the ledge. *4 bolts (55')*

Descent: Rap the route with a 70m rope, or rap to the top of P3 for your first rap, then double rope rappel 200 feet to the base of the wall.
FA: Darren Mabe, Peter Hunt 2004

7 Wild Child 5.11b ★★★ ☐☐

See the route description on the previous page.

8 Eye of the Beholder 5.10c ★ ☐☐

P1: 5.10c Start a few feet left of the low bolt on *Challenger* at a short, hanging, left-facing corner located 10 feet off the ground. Pull a bouldery start and face climb up to a high bolt. Pick your way up the face, moving a bit left and then back right aiming for the big roof high over head. Pull the juggy crux roof and run up to join *Wild Child* one bolt below that route's second pitch anchor. *9 bolts, rack to #4 Camalot, 2-bolt anchor (140')*

P2: 5.9 Climb P3 of *Wild Child* to the seventh bolt and then traverse hard right along a sloped ledge system to a bolted anchor at the base of a large, angling, left-facing corner. *7 bolts, rack to #2 Camalot, 2-bolt anchor (70')*

P3: 5.10c Stem the angling corner, angling left to a big roof. Pull over at a scary-looking (but seemingly solid) protruding flake and do a difficult mantel guarding the anchor. *5 bolts, 0.5 Camalot, 2-bolt anchor (50')*

P4: 5.10b Climb broken terrain straight up from the anchor to a looming wide crack splitting the edge of the steep headwall. Stem, jam, and struggle up the crack. Once over the chockstone, run up a fun finger crack to a final face section. Belay from a tree and then move right to rappel from the anchor on *Wild Child*. *Rack to #5 Camalot, tree anchor (70')*
FA: Greg Miller, Steve Johnson 08/13

Surette Headwall Routes

The following four routes are located just below the summit and begin off a massive sloped ledge known as Surette Ledge. Climb one of the previous routes to access it.

9 Unknown One project ☐☐

Climb up the overhanging face to the right of *Three Points of Contact*. It is believed this route was never red-pointed, but should go around 5.13. *5 bolts, 2-bolt anchor (55')*

10 Three Points of Contact 5.13c ★ ☐☐

The only actually established route on this overhanging, upper head-wall features challenging movement with great exposure. Tackle burly moves throughout the route, with a very tough sequence pulling past the third bolt. Even with some glue to re-inforce a few holds, much of the rock is still crumbly.
6 bolts, 2-bolt anchor (60')
FA: Jim Surette 1991

11 Unfinished ☐☐

Clean up the unfinished route to the right of *Three Points of Contact*. *2 bolts*

12 Unknown Two project ☐☐

There is another line on the right side of the overhanging face, which has crumbly rock through 5.13-ish climbing. *6 bolts, 2-bolt anchor (55')*

The Right Side of Mission Wall

These routes are easily found by the large, right-slanting white rock band which *Challenger* climbs up on the right side of the wall.

13 Challenger 5.11b ★ ☐☐

Face climb up the white, right-angling pegmatite band. The rock quality is not great, but it's still kinda fun. Share anchors with *Ground Control*. *6 bolts, 2-bolt anchor (60')*
FA: Rob Pizem 2000

14 Ground Control to Gumby One 5.10a ★★ ☐☐

Move right from *Challenger*, going around a small pillar. Jug-bash up the steep face to a crux pulling over the final bulge. The anchor needs some chains. *6 bolts, 2-bolt anchor (60')*
FA: Braden Peters 2000

15 Floorshow 5.12d ★★ ☐☐

A hardman's test piece for the wall contains very challenging and sustained face climbing up high.

P1: 5.10d Start on the face to the right of *Ground Control to Gumby One*. Pull a difficult sequence and mantel over the roof to the anchor above, although it can easily be linked with pitch two. *5 bolts, 2-bolt anchor (70')*

P2: 5.10c Continue up the lichen-covered face to a confusing couple of moves past some pegmatite rock. The anchor is straight up on the ledge. *4 bolts, 2-bolt anchor (65')*

P3: 5.12c Climb the face past a small right-facing dihedral on the left side of the roof to get to some technical face climbing, which contains a few manufactured holds. Finish at a hanging belay below the steep face. *12 bolts, 2-bolt anchor (90')*

P4: 5.12d Exposed climbing up the steep face involves pulling over a small bulge to get to some pumpy and technical face climbing. Hold on tight as it eases off towards the top. *8 bolts, 2-bolt anchor (80')*

Descent: Rappel the route with a 60-meter rope.
FA: Steve Landin 1996

16 Behind the Sun 5.12b ★★★ ☐☐

Be sure to sample this fantastic multi-pitch route with quality climbing on the upper headwall.

P1/P2: 5.10d Climb the first two pitches of *Floorshow*, but once you reach the ledge, traverse up and right to an anchor below the third pitch.

P3: 5.12b An excellent pitch! You'll encounter a short boulder problem to a good rest repetitively until reaching an exciting technical crux pulling over onto the face towards the top. *10 bolts, 2-bolt anchor (95')*

P4: 5.10d Start up the small, blocky, right-facing corner to pull over into a large left-facing dihedral. Finish the route at the top of the dihedral. This long pitch is a fun way to finish the route. *11 bolts, 2-bolt anchor (90')*

Descent: Rappel down P4/P3 to the ledge, and then traverse left to *Floorshow*'s anchor and rappel the first two pitches on *Floorshow*.
FA: Greg Purnell, Richard Wright 2000

Funyun Wall

15-20min

ALL DAY

1 Route

≤5.8　5.9　5.10　5.11　5.12　5.13　5.14　proj

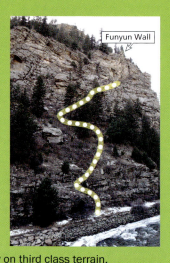

Funyun Wall

Crag Profile: This little crag popped up in 2013 and currently has only one route on it. However, there may be another route or two on it in the future. The wall sits high on the rim of the canyon, up and to the right of Mission Wall, and has some excellent exposure. Be aware that you should exercise caution while hanging out at this cliff as there is only a small ledge to belay from and a big fall potential. The wall faces north and receives shade all day.

Approach: Getting here actually isn't that bad once you are on the other side of the creek. Following the same approach as for Mission Wall (p114), use the tyrollean to get across the creek, then continue east on the creek side trail. Find a slight break in the hillside and follow a weakness and a switchback up and making your way up and to the right to get to the cliff. The final 20 yards are exposed and potentially on third class terrain.

Funyun Wall

(1) Project project ★★

This is currently the only bolted route on the wall and it climbs up the right side. Pull a hard sequence past the initial bulge to fun and featured climbing above. Finish on the anchor up and to the left.

7 bolts, 2-bolt anchor (65')
Equipper: Derek Peavey 2013

Capitalist Crag

 10-15min

 A.M.   P.M.

16 Routes

≤5.8 5.9 5.10 5.11 5.12 5.13 5.14 *proj*

Crag Profile: This is a fun wall to come to because it's tucked in by Tunnel 3, so you can barely hear the sound of cars. And when the creek is high, you can barely hear anything at all. It also has a quick and easy approach. Capitalist Crag is split into Upper Capitalist and Lower Capitalist, each with their own overview descriptions. The wall faces east and gets morning sun in the summer.

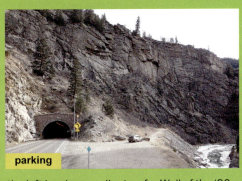

parking

Approach: Drive just past Tunnel 2, going 6.5 miles up canyon, and park immediately on the left in a large pullout as for Wall of the '90s. From the parking area, walk on the roadside trail, heading west along the south (left) side of the road towards Tunnel 3. The trail will curve you to the south before spotting Capitalist Crag.

Capitalist Crag overview

LOWER CAPITALIST

Overview: The Lower Capitalist has a large concentration of fantastic 5.10s, including *Lunchmoney*, which is a classic for the canyon. To get here, continue down the trail until it gets close to the creek where you can see *High Tides*, a three-bolt sport climb by the creek. From here, continue up and right on a small ledge. You might want to have your belayer anchored in for a few of the routes on the left side of the wall.

① **Vitamin N** 5.9 ★★

This is the last route you will find walking up the left-trending ledge system. Start up and right with techy slab moves before busting up and left into a mini-flake roof.
9 bolts, 2-bolt anchor (95')
FA: Darren Mabe 2005

② **Mounty** 5.8 ★

This moderate trad climb is not super classic, as it wanders quite a bit, but it's worth it if you need a trad fix.
1 fixed pin, rack to #3 Camalot, slings, 2-bolt anchor (95')   *FA: Darren Mabe*

③ **Aries** 5.10d ★

A fun and engaging line features a sloper boulder problem off the ground. Arrive at a great sequence around the fourth bolt. Easier climbing sets in for a while until the final challenging moves going through the last few bolts.
10 bolts, 2-bolt anchors (100')
FA: Darren Mabe

④ **Cheap Labor** 5.10a ★★★

Originally done as a traditional lead, this route sees many more ascents now with it's addition of bolts. Scamper up zig zaggy ledges to a stellar thin seam on the second half of the route where you can practice your finger locks. ***9 bolts, 2-bolt anchor (85')***
FA: Casey Bernal, Darren Mabe 2003

⑤ **Five Finger Discount** 5.9+ ★★

Begin 10 feet to the left of *Lunchmoney* and ascend the ledgy, featured rock to a small bulge and face climbing up high.
9 bolts, 2-bolt anchor (85')
FA: Ryan and C. Laird

⑥ **Lunchmoney** 5.9+ ★★★★

Wow, the best 5.9 in the canyon! This is the first route you encounter up the ramp. Climb up the steep, well-featured lower section to a small slab and onto the beautiful smooth headwall above.
10 bolts, 2-bolt anchor (95')
FA: Brandon Patterson, Darren Mabe 2002

Lower Capitalist

7 High Tides 5.11a ★★

As you approach Lower Capitalist, head down and left towards the creek to find a nice little beach where *High Tides* sits. From the ledge by the first bolt, decide if you wanna climb the wide crack, lie back, or climb the thin face up and left. However you do it, it's a fun little climb!
4 bolts, 2-bolt anchor (25')
FA: Dave Montgomery 2010

8 Contra 5.11a ★

Located on a ledge above *Vitamin N*, this route can be alternatively accessed via a grassy ledge system around to the left. It's a good climb with a tough crux near the end that can make the route feel harder than it is. A touch reachy.
4 bolts, 2-bolt anchors (50')
FA: Darren Mabe 2002

Note: The next few climbs are located up and right of *Lunchmoney*. *Downsizing* starts just off the trail while *Stoh's* and *Venture Capital* are on a ledge system. Be careful not to knock any rock on the climbers below you.

⑨ Venture Capital 5.11a ★★ ☐☐
Locate this climb on the far left end of the grassy ledges past *Stroh's*, or just climb *Lunchmoney* as a warm up and find yourself at the start of *VC*. This pretty fun route has it all; crimps, jugs, and small feet... as well as some less than perfect rock.
7 bolts, 2-bolt anchors (60')
FA: Vaino Kodas, Mary Zuvela 2004

Note: to the left of *Stroh's* is an unfinished/abandoned route with no hangers currently called *Stroh's Lite.*

⑩ Stroh's 5.11a ★★   ☐☐
Recommended. Access this route by scrambling up the loose but easy ramp from the right, or climb *Downsizing*. Start on the right side of the large ledge near a boulder. Climb up a challenging start on thin crimpers to fun, varied climbing.
6 bolts, 2-bolt anchor (60')
FA: Darren Mabe 2002

⑪ Downsizing 5.10a ★   ☐☐
Dirty but still not a total waste as it is a decent way to warm up for *Stroh's* since you can climb the first half to gain the *Stroh's* ledge. Rock quality marginally improves as you get higher. *12 bolts, 2-bolt anchor (100')*
FA: Vaino Kodas 2004

UPPER CAPITALIST

Overview: Most of the harder routes on this wall are found up the hill on the steep wall with tiered roofs. Aside from some of the easier routes on the right side, routes like *Free Enterprise* (5.12a) and *Entrepreneur* (5.11c) are sure to challenge your climbing ability. As you approach the wall, take the loose trail uphill to the right and arrive at *Get Rich*. Traverse the small ledges to get from route to route, there are belay anchors on the routes to the left.

⑫ Free Enterprise 5.12a ★★☐☐
This is the furthest bolted route on the left side, which starts from a bolted belay anchor. Interesting and crimpy face climbing leads to a decent shake before pulling the long reaches of the small roof and on the headwall. *7 bolts, 2-bolt anchor (70')*
FA: Alan Nelson, Richard Wright 1993

⑬ Entrepreneur 5.11b ★★ ☐☐
Fifteen feet right of *Free Enterprise* is another two-bolt belay anchor. From here, climb up and left to the fun and moderate right-facing corner to gain a great rest before pulling the roof move over the lip to the upper wall. *6 bolts, 2-bolt anchor (65')*
FA: Alan Nelson, Richard Wright 1993

⑭ Fire the Boss 5.11c ★   ☐☐
Start at the same belay anchor as *Entrepreneur* but climb straight up the face to the bulgy and awkward climbing higher on the route. Also share an anchor with *Entrepreneur*. *6 bolts, 2-bolt anchor, (65')*
FA: Alan Nelson, Richard Wright 1993

15 Hours for Dollars
5.10c ★★   ☐☐
Just left of *Get Rich* is this route, which climbs just left of its counterpart until the two routes join each other just after the roof.
7 bolts, 2-bolt anchor (75')
FA: Alan Nelson, Richard Wright, 1993

16 Get Rich 5.10a ★   ☐☐
Find this route on the right side of the small ledge at the top of the loose trail. There is large gap between bolts one and two, which can be protected with a #1 Camalot. This is a good route despite needing some rebolting. *7 bolts, 2-bolt anchor (75')*
FA: Alan Nelson, Richard Wright, 1993

Upper Capitalist

Socialist Crag

 20min   A.M.   P.M.

3 Routes

≤5.8 5.9 5.10 5.11 5.12 5.13 5.14 proj

Crag Profile: This wall is located directly across the creek from Capitalist Crag. Getting here is much more difficult than Capitalist, but you will see far less people. Socialist Crag currently has only a couple of routes at it, but there is plenty of room for development of some more moderates. By the time this book comes out, it wouldn't be surprising if a few more routes popped up on the wall. The crag faces west and gets shade in the mornings.

Approach: Drive just past Tunnel 2, going 6.5 miles up canyon, and park immediately on the left in a large pullout as for Wall of the '90s. Walk along the river, going past the Wall of the '90s left-hand turnoff. Head down a scree slope to the river, and spot a steel cable going across the river. The steel tyrol will trash a carabiner, so either bring a junk biner,

approach

steel carabiner, or better yet, a pulley. You can also wade across the creek in low water. Once across the river, turn right and walk about a quarter mile upstream (going past Mission Wall) until you're about level with Capitalist Crag. The wall will be uphill to your left from here. Find a faint approach trail on your left with cairn to take you up to the crag.

1 Capitalist Pig 5.10b ★★ ⬜
Climb the steep face on the left side of the wall. Consistent climbing leads to a slab finish.
9 bolts, 2-bolt anchor (85')
FA: Alex Andrews, Joe Yantis 2013

2 The Marxist 5.11a ★★ ⬜
Start in the corner to the right of a chimney/gully system and then climb up on the face and into a left-facing dihedral. Finish at the anchors above the small corner. There is another set of anchors at the top of the cliff for a potential second pitch.
8 bolts, 2-bolt anchor (75')
FA: Alex Andrews, Rob Bauer 2013

Socialist Crag

CHUCK FRYBERGER HAS THE WALL TO HIMSELF DURING A NIGHTTIME ASCENT OF ANARCHITECT, 5.12D, P127 📷 KEITH LADZINSKI

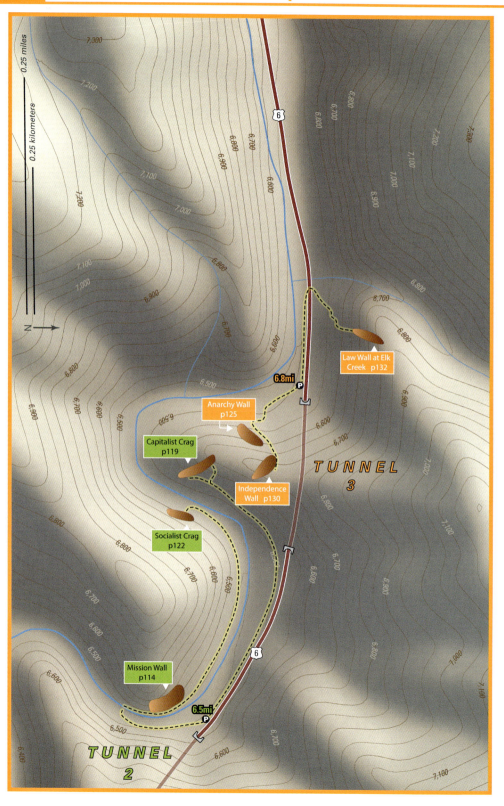

0.25 miles

0.25 kilometers

N →

7,300

7,200

7,100

7,200

7,100

7,000

7,100

7,000

6,900

6,800

6,700

6,900

7,000

6,800

6,700

6,600

6,900

6,800

6,700

6,600

6,900

6,800

6,700

6,600

6,500

6,600

6,800

6,700

6,600

6,500

6,700

6,600

6,500

6,600

6,500

6,400

6,800

6,700

6,600

6,500

6,600

6,700

6,800

6,600

6,700

6,800

6,900

7,000

7,100

7,200

7,300

6,800

6,900

7,100

7,000

6,800

6,700

6,600

6,500

6,600

6,200

6,800

6,700

6,600

6,500

7,100

6

6

Law Wall at Elk Creek p132

6.8mi P

Anarchy Wall p125

Capitalist Crag p119

Independence Wall p130

T U N N E L 3

Socialist Crag p122

Mission Wall p114

6.5mi P

T U N N E L 2

Anarchy Wall

5-10min   A.M.   P.M.   ≤5.8 5.9 5.10 5.11 5.12 5.13 5.14 proj   **17 Routes**

Tunnel Three (west side)

Anarchy Wall

parking

Crag Profile: Slopers, slopers, and may-be a crimp or two. This wall has a variety of classic lines such as *Anarchitect* (5.12d), *Power Trip* (5.12a), and *Maestro* (5.12d), with a couple of fun boulder problems on a rope like *Question Authority* (5.12b) and *Chaos* (5.13a). In the summer, this wall gets baked with afternoon sun and slopers don't feel as good when they're greasy. The entire wall was rebolted in the summer of 2013 thanks to the Boulder Climbing Community and Fixed Pin Publishing.

Approach: To get to Anarchy Wall, park just west of Tunnel 3 at mile 6.8 on the south (left) side of the road. Look up at the wall to the east of the parking area to find the beautiful stone and you will probably see chalked holds on the classic, *Anarchitect*. You can find the trail to the wall about 40 yards south of the parking area.

1 Hazardous Waste 5.11d ★★

Climb the leftmost bolted route on the wall. While it's kind of a warm-up, it does have a pretty stiff and reachy sequence before clipping the anchor.
5 bolts, 2-bolt anchor (40')
FA: Alan Nelson, Pete Steres 1990

2 Power Trip 5.12a ★★★

One of the more popular routes on the wall has fun movement on great stone and a challenging, but non-reachy crux. It's probably the best warm-up on the wall, even though it is not the easiest route.
6 bolts, 2-bolt anchor (40')
FA: Alan Nelson 1994

3 Anarchy in the U.K. 5.12b ★★

After clipping a high first bolt, pull on small crimpers to a rest before a hard mantel below the anchor. You do not have to clip all of the bolts on this route – some are for *Anatomic* (the traverse link-up).
6 bolts, 2-bolt anchor (40')
FA: Kurt Smith 1990

Independence Day Wall

Anarchy Wall

Anarchy Wall

to Independence Day Wall

Anarchy Wall

4 **Anarchy Rules** 5.12b ★★ ☐☐
A bouldery start leads to a pumpy couple of bolts. After the second bolt, climb up and right on small edges to a high third bolt.
5 bolts, 2-bolt anchor (40')
FA: Alan Nelson 1990

5 **Monkey Wrench** 5.11c ★ ☐☐
This is the first route left of the slight break in the middle of the wall that separates the shorter routes to the left and the taller routes to the right. Climb the left-leaning slopey ramp to a couple of difficult moves and a mantel. **5 bolts, 2-bolt anchor (40')**
FA: Alan Nelson, Kurt Smith 1990

6 **Anatomic** 5.12c ★★★   ☐☐
This link-up climbs through some of the best moves on the left side of the wall. Start on *Monkey Wrench* and climb left along a line of crimps, a couple slopers, and a jug or two for a well-protected traverse before finishing on *Hazardous Waste*.
10 bolts, 2-bolt anchor (45')

7 Matriarch 5.12d ★★
A stout, tensiony start leads to a small rest before pulling the sloper crux. There are plenty of lay down rests towards the top of this route; be sure to take them because it's not over until you clip the anchor.
7 bolts, 2-bolt anchor (70')
FA: Alan Nelson 1992

8 Presto 5.12c ★★
Start on *Maestro*. After a quick pump on the first part, bust up and left to finish on *Matriarch*. Take advantage of the rest before making the final moves to the anchor.
8 bolts, 2-bolt anchor (70')
FA: Alan Nelson, Kurt Smith 1990

9 Maestro 5.12d ★★★
Climb fun and interesting moves to a hard crux up high. It's not as good as its classic counterpart, but it's still definitely worth climbing.
6 bolts, 2-bolt anchor (65')
FA: Alan Nelson, Kurt Smith 1990

10 Anarchitect 5.12d ★★★★
A classic for the canyon and a benchmark at 12d. Start at the lowest point in the center of the wall. This route has it all, slopers, tiny worm-like pinches, big moves, technical footwork, and beautiful stone. Cooler temps can make the slopers feel more like holds. As a side note, this has been lead by Matt Lloyd without using the bolts as an R/X trad climb.
7 bolts, 2-bolt anchor (70')
FA: Alan Nelson 1990

11 Crackpot 5.12c ★★
Start on the chalky crack to the right of *Anarchitect* and traverse left until you find a happy ending on either *Anarchitect*, *Presto*, or *Maestro*.
10 bolts, 2-bolt anchor (80')
FA: Alan Nelson 1994

12 Unfinished project
A project with a couple of spaced out bolts and two cold shuts exist to the left of *Chaos*. These bolts were not updated when the wall was re-equipped.

13 Chaos 5.13a ★★
Start up on the ledge to the right of *Anarchitect*. A stiff sequence down low on razor sharp crimps leads to slightly easier climbing above the third bolt. This route is often climbed with the third bolt stickclipped for safety purposes.
4 bolts, 2-bolt anchor (30')
FA: Alan Nelson 1990

14 Question Authority
5.12b ★
Climb the rightmost bolted line on the wall. Encounter a couple of powerful, crimpy moves on this shorty.
3 bolts, 2-bolt anchor (25')
FA: Alan Nelson 1992

15 Power Rules 5.12a ★
This route is up and right of the main part of Anarchy Wall. Climb the ledges up to the right of *Question Authority* to find a small face. A couple of powerful moves get lead to a tricky mantel below the anchors.
3 bolts, 2-bolt anchor (20')
FA: Alan Nelson 1992

Cool Thing

16 Halloween 5.8 ★★
From the parking area, walk downstream to the small, well-protected face. This is probably the easiest climb in the area and can be great for warming up.
4 bolts, 2-bolt anchor (40')
FA: F. Zieve, S. Reardick 1992

17 Cool Thing 5.13a ★★★
This route sits across the other side of the river from Anarchy Wall on a west-facing, overhanging wall. The route is great, although it might not look like it. Climb the sustained, difficult, edge-pulling overhang to a complex and reachy crux at the end. Full value. *6 bolts, 2-bolt anchor (40')*
FA: Pete Zoller 1992

Josh Brossman on a *Power Trip*, 5.12a, p125.
📷 Jay Samuelson

Independence Day Wall

 10min

ALL DAY

≤5.8 5.9 5.10 5.11 5.12 5.13 5.14 proj

6 Routes

Crag Profile: This wall offers a few vertical routes that can serve as a nice warm-up for some of the harder lines at Anarchy Wall. The cliff faces north and sees shade most of the day.

Approach: To get here, use the same approach as Anarchy Wall (p125) and hike up and left past Anarchy on a loose trail to find some routes uphill towards the ridge.

1 **Independence Day** 5.9
The leftmost route on the wall starts at the top of the ridge and climbs the blocky face.
2 bolts, 2-bolt anchor (20')
FA: Alan Nelson 1997

2 **Rock the Vote** 5.9+ ★
The second route from the left shares an anchor with *Independence Day*.
3 bolts, 2-bolt anchor (30')
FA: Alan Nelson 1997

3 **Campaign Trail** 5.10d ★
Climb the seam just left of the bolt line. If you're bored, you can climb only to the right of the bolt line for an eliminate called *Lady Liberty*.
4 bolts, 2-bolt anchor (35')
FA: Alan Nelson 1997

4 **Party Line** 5.10d ★
Work past the first bolt and ledge to a right-angling crack that delivers some strong 5.10 cruxes. Share anchors with *Fat Democrat* to the right.
4 bolts, 2-bolt anchor (40')
FA: Alan Nelson 1997

5 **Fat Democrat** 5.11b ★
Start behind a tree to the left of *Right to be Wrong*. Follow mostly 5.10 climbing to a balancy crux towards the top. *4 bolts, 2-bolt anchor (40')*
FA: Alan Nelson 1997

6 **Right to be Wrong**
5.11a ★★
This is a great route for the wall, and is possibly the best line at Independence Day Wall. Sustained climbing on incut holds offer a little bit of a pump. This is the first route you encounter when walking uphill to the wall. *6 bolts, 2-bolt anchor (45')*
FA: Alan Nelson 1997

Independence Day Wall

Right to be Wrong

Law Wall at Elk Creek

15min A.M. P.M.

≤5.8 5.9 5.10 5.11 5.12 5.13 5.14 proj

6 Routes

Crag Profile: Little is known about the history of this wall other than the fact that it is home to a few moderate to hard routes with some unfinished/abandoned projects mixed in. The rock is generally crumbly and fractured, but the routes are worth checking out. Bring a helmet, there is loose rock, with traffic and time this will improve. This wall faces east and receives morning sun with some nice afternoon shade.

Approach: To get here, drive 6.8 miles up the canyon and park just west of Tunnel 3 on the south side of the road. From the parking area, look up to the northwest and spot this crag on the hillside. There is not a great way to get here, but the best way is to hike just west of the parking area for a couple hundred feet to get to a bridge and the Elk Creek drainage. Scramble up the creek and then cut back to the right to get out of it. From here, continue uphill to the left slightly to get to the wall.

Elk Creek

parking

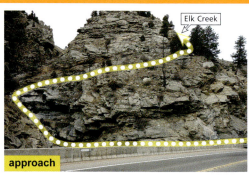

Elk Creek

approach

1 Wolf Pack 5.11a ★
Climb the leftmost bolted line on the wall. *8 bolts, 2-bolt anchor (75′)*
FA: Keith North 06/14

2 Evolvlution 5.11a ★★
Climb the start of *Extradition* to the first little roof then traverse left until you can clip the left line of bolts. Loose, friable stone leads to excellent climbing above with great holds on the overhang right before the chains. It's worth climbing but like everything here, it's dirty.
9 bolts 2-bolt anchors (80′)
FA: Todd Smith 2014

3 Magic Rat Tail 5.10b ★★
This line is located on the first wall you arrive at after huffing up the hill. Currently, you can climb straight up these bolts. This route is long and varied. While it's very dirty, it will clean up to become a CCC classic, just not yet.
8 bolts, 2-bolt anchors (70′)
FA: Todd Smith 2013

4 Order 5.11d ★★
Dirty climbing down low leads to perfect stone up high. Interesting moves on diagonal cracks on the second half. *6 bolts, 2-bolt anchor (40′)*
FKA: Matt Lloyd 2014

5 Unknown project
As of now, there are no hangers on this line, just bolts, although it looks good. It will probably go at about 5.12 when finished. *(40′)*

6 Council 5.11c ★
Good steep climbing on weak stone. It's shorter and thinner than its neighbor to the left. Clipping the chains is the crux.
4 bolts, 2-bolt anchor (30′)

Evolvlution

Order

JON CARDWELL ON STONE COLD MODERN, 5.13B, SEX CAVE, P135. Ⓞ SCOTT CLARK

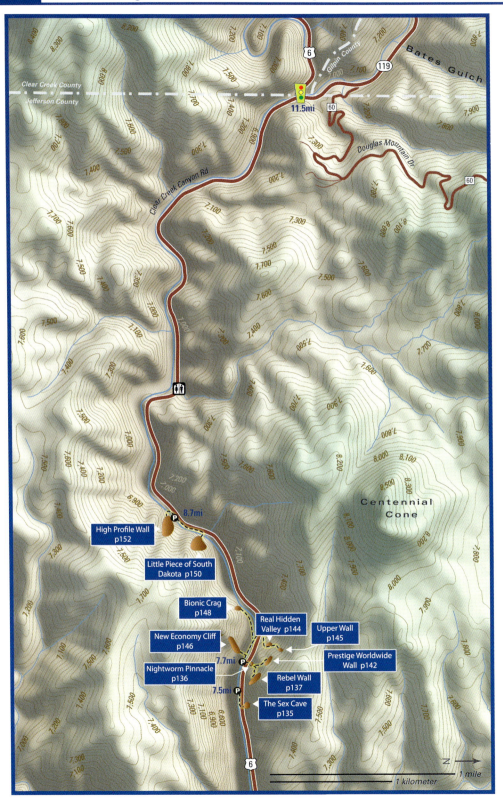

Bates Gulch

Gilpin County

6

119

Douglas Mountain Dr.

60

60

11.5mi

Clear Creek County
Jefferson County

Clear Creek Canyon Rd

Centennial
Cone

8.7mi

High Profile Wall
p152

Little Piece of South
Dakota p150

Bionic Crag
p148

Real Hidden
Valley p144

Upper Wall
p145

New Economy Cliff
p146

Prestige Worldwide
Wall p142

Nightworm Pinnacle
p136

7.7mi

Rebel Wall
p137

7.5mi

The Sex Cave
p135

6

N

1 mile

1 kilometer

Sex Cave

Mile Marker: 264

 5min

 ALL DAY

3 Routes

≤5.8 5.9 5.10 5.11 5.12 5.13 5.14 proj

Crag Profile: This is for the gym rats as the cave is steep and powerful with a short approach. The routes are bouldery and many link-ups exist to keep you busy. This wall gets sun all day most of the year, making it a great winter spot.

Approach: Park at the on the south (left) side of the road 7.5 miles up the canyon. Walk down stream about 50 feet or until a faint trail can be seen on the north side of the road; the crag will be visible just uphill.

parking

① Head Like a Hole
5.12d ★★★

This classic starts up the left side of the cave on easy but sometimes suspect rock (the holds are secure though). Take a rest and then fire right under the roof on sloper jugs to a crux (and a kneebar) rounding out onto the face for a final technical boulder problem.
6 bolts, 2-bolt anchor (40')
FA: Pete Zoller 1991

①a Head Cold 5.13b ★★

A less than fantastic link-up climbs the so/so beginning of *Head Like a Hole* and then busts up the hard crux of *Stone Cold Modern*.
7 bolts, 2-bolt anchor (40')

② Stone Cold Modern
5.13b ★★★

If you like power, then this route's for you. Start up the middle of the cave using drilled pockets and jumping to "the basketball." Use ninja beta to mitigate this awesome mini crux and get to the base of the roof to try and rest. Make sure your biceps are strong to pull the extremely powerful boulder problem below the chains that are just around the roof to the left. *7 bolts, 2-bolt anchor (40')*
FA: Pete Zoller 1991

②a Stone Cold Head
5.13a ★★★

This excellent link-up is perhaps better than either of its original lines. Climb up the excellent start of *Stone Cold Modern* to the roof, but instead of climbing left, finish out *Head Like a Hole*. *8 bolts, 2-bolt anchor (40')*

③ Rubble 5.13c ★★

This one is tough, but good! I have watched 5.14c climbers flounder on this route. With good beta it goes, but doesn't go too often according to 8a.nu. A hard boulder problem guards the beginning of this route.
8 bolts, 2-bolt anchors (40')
FA: Pete Zoller 1991

Sex Cave

Nightworm Pinnacle

0.2mi past mm264   5min   ALL DAY   ≤5.8 5.9 5.10 5.11 5.12 5.13 5.14 proj   **3 Routes**

Crag Profile: This crag is defined by having a splitter hand crack up the middle of it. The Nightworm Pinnacle has a few routes with a short approach. If you're looking for a fun gear-protected route like *Nightingale* (5.8), or a short little sport climb like *Worm Skin* (5.11a), this might be your wall. With its openness and south-facing angle, you will be sure and catch the sun on a cold winter day.

Approach: Park in the dirt pullout 7.7 miles up the canyon on the south (left) side of the road. Look across the road to find a pinnacle with a single hand crack up the center of it, 100 feet uphill on the north side of the road.

❶ Night Crawler 5.8+ R ★
Start just left of *Nightingale* and climb past the hollow, blocky flakes, going up around the arête to the top. Most people set up a toprope on this route for safety.
Light rack, no anchor (70')

❷ Nightingale 5.8 ★★
Fun crack climbing up the splitter hand crack. Start on the face below the crack and pull a couple slab moves through blocky underclings. From here, you are rewarded with a bomber hand crack to the top. Use *Worm Skin*'s anchor to the right.
Rack to #3 Camalot, 2-bolt anchor (70')

❸ Worm Skin 5.11a ★★
This is the bolted line on the right side of the wall. Climb up the face to be challenged on some thin moves towards the top. It's kind of fun for being so close to the road. The fixed pins can be backed up by a micro cam in a small flake in between the two pins, or in the undercling flake up and right with a #1 Camalot.
5 bolts, 2 fixed pins, 2-bolt anchor (70')

Nightworm Pinnacle

Rebel Wall

0.2mi past mm264

 15min

 ALL DAY

21 Routes

≤5.8 5.9 5.10 5.11 5.12 5.13 5.14 proj

Crag Profile: While Clear Creek Canyon isn't typically known for its large amount of traditional climbs, Rebel Wall is one of the many walls where you can find some fun gear routes. It's hard to come to Rebel Wall and not climb the beautiful *Body English* (5.9) dihedral, or even test your mental composure on routes like *Jump Start* (5.11c R) or *Down to the Wire* (5.11c R). This wall faces south, is high in the canyon, and gets sun most of the day, especially midday, making it a great wall to find some warm sun in the winter.

Rebel Wall approach

Approach: Drive 7.7 miles up the canyon and park on the south (left) side of the road in a large dirt parking area. Locate the Nightworm Pinnacle (previous page), then hike up and to the right of it. Follow a gully uphill for about 50 feet, then angle up and to the right for a few switchbacks to get to the left side of the wall.

① Learner's Permit
5.7 PG13
Work your way up the squeeze chimney on the far left side of the wall. Locate two, wide parallel crack systems; this is the right one. Be careful of loose chockstones in the chimney. Belay on gear and walk off to the left.
Rack to #4 Camalot, no anchor (100')

② Dirty Girl 5.9+ ★
Start on the face to the right of a short, right-facing corner. A few tricky sequences on suspect rock lead past four bolts and a fixed pin (that can be backed up by a 0.4 Camalot). From here, easier, gear-protected climbing brings you up to the anchor.
4 bolts, 1 fixed pin, rack 0.4 - #3 Camalot, 2-bolt anchor (65')

③ Wide Fetish 5.10b
Climb the crack in the large, right-facing dihedral that leads out the roof. Jam past the roof, heading up and left to finish on *Dirty Girl*'s anchor. This route is dirty, and goes through a few bushes.
Rack to #4 Camalot, 2-bolt anchor (65')

Matt Lloyd on *Winter Kill*, 5.12c, p141.
📷 Bethany Lukens

Rebel Wall - left side

4 Large Crack 5.9+ ★
This route goes through the slot on the right side of the roof. Pull the steep moves over to lower angled climbing, then bust up and right and finish at an anchor below a large roof. You also have the option to continue up left and walk off.
Rack to #3 Camalot, 2-bolt anchor (90')
FA: Mark Pell, Alvino Pon 1994

5 Mama Said Knock You Out 5.11c ★★
Start in a shallow left-facing corner and climb up a dirty crack system to get to the base of an off-hands roof crack 25 feet up. Powerful climbing through the roof takes you to a thank-God jug to mantel over on. Somewhat easier climbing leads to one more challenging section through a small roof before going to the anchors on the underside of a massive roof.
Rack doubles to #3 Camalot, 2-bolt anchor (90') *FA: Mark Pell, Alvino Pon 1994*

6 The Curse of Eve project
Climb any of the surrounding routes to get to the base of a large roof and a belay anchor. Climb up the steep face. This route is in project status and is more of a toprope line. There is a 2-bolt anchor at the top of the route. *(50')*

7 Epidote 5.11a ★★

Begin right of *Mama Said Knock You Out* and jam the crack over a small roof crux at the start with a difficult mantel move. Continue up and left along the hand crack to meet up with *Mama Said Knock You Out*.
Rack to #3 Camalot, 2-bolt anchor (90')

8 South Paw 5.10a ★★

As a new addition to the wall, this bolted sport climb offers a nice alternative to a largely traditional wall. Start on the face left of *Body English* and climb up some interesting and at times harder-than-it-looks climbing to the anchors above.
11 bolts, 2-bolt anchors (90')
FA: Ryan and C. Laird 2008

9 Body English 5.9 ★★★

This is the climb to do at Rebel Wall. While not the most classic crack, it certainly is fun and engaging and climbs much better than it looks. Find the large right-facing dihedral in the middle of the wall. Climb up through some interesting roofs using stemming techniques to a nice ledge. From here, rap or continue on *Upper Cut* to top it out. *Rack doubles to #3 Camalot, 2-bolt anchor (90')*
FA: Mark Pell, Alvino Pon 1994

10 Upper Cut 5.10b ★★

A stout roof sequence leads to easier climbing above. Located up and to the left of the anchors of Body English, this is the best way to top out the wall. Climb through a stout roof sequence in the right-facing dihedral to easier climbing above. Walk off to the north or rap from anchors down and left. *Rack to #3 Camalot, 2-bolt anchor. (70')*
FA: Mark Pell, Alvino Pon 1994

11 Make It So 5.10a PG13 ★

Move 15 feet right of *Body English*. Hard moves up the face past a couple of bolts lead to a great .75 Camalot placement. After clipping the third bolt, step left, then up right to find a few placements in the flaring flakes. From here, take the seam to the top to get to lower angled terrain. At the top of the seam, traverse 15 feet right to a two-bolt anchor, or traverse left and continue on to *Make it Go*.
3 bolts, rack to #1 Camalot, 2-bolt anchor (75') *FA: Mark Pell, Alvino Pon 1994*

Ryan Fiore on *Tumbling Stock*, 5.12a, p147. 📷 Dan Gambino

12 Make It Go 5.9+ R

P1: This is the not-so-well-protected extension to *Make It So*. When you place your last piece on *Make It So*, traverse up to the left and make a belay at a weakness in the wall.
P2: Climb straight up through a bulge and place gear when you can. Build an anchor and walk off.
Rack to #3 Camalot, no anchor (75')

13 Only the Strong 5.11c ★★

Start in the left-facing corner that climbs up a crack and through a slot at the beginning of the route. Climb the crack straight up and be diligent with your placements before the crack ends and turns into a slab. A bolt protects a thin slab crux that guards the top of the route. *1 bolt, rack to #2 Camalot, 2-bolt anchor (75')*

13a Jump Start 5.11c R

As the name implies, jump start up to a lieback crack five feet left of *Only the Strong*. Pull the roof and join up with *Only the Strong* on the slab. Not recommended as a lead, but it's a decent toprope. *1 bolt, 1 fixed pin, rack to #1 Camalot, 2-bolt anchor (75')*

13b Piedmont Boulder Toad (PBT) 5.10b ★

A fun, direct start variation heads up the face just around the corner to the right of *Only the Strong*. Start down to the right of the bolt on incuts and edges and climb up to the left to join up with *Only the Strong*. This is also the recommended start to *Siouxami*, *Dreidel*, and *Shane's Addiction*. One bolt protects the start; you decide how to finish.
Rack to #2 Camalot, 2-bolt anchor (80')

Rebel Wall - right side

13c Dreidel 5.10b ★
Another fun little traversing variation to *Only the Strong* follows that route for 45 feet, after which place a finger-sized piece in a small crack and traverse up and right to a lone bolt. From here, an exciting finish takes you up and left to the anchor.
1 bolt, rack to #2 Camalot, 2-bolt anchor (80')

14 Siouxnami 5.12b ★★
How do you feel about excellent undercling traversing with smeary feet? Start on *PBT*, then take the seam traverse out right, clipping two bolts along the way and applying pressure in the underclings to keep your feet pasted on the slab. Finish on *Shane's Addiction* around the corner to the right. *3 bolts, rack to #2 Camalot, 2-bolt anchor (80')*

15 Shane's Addiction 5.11a ★
Begin on *PBT*, but after the second bolt traverse out right on the thin slab to get to a thin crack under a bulge. After placing some thin gear, continue up to an easier and more protectable finish.
2 bolts, rack to #2 Camalot with extra thin cams, 2-bolt anchor (80')

16 Winter Kill 5.12c ★★

It's a bit of a mission to get to, but it's worth it if you're in the area or it's too cold to climb anything else. This route sits in the sun all day and is high on the south side, so even on the shortest winter days it bakes! There are many ways to access this route, climb either *Last Chance to Dance* or the slightly frightening but easier *Make It So*. This three-bolt route starts from this ledge (80 feet up). The anchors were put in years ago for *Winter Kill* but only recently were bolts added and the first ascent made. Short and sweet.
3 bolts, 2-bolt anchor (25')
FA: Matt Lloyd 2013

17 Last Chance to Dance
5.12a PG13 ★

Challenging face climbing to the right of the arête involves pulling onto the wall by the first bolt and then getting past bolt two. There is a good clipping hold for bolt two as well as good holds and easier climbing about five feet past the second bolt. While you will probably not hit the ground, expect to log some long falls if you whip. *3 bolts, 2-bolt anchor (80')*

18 Bust a Move 5.11b ★

Fun face climbing high on the wall serves as a second pitch to any of the following routes. From the bolted belay on the ledge, scramble up the ramp to the right to get to a short and steep headwall. An optional #1 Camalot placement is available at the start of the route. Pull onto the wall and work your way through a few face moves on decent holds, moving past a few bolts and a fixed stopper to the anchor.
3 bolts, fixed stopper, optional #1 Camalot, 2-bolt anchor (75')

19 Down to the Wire 5.11c R

This ambitious and scary route climbs up the fingernail seam on the steep slab to the right of *Last Chance to Dance*. Wiggle thin stoppers into the seam, then a bolt protects a few hard moves up higher. *1 bolt, extra thin gear, 2-bolt anchor (60')*

Floppy Boot Stamp

20 Floppy Boot Stamp
5.8 ★★

P1: 5.8 Climb the thin to hand-sized crack system on the face just right of *Down to the Wire*. After gaining a ledge 60 feet up, move 10 feet right and pull crux moves up the steep crack and continue on to easier climbing to a ledge and belay. *Rack to #3 Camalot, no anchor (90')*
P2: 5.7 Follow the hand-sized and slightly left-slanting crack to the top of the wall; belay from a small pine. *Rack to #3 Camalot, tree anchor (80')*

20a Floppy Right Start 5.8

Start in the broken, right-facing dihedral just around the corner to the right of Floppy Boot Stamp, and then join up with that route for the second half of the first pitch.
Rack to #3 Camalot (90')

21 Happy Crack 5.9 ★

P1: 5.9 Start 25 feet right of *Floppy Boot Stamp* and scramble up some easy but broken to get to the base of a hand crack on the steep face just right of an arête. Jam your way up and over to a belay ledge. *Rack to #3 Camalot, no anchor (90')*
P2: 5.8 Climb the crack inside a right-facing corner past a few questionable blocks to the top of the wall. You may also choose to go slightly left and do the second pitch of *Floppy Boot Stamp* instead. *Rack to #4 Camalot, no anchor (80')*

Prestige Worldwide Wall

0.2mi past mm264   10-15min   MOST OF THE DAY | | | | | **9 Routes**
≤5.8 5.9 5.10 5.11 5.12 5.13 5.14 proj

Crag Profile: This short wall gives you some fun, sport climbing action off the beaten path, along with some easier traditional slab/crack climbs. This seldom-climbed wall has a couple of sport climbs that are worthy of the hike uphill, including *The Gilded Lady* (5.12c) and *Bolts & Hoes* (5.11b). This wall is on the north side of the road facing southeast.

Approach: Park at mile 7.7 at a dirt pull out on the south side of the road. Across the road you will see Nightworm Pinnacle (p136); walk up and past its right side in a small gully. Continue up for another few hundred feet on switchbacks with cairns.

Prestige Worldwide Wall approach

Note: These routes are not bad if you brought some trad gear with you. The routes on the left side of the wall offer some easier climbing and a little adventure. As you approach the wall, hike up to the left. The first route with a bolt on the slab is *Tetherly*.

① Slabs 5.5-5.7
Locate the slab on the left side of the wall that is 40 feet wide and 30 feet tall. There are many different ways to negotiate the slab through cracks to the top and a standard rack should be fine for all of them.
No anchors, walk off to the left (30')

② Seams Thin 5.6 ★
Climb the thin seam 10 feet left of *Pine Tree Eliminate*. It's kind of fun for a short route. *Rack to #1 Camalot, 2-bolt anchor up and right (30')*
FA: John Garlough 2013

③ Rat Rod 5.6 ★
Climb the discontinuous crack system between the two more obvious cracks of *Pine Tree Eliminate* and *Seams Thin*.
Rack to #3 Camalot, 2-bolt anchor (30')
FA: John Garlough 2013

④ Pine Tree Eliminate 5.4 ★★
A great beginner trad lead climbs the low-angled, hand crack that ends just past at a small tree. *Rack to #3 Camalot, 2-bolt anchor up left (30')*
FA: John Garlough 2013

⑤ Tetherly 5.7 ★
As you hike uphill to the left towards the cliff, *Tetherly* is the first route on your right. Start by pulling over a small bulge and a shallow right-facing corner, then edge up the slab.
2 bolts, rack to #1 Camalot, 2-bolt anchor (40')   FA: John Garlough 2013

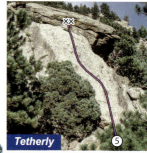
Tetherly

Rat Rod

Note: The following routes are the bolted sport climbs on the right side of the wall around the corner.

6 Catalina Wine Mixer
5.11b ★★
Cruise up the first three bolts on *The Gilded Lady*, then bust out left and up the slab for an easier finish.
4 bolts, 2-bolt anchor (40')
FA: John Garlough, Henry Maxfield 2011

7 The Gilded Lady 5.12c ★★
This fun, overhanging route is just left of *Bolts & Hoes*. Powerful climbing leads to a quick shake before a short, but hard boulder problem to gain the lip. *4 bolts, 2-bolt anchor (40')*
FA: John Garlough, Henry Maxfield 2011

8 Bolts & Hoes 5.11b ★
Climb the prominent overhanging corner. Stemming up the slightly overhanging dihedral provides a solid pump before pulling a beached whale move to mantel onto the ledge. It's a good warm up for its neighbor, but also a proud tick itself. A bit crumbly in spots.
5 bolts, 2-bolt anchor (45')
FA: John Garlough, Henry Maxfield 2011

9 Mud Bath 5.10a
This is the right-leaning hand crack 10 feet right of *Bolts & Hoes* that has a challenging start. Jam up the dirty, muddy, crumbly, and flaring crack to a large tree at the top. Build an anchor on the tree and walk off.
Rack doubles 0.5 - #3 Camalot, no anchor (45')   *FA: Kevin Capps 2012*

walk off

Prestige Worldwide Wall - right side

📷 Dan Gambino

Real Hidden Valley

0.2mi past mm264   10-15min   A.M. ☀   P.M. ☁   **11 Routes**

≤5.8 5.9 5.10 5.11 5.12 5.13 5.14 proj

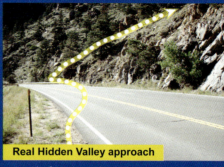

Crag Profile: This wall is fun mainly for one reason: it is way off the beaten path and you may never see anyone at this wall. So, when you get tired of the crowds at Wall of the '90s or High Wire, take a short hike up the hill and come to this beautiful sanctuary. It is higher in the canyon and offers great views. All of the climbs here are bolted slab routes, the best of which is probably *Paper Tiger* (5.10b). The wall is newly developed, so there are still a lot of flakes and crumbly rock that may clean up one day. The wall faces east and gets morning sun and afternoon shade.

Real Hidden Valley approach

Approach: Drive 7.7 miles up canyon and park in a dirt pullout on the south (left) side of the road. Cross the road and hike west along the road passing a guardrail and finding a drainage gully up to the right. Hike about 100 feet up the gully up and right, then take a solid right and hike east past a small ridge. When you are about level with the parking lot again, find a gully and take this uphill until finding the cliff on your left.

1 Tropicala 5.9

This short route is found on a separate block in front of the main wall. It climbs up the right side of the schist face. Not recommended.
3 bolts, 2-bolt anchor (30')
FA: John Garlough 2013

2 Paper Tiger 5.10b ★★

Fun and sustained slab climbing starts on the steep slab to the right of the arête. Continuous slab moves stay on you the whole way until culminating with a spectacular finish on the arête that is reminiscent of *The Edge of Time* in Estes Park.
7 bolts, 2-bolt anchor (65')
FA: John Garlough 2013

3 Calm Power 5.10c ★

Belay on the steep, rocky ledges just left of a wide, bushy crack. It's a little rough at the start, but it leads to a fun slab mantle on a big black plate like hold. Watch out for the technical slab crux traversing up and left.
7 bolts, 2-bolt anchor (65')
FA: John Garlough 2013

4 Odelay 5.10c ★

Start in the right-leaning ramp/wide crack, then pull multiple slab cruxes to get to the chains. It will probably get better when it cleans up a bit.
7 bolts, 2-bolt anchor (65')
FA: John Garlough 2013

Real Hidden Valley

Upper Wall of Real Hidden Valley approach

⑤ Debra 5.10d ★★ ⬜⬜
A technical and slightly reachy crux on the first half gets you to a ledge rest before conquering the easier climbing in the chimney on the second half. Take in the great views from the anchor. *8 bolts, 2-bolt anchor (70')*
FA: John Garlough 2013

UPPER WALL
To get to the Upper Wall, continue uphill past Real Hidden Valley for about 200 yards. You will spot the wall up to your right on the hillside. The views and solitude up here are amazing.

⑥ Prissy Prancin' 5.8 PG13 ⬜⬜
Mostly face climbing to the left of *Streakers* involves challenging moves on the steep face up high with decent gear. *Standard rack, with extra small pieces, tree anchor (40')*
FA: John Garlough 2013

⑦ Streakers 5.10a ★ ⬜⬜
This interesting route climbs up the grooved streak on the left side of the wall. Climb just slightly right of the bolt line to find better holds. Belay at a tree and walk off.
4 bolts, no anchor (40')
FA: John Garlough 2013

⑧ Valley Boys 5.6 ⬜⬜
Climb the ledgy crack system to the right of *Streakers*. Use the tree to belay and walk off.
Rack to #3 Camalot, no anchor (40')
FA: James Dickson 2013

⑨ Tetherly Designs 5.10a ★ ⬜⬜
Start just left of *Battle* and enjoy moderate climbing with a bit of a challenge just before the shared anchor. Small to medium-sized cams are necessary for the finish. *2 bolts, rack to #3 Camalot, 2-bolt anchor (40')*
FA: Lincoln Tetherly 2013

⑩ Battle of the Bulge
5.11c ★★ ⬜⬜
Power over the roof bulge at the start to gain some thin face climbing above. Small to medium-sized cams can protect the start (under the roof) and then going to the second bolt, or a stick clipping the first bolt works as well. *3 bolts, rack to 0.4 Camalot, 2-bolt anchor (40')*
FA: John Garlough 2013

⑪ Tower Dogs 5.10b ★ ⬜⬜
This is the rightmost bolted line. Start in the right-angling crack and place some gear to protect getting to the first bolt. Fun slab climbing up higher leads you to the top.
3 bolts, rack 0.4 - .75 Camalot, 2-bolt anchor (40')   FA: James Dickson 2013

Real Hidden Valley - Upper Wall

New Economy Cliff

0.2mi past mm264 10min

ALL DAY

15 Routes

| ≤5.8 | 5.9 | 5.10 | 5.11 | 5.12 | 5.13 | 5.14 | proj |

Crag Profile: New Economy is a great wall that's full of shaded moderates that will keep you busy on a hot, summer day. This cliff is great for the climber wanting to climb some fun 5.11/5.12s without the crowd. Routes like *Leading Indicators* (5.12c) and *Inflation* (5.12b) give an especially hard challenge for the 5.12 climber. This north-facing/shaded wall is perfect for late summer into fall when the water levels in the creek are lower, making it easier to cross the creek. Do not attempt to cross the creek during high water, it is faster and more dangerous than it looks.

Approach: Park in a dirt pullout on the south (left) side of the road after driving 7.7 miles up canyon. Look to the south side of the creek to spot the cliff. The only approach to this crag is wading the creek during low water, or walking across an ice bridge in the winter. However, you wouldn't want to climb here in the winter because it receives zero sun. After crossing the creek follow a faint trail to the cliff.

❶ Online Trading 5.11d ★
Find this route by itself downhill to the left from *Buy Gold*. Power past the first part of the route to gain a nice ledge rest, then easier climbing takes you to the top.
4 bolts, 2-bolt anchor (45')
FA: Vaino Kodas, Bob D'Antonio 2001

❷ Buy Gold 5.12a ★
Bushy ledges will lead you to a rest before conquering the steep face on the second half of this route. A fun way to climb this is to do *Buy Low, Sell High* until the upper headwall, then move left to do *Buy Gold*'s crux.
11 bolts, 2-bolt anchor (90')
FA: Vaino Kodas, Bob D'Antonio 2001

❸ Buy Low, Sell High
5.11c ★★★
Moderate climbing on the slab gets you warmed up for the fun, steep, and technical face on the upper headwall. *11 bolts, 2-bolt anchor (80')*
FA: Vaino Kodas, Bob D'Antonio 2000

New Economy overview

4 Inflation 5.12b ★★★   ☐☐

Has a dwindling economy ever been so much fun? Find this hidden gem by walking left from where the trail meets the cliff. Climb the easy, low-angled start just left of *Market Meltdown*. Ascend jugs to a rest below the overhanging wall above. From here, bust big moves on perfect stone to a tricky sequence at the lip. Fantastic! *11 bolts, 2-bolt anchor (80')*
FA: Vaino Kodas, Bob D'Antonio 2000

5 Market Meltdown 5.10d ★☐☐

This is a good route to do after warming up on *Undervalued*. Start up left of the white rock/dike.
9 bolts, 2-bolt anchor (80')
FA: Vaino Kodas, Bob D'Antonio 2000

6 Leading Indicators 5.12c ★★   ☐☐

A technical start climbing past the seam using small crimps on the blank, vertical wall leads you past the fourth bolt and into easier 5.10 climbing above. It's a little reachy, and probably solid 12c for shorter people. *9 bolts, 2-bolt anchor (75')*
FA: Vaino Kodas, Bob D'Antonio 2000

7 Undervalued 5.10a ★★   ☐☐

The rightmost route on the lower section has fun climbing on good stone with a couple of tougher sequences separated by small ledges. A great warm up for the wall.
7 bolts, 2-bolt anchor (75')
FA: Vaino Kodas, Bob D'Antonio 2000

8 On the Margin 5.10c ★   ☐☐

Although it's a bit short, this is an enjoyable climb with a hard move around the second bolt.
5 bolts, 2-bolt anchor (40')
FA: Vaino Kodas, Bob D'Antonio 2000

9 Tumbling Stocks 5.12a ★★   ☐☐

Soft for the grade. Interesting climbing leads to a great crux on gym-like holds. The first move can be a bit of a reach; consider using a stickclip.
7 bolts, 2-bolt anchor (40')
FA: Vaino Kodas, Bob D'Antonio 2000

10 Consumer Confidence 5.11c ★★   ☐☐

A short, low crux on side pulls leads to easier climbing above.
4 bolts, 2-bolt anchor (40')
FA: Vaino Kodas, Bob D'Antonio 2000

New Economy - left side

11 Selling Short 5.11c ★   ☐☐

Similar to its lefthand neighbor, *Selling Short* busts through the underclings. It's all over after the third bolt.
4 bolts, 2-bolt anchor (40')
FA: Vaino Kodas, Bob D'Antonio 2000

12 High Tech Sector 5.10c   ☐☐

It's long – that's about all this route has to offer. Dirty and fragile holds down low lead to discontinuous but much better climbing above.
11 bolts, 2-bolt anchor (95')
FA: Vaino Kodas, Bob D'Antonio 2000

13 Portfolio 5.11b ★   ☐☐

Scramble up to the start of the route and climb the face to the right of the white rock. Trend up to the right before shooting up to the anchors straight up. *8 bolts, 2-bolt anchor (75')*
FA: Vaino Kodas, Bob D'Antonio 2000

14 High Return 5.12a   ☐☐

This not-so-great route has a couple of hard little sequences.
8 bolts, 2-bolt anchor (75')
FA: Vaino Kodas, Bob D'Antonio 2000

15 Interest Rate 5.12a ★   ☐☐

The rightmost route climbs up the featured rock to a ledge and past a crack to scope out the steeper climbing above. Sustained face climbing with a few difficult moves brings you to the top. *8 bolts, 2-bolt anchor (75')*
FA: Vaino Kodas, Bob D'Antonio 2000

Bionic Crag

west of mm264   10min

ALL DAY   Some P.M. in Summer

5 Routes

≤5.8 5.9 5.10 5.11 5.12 5.13 5.14 proj

Crag Profile: This wall can be a little bit of a challenge to get to, and the climbing isn't ex-actly classic, but it might offer some seclusion on a busy day in the canyon. There are only two sport routes here, but with a few small to medium-sized cams, you can climb all the routes.

Approach: Drive 8.1 miles up the canyon and park on the south (left) side of the road in a small dirt pull off. Hike down to the creek and wade across at its lowest point. A short hike up-hill will take you to the base of the crag. You may also park 7.7 miles up the canyon on the south side of the road in a large dirt parking area, walk across the creek there, then hike upstream about 200 yards or so, to get to Bionic Crag.

1 Blade Runner 5.12b ★★
An interesting route fires up the over-hanging face to the left of the arête. Nasty rock quality on the first half brings you to a wildly interesting crux with a powerful lieback that rides the fin to the left of the arête. It's worth climbing if you're already at the wall, and would be four stars if the rock down low was better.
8 bolts, 2-bolt anchor (50')
FA: Mark Tarrant, Richard Wright 2008

2 The Shaft 5.11b ★★
Climb up the small, left-facing dihe-dral to the right of the arête. Lieback up steep rock to get to a balancy tra-verse up and left to *Blade Runner*'s anchor. *7 bolts, 2-bolt anchor (50')*
FA: Mark Tarrant, Richard Wright 2008

3 Ti'ed 5.11a ★
This is a mixed line that climbs up the crack to the right of *The Shaft*. A bolt protects the start before climbing up the crack. Another bolt protects the face moves up higher before going up and right to the anchor.
2 bolts, small to medium-sized cams, 2-bolt anchor (50')
FA: Mark Tarrant, Richard Wright 2008

4 Replicants 5.11b ★
Steep face climbing using sidepull flakes leads up to a big move out left by the third bolt. Follow climbing past the fourth bolt while placing gear as you move up and right towards the anchors on *Electric Sheep*. *4 bolts, rack to #1 Camalot, 2-bolt anchor (50')*
FA: Mark Tarrant, Richard Wright 2008

Bionic Crag

5 Electric Sheep 5.11a ★★
The rightmost route on the wall fea-tures technical climbing up the shal-low dihedral. Clip bolts up to a finger crack and follow it to the top.
3 bolts, small to medium sized gear, 2-bolt anchor (50')
FA: Mark Tarrant, Richard Wright 2008

Kevin Capps feels the *Inflation*, 5.12b, New Economy Cliff, p147. 📷 Dan Gambino

Little Piece of South Dakota

Mile Marker: 263

 15min

 A.M.

 P.M.

≤5.8 5.9 5.10 5.11 5.12 5.13 5.14 proj

5 Routes

Crag Profile: This wall hosts a number of moderate to easy traditional lines and even more adventure. The most obvious routes are listed here in this book, but there are many more fun little lines that one could climb with a rack of gear. Currently, there is one bolted anchor at the top of *Ethical Gesture*, but there is almost always a tree to belay from at the top of the wall when you need one. Use the trail on the left side of the wall to walk back around to the base from the top. The wall gets afternoon sun.

Approach: Little Piece of South Dakota uses the same parking area as High Profile Crag (p152). Drive 8.7 miles up the canyon and park on the south (left) side of the road. Walk about 200 yards east/downstream until you are about even with the wall and wade across the creek to get to the crag.

parking (looking west)

Little Piece of South Dakota

approach (looking back down canyon)

Little Piece of South Dakota

1 **North Dakota** 5.7 ⭐
Belay behind a large pine tree and climb up the obvious, left-slanting crack system. Protectable climbing through ledges brings you to a belay from a small tree at the top of the wall. *Rack to #3 Camalot (90')*

2 **Little Piece** 5.8
From behind the large tree, climb up and right in the thin, right-angling seam where you can plug a couple of small pieces before pulling over onto easier terrain as you follow the weakness to the top of the wall.
Rack to #3 Camalot (95')

3 **Ethical Gesture** 5.9 ⭐⭐
Start at the lowest point in the center of the wall in a slot behind a boulder. Climb past a crack system to gain lower angled terrain up and left. Head straight up past a bolt to get to a ledge where you can continue straight up the steep prow or climb an easier variation on the lower angled face to the left. Belay from a bolted anchor. It's easiest to climb this in one long pitch. *1 bolt, rack to #3 Camalot, 2-bolt anchor (130')*
FA: Fred Knapp, S. Powers, L. Davis 1989

4 **Reds** 5.8
Head 25 feet uphill and to the right of *Ethical Gesture*. Start up the left-slanting slab and then climb the bushy, broken crack system straight up. Finish in a left-slanting crack to get to the top of the wall and a bolted anchor at the top of *Ethical Gesture*. Bring long slings to reduce drag if you're doing this in one pitch.
Rack to #3 Camalot (125')

5 **Midwestern Crack** 5.6 ⭐
Choose from one of the easy crack systems on the right side of the wall that leads up to a prominent, right-slanting parallel crack system that angles up to a tree halfway up the wall. Build an anchor at the tree, or continue up the wide crack up and left and belay from a tree at the top. Walk off to the left.
Rack to #3 Camalot (110')

Matt Lloyd on *Hungry Wolf*, 5.13a, High Profile Wall, next page.
📷 Dan Gambino

High Profile Wall

Mile Marker: 263

10-15min

MOST OF THE DAY

P.M.

4 Routes

≤5.8 5.9 5.10 5.11 5.12 5.13 5.14 proj

Crag Profile: This hardman's wall is home to two classic 5.13s that will surely feed your appetite for technical face climbing. Despite being so close to the road, it's not the easiest wall to get to considering the creek crossing and the scrambling needed to get to the base. Regardless, *Stuffed Wolf* is one of the best 5.13s in the canyon, and at 13b, it is earns every bit of the grade. This wall faces northwest and gets shade most of the first part of the day and sun in the afternoon.

parking (looking west)

Approach: Drive 8.7 miles up the canyon and park in a large dirt pullout on the south (left) side of the road. There is an ice bridge that forms in the winter, or wade the creek in the shallowest spot you can find during low water. After crossing the creek, scramble up to the right side of the wall through fourth to easy fifth class terrain to get to the base of the routes.

1 Mouse Meat 5.10b ★
This is the warm up for the wall. Carefully scramble down the ledge and to the left to a belay anchor. Climb up and left, then trend up moving around the arête and up the face to the anchor.
10 bolts, 2-bolt anchor (75')
FA: Darren Mabe 2010

2 Puppy Chow 5.11c TR
Toprope the left-slanting crack to the left of *Hungry Wolf*. (70')

3 Hungry Wolf 5.13a ★★★★
Excellent! Start in a left-slanting crack, then power up the challenging face to meet up with *Stuffed Wolf* and pull a burly redpoint crux. This was the first route established on the wall. *6 bolts, 2-bolt anchor (70')*
FA: Kurt Smith, Pete Zoller

4 Stuffed Wolf 5.13b ★★★★
Stuffed Wolf is one of the best 5.13s in the canyon. Start on the right side of the wall. Pull a few challenging, but still kind of moderate moves, to enter into a technical and powerful low crux. After making it out of the first crux alive, continue through another tough sequence with thin, crimpy moves and fight the pump all the way to the anchor. Sustained and hard for the grade.
7 bolts, 2-bolt anchor (60')
FA: Pat Adams 1994

High Profile Wall

TUNNEL FIVE

BETHANY LUKENS ON MR. MISTOFFELES, 5.9, CATSLAB, P158. 🄯 DAN GAMBINO

6

TUNNEL 6

Play Pen
p180

12.5mi

Creekside
p168

Stoked Bowl
p467

Live Action Wall
p165

tyrol from
tree to cliff

The Bunker
p78

The Doghouse
p162

12.2mi

TUNNEL 5

Cats v. Dogs
Wall p160

The Fiscal Cliff
p155

Catslab
p158

Mourning Glory
p157

11.7mi

6

N

0.5 miles

0.5 kilometers

Clear Creek County
Jefferson County

Gilpin County

11.5mi

119

6

The Fiscal Cliff

5-10min   ALL DAY   **14 Routes**

≤5.8 5.9 5.10 5.11 5.12 5.13 5.14 proj

Crag Profile: The Fiscal Cliff is a short cliff band that borders the south side of the creek just east of Tunnel 5. There has recently been some development at this wall that has made it a destination climbing area with a variety of fun routes. The rock is very featured, and on the harder routes the use of some kneebar trickery comes in handy. The wall faces northwest and might see some afternoon sun in the summer.

Approach: To get to the Fiscal Cliff, drive 11.7 miles up the canyon on Highway 6 and park on the south (left) side of the road by a guardrail. Follow the creekside trail for a couple hundred yards before coming to a short wall with bolts on your left.

Fiscal Cliff parking

❶ Mirror 5.12c ★
This is the first route you encounter when you approach the cliff. It climbs up a left-facing overhang.
5 bolts, 2-bolt anchor (30')
FA: Derek Peavey 2014

❷ Just in Time 5.12d ★
Climb the first three bolts of *Mirror*, then bust up and right.
6 bolts, 2-bolt anchor (30')
FA: Derek Peavey, Matt Samet 2014

❸ Systemic Risk 5.11b ★
This is more fun than it looks, but still not that good. Overhanging climbing on featured rock with blocky holds leads to a mantel onto a dirty ledge. Continue on to the juggy finish.
6 bolts, 2-bolt anchor (35')
FA: Thor Kiesser 2012

❹ Glitter and Doom 5.11d
Start under the small bulge to the right of Systemic Risk; this has a harder and pumpier start than its counterpart with slightly dirtier rock. Be creative on this thuggy route. There is a lone bolt in the overhang at the start, avoid this and head up and left. *7 bolts, 2-bolt anchor (35')*
FA: Mike Bronson 2012

❺ Dump Truck 5.12b ★
Start on Glitter and Doom, pull a hard boulder problem straight up over the bulge. *4 bolts, 2-bolt anchor (20')*
FA: Matt Samet, Derek Peavey 2014

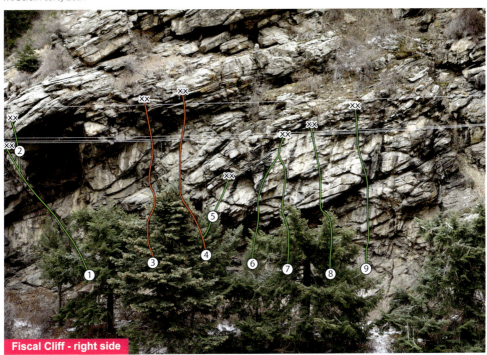

Fiscal Cliff - right side

6 Colliding 5.12b ★   ☐☐

Start just right of Dump Truck and climb straight up to the right and link up with Over the Top.
4 bolts, 2-bolt anchor (30')
FA: Derek Peavey, Matt Samet 2014

7 Over the Top 5.12a ★★   ☐☐

Though a bit dirty, this route has fun and sustained climbing with a final challenge going to the top. It will be better once it cleans up a bit.
4 bolts, 2-bolt anchor (30')
FA: Derek Peavey, Cassidy Hill 2014

8 The Road 5.12c ★★   ☐☐

A great testpiece for the wall! Start out with some okay climbing to get to a fantastic crux sequence (with a hand jam) pulling over the lip and getting established on the wall above. Enjoy great stone on the upper section. *5 bolts, 2-bolt anchor (30')*
FA: Derek Peavey 2014

9 Last Minute 5.12c ★   ☐☐

Start 10 feet to the right of The Road and climb the rightmost bolted line before the cliff breaks down for awhile. *5 bolts, 2-bolt anchor (30')*
FA: Derek Peavey, Matt Samet 2014

Note: Walk a couple hundred feet right of The Road to get to the routes on the right side of the wall.

10 Runaway Truck Ram   ☐☐
5.12a ★★

This fun little route climbs up the nice looking face on the left side of this section of the wall.
5 bolts, 2-bolt anchor (30')
FA: Derek Peavey, Cassidy Hill 2014

11 Large Marge 5.11d ★★   ☐☐

Climb out multiple roof cruxes separated by nice rests. Very bouldery and fun, it's just a bit awkward clipping the fourth bolt.
5 bolts, 2-bolt anchor (40')
FA: Derek Peavey 2014

Fiscal Cliff - left side

12 Joppa Road 5.12a ★   ☐☐
A bit of a squeeze; climb up through two small roofs.
6 bolts, 2-bolt anchor (30')
FA: Derek Peavey 2014

13 Lot Lizards 5.11c ★★   ☐☐
Start just left of Joyride and climb up and pull a small roof before engaging in a crux establishing yourself on the face above the second roof.
6 bolts, 2-bolt anchor (45')
FA: Derek Peavey 2014

14 Joyride 5.8 ★★★   ☐☐
An excellent warm up for the area. Start on the left side of the black water streak and enjoy good holds the whole way as you climb to the anchor up and slightly left.
6 bolts, 2-bolt anchor (45')
FA: Derek Peavey 2014

Mourning Glory Wall

 15-20min

A.M.   MOST OF THE DAY

2 Routes

≤5.8 5.9 5.10 5.11 5.12 5.13 5.14 proj

Crag Profile: Mourning Glory is a newer wall that holds one of the hardest Front Range test pieces, *Mourning Glory* (5.14c). Originally developed by Darren Mabe and his futuristic vision for hard lines. By finding *Mourning Glory*, he set a new standard for hard climbing in Clear Creek Canyon. This wall is situated high in the canyon and offers some amazing exposure for single pitch sport climbs. The wall is west-facing and gets morning shade.

Mourning Glory Wall and Fiscal Cliff parking

Approach: After making the left turn at the light, continue for just a bit before pulling off on the south (left) side of the road, driving a total of 11.7 miles up the canyon. Take the creekside trail west until finding some cairn with a faint slanted trail going uphill to your left; if you see the Fiscal Cliff then you have gone too far. Hike uphill via a few switchbacks and slanting to the right as you wrap around the hillside. This will bring you to the base of the left hand side of the cliff and *Sweet Tides*.

❶ Sweet Tides 5.11c ★★
Fun climbing goes up the prow-like formation to some steeper climbing above. A technical crux in the beginning leads to fun and pumpy climbing going to the top. Great views and exposure. *9 bolts, 2-bolt anchor (85')*
FA: Darren Mabe 2009

❷ Mourning Glory
5.14c ★★★★
One of the best hard lines in the canyon climbs out the center of the large roof. Scramble up the fourth class ledges to a belay bolt at the start. Begin with some 12b climbing to get towards the base of a 35-foot roof section, and then climb through multiple powerful and dynamic cruxes before reaching the chains. Originally called *Belays of Glory* after Darren Mabe made his solo-equipping ascent.
11 bolts, 2-bolt anchor (75')
FA: Daniel Woods 2012;
Equipper: Darren Mabe 2009

Mourning Glory Wall

Fiscal Cliff

Mourning Glory Wall and Fiscal Cliff approach

Mourning Glory Wall

Catslab

 10-15min A.M. MOST OF THE DAY

10 Routes

≤5.8 5.9 5.10 5.11 5.12 5.13 5.14 *proj*

Crag Profile: This is where you will find most of the 5.7-5.10 climbers on a Saturday afternoon, and for good reason. Catslab has some of the finest and safest moderates in the canyon, and the best part is you can't even hear or see the road! This peaceful sanctuary of slab climbs hosts a handful of classics, as well as a 5.4 sport climb that is perfect for your first lead. Land ownership issues in the past have halted climbers from coming here, but in 2010 Catslab became part of Clear Creek County Open Space and is open for climbing.

Catslab, Cats vs Dogs Wall, Dog House, Live Action Wall, and Stoked Bowl parking

Approach: Park on the west side of Tunnel 5, on the south (left) side of the road after driving 12.2 miles up the canyon. Walk across the bridge towards Tunnel 5, and then take the generally flat trail on the south side of the road for a little less than a quarter mile before reaching the distinct, clean slab on your left.

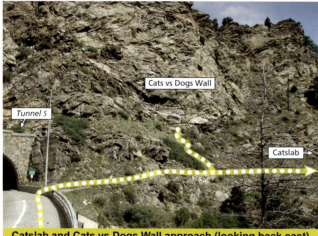

Catslab and Cats vs Dogs Wall approach (looking back east)

1 Skimbleshanks 5.8 ★★★★ ☐☐
Skimbleshanks is one of the best moderates in the canyon. There's a lot of variety in this one, with a slab down low and featured rock up higher. Watch out for some loose rock two-thirds of the way up the route. A 60-meter rope will just barely make it. *14 bolts, 2-bolt anchor (105')*
FA: Richard Wright, Anna Brandenburg-Schroeder 1997

2 Old Deuteronomy 5.10a ★★★ ☐☐
Climb the overhang and mantel onto the slab. Fun friction movement gains some great quartz blocks. A 60-meter cord just makes it; be careful when lowering if you have trimmed your rope. *10 bolts, 2-bolt anchor (102')*
FA: Richard Wright, Anna Brandenburg-Schroeder 1997

3 Mungajerry 5.10a ★★ ☐☐
Climb through the small bulge to a slab crux towards the top of the route. The crux can be skipped by moving left or right, making the route a little contrived. Even so, it's good climbing. *12 bolts, 2-bolt anchor (102')*
FA: Richard Wright, Anna Brandenburg-Schroeder 1997

4 Rumple Teaser 5.10b ★★★ ☐☐
This route has one of the harder slab cruxes on the wall. Sustained, technical movement brings you to a sequence towards the top where all of the holds disappear, making your footwork very important. Trust your feet! *12 bolts, 2-bolt anchor (102')*
FA: Richard Wright, Anna Brandenburg-Schroeder 1997

5 Mr. Mistoffelees 5.9 ★★★★ ☐☐
An easy and ledgy start leads to a challenging slab sequence that follows a seam for hands as you smear your feet on the face. Climb a fun, blocky quartz band to finish it off. A great climb for the wall. *12 bolts, 2-bolt anchor (110')*
FA: Richard Wright, Anna Brandenburg-Schroeder 1997

6a Gumby Cat 5.4 ★★ ☐☐
This is a great first lead due to its easy, straightforward climbing. This is also the first part of *Jellicle Cats*. *5 bolts, 2-bolt anchor (50')*
FA: Richard Wright, Anna Brandenburg-Schroeder 1997

Catslab

6 Jellicle Cats 5.10a ★★   ☐☐
Great climbing gains in difficulty on the second half. Climb past the anchors of *Gumby Cat* and into the slab crux of this route for one long pitch. *14 bolts, 2-bolt anchor (135')*
FA: Richard Wright, Anna Brandenburg-Schroeder 1997

7 MacCavity 5.10a ★★★★   ☐☐
Moderate slab climbing leads to a crimpy crux pulling up and over the left-facing dihedral roof. Fun climbing just right of the bolt line takes you to the top. *13 bolts, 2-bolt anchor (125')*
FA: Richard Wright, Anna Brandenburg-Schroeder 1997

8 Grizabella 5.7 ★★★   ☐☐
This is the rightmost bolted route that you can start from the bottom of the wall. Ledgy slab climbing leads to some thinner moves on the second half. *10 bolts, 2-bolt anchor (95')*
FA: Richard Wright, Anna Brandenburg-Schroeder 1997

9 Rum Tum Tugger 5.11b ★ ☐☐
This route is the total opposite of everything else at Catslab. Begin from the top of *Grizabella* on the far right side of the wall. From the belay anchors, head up and right until it is possible to climb straight up the very overhanging wall above. Four star climbing on zero star rock is the best way to describe this worthwhile climb. Be careful when lowering as it is possible to lower your climber to a ledge below the start of the climb where down climbing is possible. *10 bolts, 2-bolt anchor (75')*
FA: Richard Wright, Anna Brandenburg-Schroeder 1997

10 Gus 5.10b ★★   ☐☐
Scramble up the easy and loose slab to the two-bolt anchors at the start of this line. Like the route to the left of this one on the upper right side, it ascends the overhanging (and sometimes chossy) rock and finishes just right of *Rum Tum Tugger*. Good climbing on bad stone. *11 bolts, 2-bolt anchor (95')*
FA: Richard Wright, Anna Brandenburg-Schroeder 1997

Jamie Gatchalian on *Rum Tum Tugger,* 5.11b.   📷 Dan Gambino

Cats vs Dogs Wall

 5-10min
MOST OF
THE DAY

4 Routes

≤5.8 5.9 5.10 5.11 5.12 5.13 5.14 proj

Crag Profile: There is a plethora of classic climbing on the west side of Tunnel 5, including walls like Catslab, The Dog House, and Creekside. If you have already climbed on those walls more than enough times, head over to Cats vs Dogs Wall. This is the west-facing wall on the west side of the tunnel and a few hundred feet south (downstream) of the road. While the rock quality isn't great at this wall, the movement on the routes is fun and thoughtful.

Approach: Park 100 yards west of Tunnel 5 on the south (left) side of the road after driving 12.2 miles up canyon. This is the same parking as for Catslab. From here, walk back towards Tunnel 5 and look up to see the chossy wall a few hundred feet to the right of the tunnel on the south side of the road. Use the main approach trail on the south side of the road until you are about even with the wall, then hike up switchbacks to the base.

1 **Beer for Life** 5.10d ★
The leftmost bolted line starts up and left of *Into the Black* on a ramp. Climb to a steep upper wall and through a bulge.
9 bolts, 2-bolt anchor (85')
FA: Chuck Fitch, Adam Huxley 2013

2 **Into the Black** 5.10c ★
A powerful and kind of reachy crux pulling past the roof at the start leads to more moderate terrain on the rest of the climb.
10 bolts, 2-bolt anchor (90')
FA: Chuck Fitch, Adam Huxley 2013

3 **Out of the Blue** 5.8+ ★★
This moderate goes up the center of the wall. The first pitch has the better climbing on it. Both pitches can be done in a long pitch with slings. Make two rappels if you only have one rope.
P1: 5.8+ Tiptoe up the broken, right-angling ramp to a high first bolt. Fun climbing, that gets steeper towards the top, leads to a good belay ledge. *8 bolts, 2-bolt anchor (90')*
P2: 5.7 Climb easier terrain on dirty rock. *8 bolts, 2-bolt anchor (70')*
FA: Chuck Fitch, Adam Huxley 2013

4 **Stray Cat** 5.8 ★
The rightmost bolted route follows super-featured rock through crumbly pegmatite bands on the second half. You will find the anchor up and to the left. Bring a sling for the fourth bolt to reduce rope drag.
8 bolt, slings, 2-bolt anchor (80')
FA: Chuck Fitch, Adam Huxley 2013

Cats vs Dogs Wall

Jamie Gatchalian on *Mungajerry*, 5.10a, Catslab, p158. 📷 Dan Gambino

The Dog House

10-15min

ALL DAY

≤5.8 5.9 5.10 5.11 5.12 5.13 5.14 proj

10 Routes

Crag Profile: What's not to love? The routes are overhanging, dynamic, and always a good time. This wall is high in the canyon and gets afternoon sun. With thuggy classics like *Mighty Dog* (5.12c) and *Big Dog* (5.12b), you can test your power even through the winter months. However, virtually all the 5.12s here have man-ufactured/drilled holds on them.

The Dog House approach

Approach: Drive 12.2 miles up canyon along US-6 and park about 100 yards west of Tunnel 5 on either side of the road. This is the same parking area as for Catslab (p158). From here, look up the hill to the north (right) side of the road and spot a huge roof jutting out of the mountain. Hike back towards Tunnel 5 and find a trail on the north side of the road that will take you uphill on switchbacks.

The Dog House

1 Snoopy 5.9+ ★★
The leftmost route works over a small bulge to a ledge, and then fires up the left-facing dihedral to the top. *12 bolts, slings, 2-bolt anchor (95')* FA: Kirk Miller 2005

2 Li'l Dog 5.11b ★★
Moderate climbing leads to an over-hanging prow towards the top of the route. This is a good way to warm up for some of the harder routes on the wall. *12 bolts, 2-bolt anchor (90')* FA: Kirk Miller 2005

2a Li'l Snoopy 5.9- ★★
Follow *Li'l Dog* to the sixth bolt, and then angle up and left to finish in the *Snoopy* dihedral. *11 bolts, 2-bolt anchor (95')* FA: Kirk Miller 2005

3 Black Dog 5.9+ ★
A crimpy sequence with a long reach leads to more moderate climbing above. *10 bolts, 2-bolt anchor (75')*

4 **Dog Breath** 5.10a ★★
Climb the face to a juggy seam on the left side of the big roof. Fun climbing leads to an anchor at about 40 feet.
5 bolts, 2-bolt anchor (40')
Dog Breath Extension 5.10d
Continue above the low anchor for some more face climbing to *Black Dog*'s anchor.
10 bolts, 2-bolt anchor (75')
FA: Alan Nelson 1999

5 **Hot Dog** 5.11b ★★★
Work up the face to a thuggy, over-hanging, right-leaning traverse on positive holds with smeary feet. There are two sets of anchors; climb-ing to the higher one doesn't add much to the route.
8 bolts, 2-bolt anchor (55')
FA: Alan Nelson 1999

6 **Fiddler on the Woof**
5.12b ★★
Technical face climbing leads to a short rest before conquering the drilled pockets moving through the steep roof. Although it's drilled and manufactured, it's still kind of fun.
9 bolts, 2-bolt anchor (50')
FA: Alan Nelson 1999

7 **Mighty Dog** 5.12c ★★★
Intimidating and awesome, *Mighty Dog* climbs out the steepest part of the roof. After leaving the slab, pumpy and sustained climbing takes you to a powerful crux sequence out right to a jug before pulling over the roof. Kneebar trickery can reduce the pump on the first half.
8 bolts, 2-bolt anchor (60')
FA: Alan Nelson, Jimmy Menendez 1999

7a **Mighty Variation**
5.12c ★★
Instead of mantling over the roof after pulling the crux, traverse out right where vertical climbing brings you past a couple more bolts to an anchor. This is a slightly easier finish that can make the route soft for the grade depending on your style.
10 bolts, 2-bolt anchor (65')

8 **Big Dog** 5.12b ★★★
Start on the steep arête just to the right of *Mighty Dog*. Powerful moves on good holds lead to a high-tension sequence before moving up and right to more vertical terrain with a few active rests. After shaking out, finish straight up on the sustained face. There are a few manufactured holds on this one.
10 bolts, 2-bolt anchor (70')
FA: Mark Rolofson, Alan Nelson 1999

The Dog House - right side

8a **Big Run** 5.12b ★★
A fun variation adds another 12- crux to *Big Dog* before clipping the chains. Start on *Big Dog*, power past the opening roof and crux, and then cop a quick rest before moving out right and finishing on *Dog Run*.
10 bolts, 2-bolt anchor (70')

9 **Dog Run** 5.12b ★★
Start up on the slab in the gully to the right, then climb up and left out the small roof past a quick 12a se-quence to establish yourself on the headwall. A good shake on a jug lets you prepare for some challeng-ing moves, utilizing a couple drilled pockets before gaining the anchors.
8 bolts, 2-bolt anchor (70')
FA: Alan Nelson 1999

10 **The Underdog** 5.12c
The rightmost line heads up the gul-ly, then steps left on the overhang when you feel comfortable taking on a tough sequence with crumbly holds to get to an overhanging crack. Jam in the steep hand crack to the top, which will feel hard for the grade if you can't jam.
10 bolts, 2-bolt anchor (70')
FA: Alan Nelson 1999

Alan Nelson on his route, *Fiddler on the Woof*, 5.12b. 📷 Kirk Miller

Live Action Wall

 20min

 MOST OF THE DAY

 P.M.

5 Routes

≤5.8 5.9 5.10 5.11 5.12 5.13 5.14 proj

Crag Profile: This is a new wall with a few cool routes including the classic *Live Action* (5.12c). The wall is high in the canyon and offers great views with a bit of seclusion. There is a lot of potential for some fun moderates at this wall, and I wouldn't be surprised if by the time this book came out there would already be a few more bolted routes. It faces southeast and is very exposed to sun most of the day until it receives afternoon shade.

Approach: Park on either side of the road after driving 12.2 miles and going through Tunnel 5 to the west side. Walk towards the tunnel and across the bridge to find a trail on the north side of the road that takes you west by the stream as if you were going to Creekside. At the first main gully to your right, follow switchbacks and cairns up a few hundred feet before cutting left to find Live Action.

1 Gator Boy 5.9+

Clip the first bolt on *Turtleman*, then bust up and left to follow the small, right-facing corner. *1 bolt, rack to #3 Camalot, 2-bolt anchor (95')*
FA: Kevin Capps 2013

2 Turtleman 5.10b ★★

Climb easy terrain to a high first bolt. Continue on the fun, moderate slab to a couple of challenging moves to get past the headwall, then finish with some delicate slab moves as you go towards the anchor.
10 bolts, 2-bolt anchor (95')
FA: Kevin Capps 2013

3 Live Action 5.12c ★★★★

This excellent line is worthy of the hike uphill. Scramble up fourth class terrain to a ledge where you can clip the first bolt. Moderate climbing brings you to the slightly overhanging, intimidating headwall. Powerful and technical moves take you up the seam past the crux to a final mantel move before easier 5.10 climbing leads you to the anchors.
10 bolts, 2-bolt anchor (90')
FA: Luke Childers 2013

4 Mellow Action 5.5 ★

Climb the cracks that go up the low-angled slabs on the right side of the wall. About halfway up the wall gets steep for a small section; pick a crack and climb it to the top. Belay at a tree and walk around the right side of the wall. *Rack to #1 Camalot (90')*

5 Call of the Wildman
5.11b ★★★

Sustained climbing in the thin crack on the right side of the wall involves a tough sequence moving past the second bolt. Gain some better holds

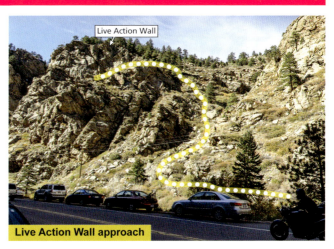

Live Action Wall approach

Live Action Wall

and a decent rest before the bulge at the top and the spicy finish.
5 bolts, 2-bolt anchor (45')
FA: Kevin Capps 2013

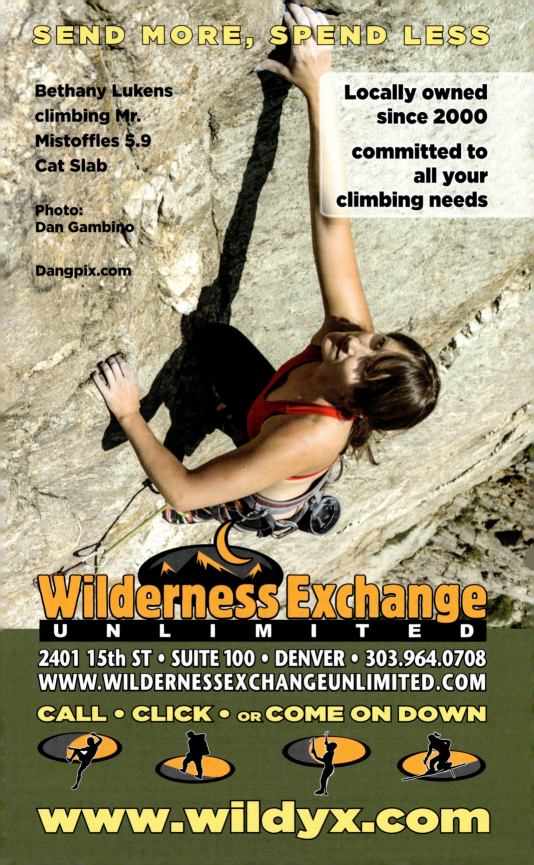

Stoked Bowl

 25min   A.M.   P.M.   **1 Route**

≤5.8 5.9 5.10 5.11 5.12 5.13 5.14 proj

Crag Profile: This newly developed area came into existence due to the popular sport of highlining. There is not much development at this wall, but it's worth mentioning. The wall faces south to southwest and gets midday sun due to its position in the gully.

Approach: Park on either side of the road on the west side of Tunnel 5, driving 12.2 miles up the canyon. This is the same as for Live Action Wall. Walk towards the tunnel and across the bridge to find a trail on the north side of the road that takes you west by the stream as if you were going to Creekside. At the first main gully to your right, follow switchbacks and cairns up a few hundred feet before cutting to your left and finding a trail to take you uphill. This trail will level out and bring you across a ridge to the gully where you will find Stoked Bowl.

① Try These Nachos 5.9+ ★ ☐☐
Hike to the top of the gully to find this south-facing route. A crumbly patch at the bottom leads you into more enjoyable moderate climbing above.
7 bolts, 2-bolt anchor (60')
FA: Scott Turpin 2012

Stoked Bowl

Luke Childers on *Live Action*, 5.12c, p165.   📷 Kevin Capps

Creekside

20min

MOST OF THE DAY

P.M.

28 Routes
≤5.8 5.9 5.10 5.11 5.12 5.13 5.14 proj

Crag Profile: Searching for a little adventure in Clear Creek? While Creekside is still close to the road, it may be what you're looking for to push your limits and gain a little exposure. Creekside is a 400-foot piece of rock shooting up on the north side of the creek just east of Tunnel 6. There is a variety of single and multi-pitch classics at this wall. One can't help but look up at the daunting upper headwall of *Solid Gold* (5.12a) when driving up the canyon. If you are a climber, you are drawn to the clean, aesthetic face starting 300 feet above the canyon floor. While some of the routes on the right side get blasted by morning sun, there is plenty of shade in the evening, making this a good place to climb in the winter or summer. Overall, the wall has a southeast aspect.

Approach: There are three different approaches depending on where you are climbing.
Hike in to the Solid Gold Area: Drive 12.2 miles up canyon and park just west of Tunnel 5 on either side of the road. Walk back towards the tunnel and across the bridge to find a trail on the north side of the road. Take this trail west (up canyon) as it follows the creek to get to a small, flat area with the start to *Solid Gold*. 10-15 min
Tyrolean to the Guppy Area: To get to routes like *Rhett Wench, Guppy,* and *Crackside*, use the tyrolean approach. Park 12.4 miles up the canyon on the north (right) side of the road, just before (east of) Tunnel 6. Walk downhill towards the creek to locate a tyrolean high in a tree. Climb the tree and pull across. 10 min

Wade the Creek for Brennivin Roof: For routes in the Brennivin Roof area, the best approach is to wade the creek during low water. Drive 12.5 miles up canyon and park just before (east of) Tunnel 6 on the north (right) side of the road. Hike upstream until finding the best spot to wade across the water at. 10 min
Climb Shenanigans to Brennivin Roof Area: Take the tyrol across the creek to the Guppy area, and then climb *Shenanigans* to traverse to the left side of the wall. 15-20 min

walkoff

Are There Bolts Up There?

Note: Routes 1-8 are on the left side of the wall in what's known as the Brennivin Roof Area. Wade across the creek or climb *Shenanigans* to get to these routes.

1 Are There Bolts Up There? 5.10a (5.8 R)

P1: 5.10a Climb the wide, right-slanting crack to the left of *Winterfest*. Find good gear and jams despite the dirty rock. Belay at a flake on a small ledge up and right. *Rack to #4 Camalot (120')*

P2: 5.5 Continue up the ledgy, broken rock until the climbing gets steeper up and right. *Rack to #4 Camalot (150')*

P3: 5.8 R Traverse right and head up the steeper (and quite runout) terrain to the top of the wall. Belay at a tree at the top. *Minimal gear (100')*

Decent: Hike off the backside for an adventure. It's best to hike down so you are to the left side of the wall. If you go straight back and slightly left you can scramble down the hillside.
FA: James Bellamy, Noah McKelvin 2012

2 Winterfest 5.9+ ★★

Start 15 feet right of the white rock band. Follow good and consistent moderate climbing all the way to the top. *7 bolts, 2-bolt anchor (65')*
FA: Dave Montgomery 2009

3 Rumpleminze 5.10d ★

Reachy moves at the start bring you to some awkward moves negotiating around the third bolt. Share anchors with *100 Proof*.
7 bolts, 2-bolt anchor (70')
FA: Dave Montgomery, Mike Sheridan 2009

4 100 Proof 5.12a ★★★

Fantastic face climbing! Crimpy and delicate moves bring you up into the white rock band. A technical crux with just enough holds hits you as you move up and left. It's a bit reachy at first, but after figuring it out, it gets better. There is a bolt moving up and right near the finish for a link up into *Macho Borracho*.
8 bolts, 2-bolt anchor (70')
FA: Dave Montgomery, Kristin McIlrath 2009

5 Approach Left 5.10c ★★★

A super fun 5.10 is a great start to get to the routes in the roof. Crimps, jugs, and steep rock make for a nice and moderate pitch.
7 bolts, 2-bolt anchor (75')

The Brennivin Roof Area

6 Approach Right 5.10b ★★

This is the bolted line to the right of the *Approach Left*, which cruises up and left on crimps for a slightly easier but less direct 5.10 approach to get to *Macho Borracho* or Brennivin.
9 bolts, 2-bolt anchor (75')

7 Macho Borracho 5.12c ★★★★

Big and committing moves on a large, juggy, exposed roof is one way to describe this Clear Creek classic. Climb *Approach Left* to a bolted belay. Then cruise up on ok climbing to a massive roof. A series of good holds brings you into a huge move/dyno to hit the lip, then better holds and one more hard sequence brings you up and right to the chains. Amazing and exposed! *8 bolts, 2-bolt anchor (55' or 125' to the ground)*
FA: Darren Mabe, Dave Montgomery 2010

8 Brennivin 5.12d ★★★★

This route climbs the ominous-looking crack going out the center of the massive roof. Climb one of the approach pitches to a bolted belay to the left of the base of the route. From the belay, climb up the ramp on good holds, going past a bolt to get to a long deadpoint crux to get into the crack. Hold on tight and fight the pump in the crack to get to the top. There is some fixed gear and stoppers on this route, but most of it can be backed up with your own gear. *1 bolt, slings, rack 0.5 – 2 Camalot, 2-bolt anchor (60' or 130' to the ground)*
FA: Pete Takeda, Eric Greene 2002

Matt Lloyd goes big on *Macho Borracho*, 5.12c, previous page. 📷 Dan Gambino

Note: For routes 9-12, use the tyrolean high in the tree to access the small ledge across the creek. These are located in the lower center of Creekside.

9 Shenanigans 5.6

This is an approach route to get to the Brennivin Roof routes and the left side of the wall. Take the tyrolean over the creek to the Guppy pod. Climb the first pitch of *Rhett Wench* to the bolted anchor, then traverse about 15 feet left, clipping a bolt along the way. From there, you can rappel down to the left to gain a ledge at the base of the cliff. On the way back, climb up and right past five bolts to get to the anchor and then rappel back to the Guppy pod from there. *7 bolts, 2-bolt anchor (65')*
FA: Darren Mabe 2009

10 Rhett Wench 5.11d ★★★

P1: 5.6 Start 15 feet left of the Guppy pod, and enjoy mellow slab climbing up and left to a small ledge with an anchor. *6 bolts, 2-bolt anchor (65')*
P2: 5.11d Follow the steep lieback seam at the start of this pitch, and then continue with somewhat easier climbing to some fun and challenging moves through the roof. *12 bolts, slings, 2-bolt anchor (85')*
FA: Darren Mabe, Jerome Stiller, Casey Bernal 2005

11 Fish and Chips 5.10a ★★★

Fantastic moderate climbing brings you to a steep, exposed wall with good holds towards the top. You can go to the second set of anchors to rap to *Rhett Wench*'s midway anchor if you don't have a 70-meter rope, or if you're worried about your rope getting wet. *1st anchor: 12 bolts, 2-bolt anchor (110'), 2nd anchor: 14 bolts, 2-bolt anchor (125')*
FA: Darren Mabe 2005

12 Guppy 5.8+ ★★★★

Classic! This route lives up to the hype of being the best 5.8 in the canyon. Romp up fun and sustained climbing on excellent stone with a little bit of a crux about a third of the way. There is always a bolt and a good hold when you need one. *13 bolts, 2-bolt anchor (115')*
FA: Darren Mabe 2005

Note: For the following three routes, traverse right from the Guppy pod on fifth class terrain, going past three bolts to access a small ledge at the start of the route.

13 Clown Loach 5.8 ★

A trad line climbs up the black rock band to the right of *Guppy*. Head up the black rock band and move right to finish on the finger crack at the top of *Crackside Direct*, then clip *Guppy*'s anchor. *2 bolts, rack to #3 Camalot, 2-bolt anchor (115')*
FA: Kent Trout, Jim Jensen 1978

14 Crackside 5.9+ ★★

Jam the hand crack to a bolt, then go up and right to get to another crack. Then pull some face moves past another bolt before clipping the anchor. *3 bolts, rack to #3 Camalot, 2-bolt anchor (85')*   FA: Ken Trout, Kirk Miller, Rusty Kirkpatrick 1980

14a Crackside Direct 5.10a ★★

Climb *Crackside*, then bust up and left where you see a bolt. Climb past a thin crack and a few more bolts to finish on *Guppy*'s anchor. *4 bolts, rack to #2 Camalot, 2-bolt anchor (115')*
FA: Ken Trout, Kirk Miller, Rusty Kirkpatrick 1980

Brennivin Roof

tyrol from tree

Guppy Pod

fifth class

Guppy Pod Area

Dave Montgomery on his route *100 Proof* 5.12a, p169. 📷 Darren Mabe

Note: Routes 16-21 are on the far right side of the wall and are best accessed by hiking in from Tunnel 5. Use the approach to hike into the Solid Gold Area. Once at *Solid Gold*, traverse left via fifth class terrain, going past *The Waiting Room* to an amphitheater area. Roping up on this traverse is recommended; you can clip a bolt on *The Waiting Room* along the way.

16 **Psychotic Love** 5.10b R

P1: 5.9+ Start in a left-slanting crack to the left of *Big Bro's Watchin'*. When the crack ends, continue straight up until you reach a belay at the base of a dihedral. *Rack to #4 Camalot (150')*

P2: 5.10a R Climb up the corner, placing a finger-sized piece. Run it out and traverse up and left to eventually reach the ledge and fixed ropes where you'll reach *Fool's Gold's* P4 anchor. *Rack to #3 Camalot (160')*

P3: 5.10b Clip the first bolt of *Fool's Gold* and pull over a small bulge. From here, traverse straight left until you find a weakness above that leads to a dihedral, then climb up and right going around a bush and past a bolt to the dihedral. Finish at the top with a tree for a belay. *2 bolts, rack to #3 Camalot (70')*

Descent: Hike over to the right and rap *Solid Gold* or *Playin' Hooky*. It is recommended to be familiar with this descent before attempting it.
FA: Noah McKelvin 2012

The Solid Gold Area

17 Fool's Gold 5.12d ★★★
This is one of the most exposed 5.12s you'll ever climb and has an excellent final pitch!
P1/P2: 5.8 Climb the first two pitches of Solid Gold to get to the traverse.
P3: 5.0 From here, traverse left along the line of bolts with a fixed rope attached to them. Stay roped up and clip the bolts along the way to back up the fixed rope. *7 bolts, 2-bolt anchor (160')*
P4: 5.10b Pull around a low roof crux and some bad rock (can be avoided) to get to a nice belay ledge. *6 bolts, 2-bolt anchor (60')*
P5: 5.11b Step right from the belay and then continue back left to pull past a small overhang to a nice rest. Cop a quick rest, then pull on blocky holds to a jug before a hard sequence before gaining easier climbing and a two-bolt anchor. Instead of stopping here, continue up to the loft and belay from the three-bolt anchor as the lower anchor is to rappel from. *11 bolts, slings, 2-bolt anchor (90')*
P6: 5.12d Fantastic! Traverse out left on an incut rail to get to the most exposed arête climbing you'll ever do in the canyon. It is easiest to clean the route on toprope to avoid a long, dangerous swing. *7 bolts, 2-bolt anchor (60')*
Descent: Rap the route with a 60-meter rope to get back to the ledge traverse to get back to the Solid Gold raps at the top of the second pitch.
FA: Dave Montgomery 2011

18 Big Bro's Watchin'
5.11b ★★★
This route offers some serious adventure for CCC, and on a cold and windy day, you may just think you're on the Diamond. It is highly recommended to wear helmets.
P1: 5.9 From a belay anchor just left of the corner, scramble up and left of the bolts on *Left of Corner* (not clipping the bolts), go past a fixed pin and continue up the blocky, left-facing dihedral. At the top of the dihedral where the crack stops, clip a bolt then traverse right to an anchor. *1 bolt, 1 fixed pin, rack to #1 Camalot, 2-bolt anchor (90')*
P2: 5.9 Continue up the face past a bolt and then pull past a left-facing flake to gain the easier terrain to the ledge. *1 bolt, rack to #1 Camalot, 2-bolt anchor (70')*
P3: 5.11a Follow the ledgy face to a thin crack and short right-facing corner to start the tough climbing. A challenging sequence brings you past a bolt and a crack to get to a

few good rests before pulling over a short roof. Traverse straight left below a larger roof to get to the hanging belay anchor. *5 bolts, rack to #1 Camalot, 2-bolt anchor (115')*
P4: 5.11b From the hanging belay, there is an optional #4 Camalot placement in a horizontal crack to protect the start. Climb up to the left (ignoring the directional rap bolt straight above your head on the bulge) and pull over the bulge in the finger to hand-sized crack to get to the thin crux. A slightly height dependent sequence past a few bolts bring you to "the Loft" in the corner. *3 bolts, rack to #4 Camalot, 2-bolt anchor (75')*
P5: 5.10d The Loft pitch! Climb up the overhanging, stemming corner and jam your way through the steep section of the roof and pull over to an exposed belay. This is an excellent pitch with technical and exciting climbing. *Rack to #1 Camalot anchor (60')*
P6: From here, rap the route with a 70-meter rope or scramble to the top of the wall and hike over to the raps on the right side of the wall for *Solid Gold* or *Playin' Hooky*. If you rap the route, use a direction rap bolt above the top of the third pitch. After rappelling down the third pitch, clip into the fixed rope on the traverse ledge.
FA: Darren Mabe, Derek Lawrence 2009; aka Craig Luebben Memorial Route

19 Left of Corner 5.10c ★★
Belay from a two-bolt anchor at the base of the cliff to the left of the wide crack/corner. Climb up the face with a few technical moves, going up and left in the seam.
9 bolts, 2-bolt anchor (90')

20 Black Flake 5.10c ★
This bolted line starts immediately to the right of the corner/gully. Face moves bring you to a flake and lieback. Pull past it and gain the slab up higher. Two 0.5 Camalots can mitigate the pull onto the flake and the runout towards the end. *8 bolts, optional gear, 2-bolt anchor (90')*

21 Little Sister 5.10d ★★
Start up the face on the rounded arête-like feature to the right of *Black Flake*. Fun climbing on featured rock brings you to a challenging undercling move by the fifth bolt to get to more moderate terrain above. Share anchors with *Black Flake*. *8 bolts, 2-bolt anchor (90')*
FA: Chuck Fitch, Adam Huxley 2013

Note: The remaining seven routes are all accessed by the Solid Gold Approach, and most of these variation finishes are found by climbing the first few pitches of *Solid Gold*.

22 The Waiting Room 5.7 ★
This is a short route to the left of the start of *Furlough Day*. Traverse left to get to the first bolt, and then moderate slab climbing brings you up to a short, right-facing dihedral. This route could be a way to kill a few minutes on a busy day while you wait for other routes to open up. *6 bolts, 2-bolt anchor (60')*

23 Furlough Day 5.9 ★★★
P1: 5.9 Fun and consistent climbing involves a crux pulling a small roof. This route is similar to the first two pitches of *Solid Gold*, except harder and a little more exciting. This is a long pitch; knot the end of your 70-meter rope if you're lowering. *10 bolts, 2-bolt anchor (125')*
P2: 5.7 Easier climbing brings you up and right to get to the ledge. You can clip the last bolt of the second pitch of *Solid Gold* to ease the runout at the end. *5 bolts, 2-bolt anchor (80')*
Descent: Rap the route with a 70-meter rope, or rap the first two pitches of *Solid Gold* with a 60-meter rope. If rapping the route, knot the end of your 70-meter rope!
FA: Kevin Capps 2013

Darren Mabe on *Macho Barracho*, 5.12c, p169. 📷 Kristin McIlrath

The Upper Solid Gold Area

24 Solid Gold 5.12a ★★★★

P1: 5.8 Slab climb to the well-protected, shallow, right-facing dihedral. Belay at a hanging belay or combine the first two pitches for a 200-foot warm up pitch. *10 bolts, 2-bolt anchor (105')*
P2: 5.7 Work up the slab to a big ledge with a belay anchor. There are two sets of anchors; one is low and another is about 10 feet up. The higher anchor is newer and nice for rapping. *8 bolts, 2-bolt anchor (100')*

P3: 5.7 From the belay ledge, climb up to the left along fourth class terrain. Pass an anchor 30 feet up and continue past a few more bolts before gaining a nice little belay spot. *7 bolts, 2-bolt anchor (80')*
P4: 5.12a Crumbly face climbing leads to high quality sustained moves going past the small roofs. Super exposed and amazing! A comfy little ledge awaits you. *10 bolts, 2-bolt anchor (85')*

P5: 5.11d A few powerful sequences guards an easy finish on a slab leading to the summit. There's a spicy reach out left for bolt two; if you blow it you'll land right on your belayer. *12 bolts, 2-bolt anchor (90')*

Descent: Rap the route, stopping at every anchor unless you bring two ropes.
FA: Richard Wright, Mark Tarrant, Koko Kosila 2002

25 Spun Gold 5.12a ★★★

P1-P3: 5.8 Climb the first three pitches of *Solid Gold* to the small ledge and belay anchor.

P4: 5.11c Clip the first bolt on *Solid Gold*, then bust out right to some thin, technical face climbing that leads into a hand-sized, right-slanting crack. At the top of the crack, traverse left to a two-bolt hanging belay. Connect this into the next pitch for full value, by bringing lots of long slings and skipping the hanging belay. *10 bolts, 2-bolt anchor (80')*

P5: 5.12a Continue up to the left of the belay anchor, heading around the bulge to the right before climbing up the intimidating headwall to a fun, final crux. *11 bolts, 2-bolt anchor (85')*

Descent: Rappel the route with a 60-meter rope. You may need to clip directionals to get back to the anchor (the second can unclip them on their way down).
FA: Richard Wright, Mark Tarrant 2006

26 The Golden Hammer 5.12b ★★★★

P1-P3: 5.8 Climb the first three pitches of *Solid Gold* to the large ledge.

P4: 5.7 The traversing pitch. Clip the first bolt above the anchor with a sling, then traverse about 40 feet to the right to get to the base of the real climbing. *5 bolts, 2-bolt anchor (50')*

P5: 5.12b Balancy movement up the steep face brings you to a tricky mantel move below an intimidating roof. Cop a quick rest, then fire up positive holds and heel hooks to a final redpoint crux past the last bolt. It's a bit reachy at times, and the face below the roof still has some small crumbly flakes, but it's a fun pitch overall. *7 bolts, 2-bolt anchor (60')*

P6: 5.11d Fantastic climbing hugs the arête on the left side, which makes for a short, but technical finish to this spectacular multi-pitch climb. Finish up and left on *Spun Gold*'s anchor. If you're feeling strong, connect these last two pitches for a long, pumpy pitch. *5 bolts, 2-bolt anchor (50')*

Decent: Rappel the route with a 60-meter rope.
FA: Eric Schmeer, Chip Nakagawa 2013

Eric Schmeer on his route, *Golden Hammer*, 5.12b. 📷 Dave Montgomery

27 Creekafixion 5.11c ★★★

This is Clear Creek's version of *Rosy Crucifixion* in Eldo.

P1-P2: 5.8 Climb the first two pitches of *Solid Gold*. Combining the pitches makes for a nice warm up.

P3: 5.6 Head up and then right for the third pitch of *Playin' Hooky*.

P4: 5.11c Start up *Playin' Hooky*'s fourth pitch to the fifth bolt, and then follow the bolt line that veers up and left for a traverse above a large roof on the vertical face. It's not recommended to link this into the next pitch due to the fall potential for your follower on the technical traverse. *11 bolts, 2-bolt anchor (85')*

P5: 5.11a Continue up to the right in the corner and pull over a small roof to get to an easier slab. The anchor is up and right. *4 bolts, 2-bolt anchor (50')*

Decent: Rap the route with a 60-meter rope.
FA: Dave Montgomery, Sam Benedict, Eric Schmeer, Bruno Hache 2010

28 Playin' Hooky 5.8 ★★★★

Take the day off and play some hooky with this Clear Creek classic. This is a very popular multi-pitch moderate with its ease of accessibility and quality of climbing.

P1-P2: 5.8 Climb the first two pitches of *Solid Gold*, or combined them into one long pitch to the ledge.

P3: 5.6 From the ledge, climb up and left to a seam that brings you to another ledge with some fourth class terrain. Follow the bolt line up the slab to your right to an anchor and a small ledge about halfway up the slab. *6 bolts (including intermediate anchors), slings, 2-bolt anchor (75')*

P4: 5.8 Start up the slab five feet left of the anchor and finish on a vertical block with an anchor at the summit. *10 bolts, 2-bolt anchor (90')*

Descent: Rappel the route, stopping at every anchor with a 60m rope.
FA: Dave Montgomery, Kristin McIlrath 2010

The Bunker

 25-30min

 MOST OF THE DAY

 P.M.

8 Routes

≤5.8 5.9 5.10 5.11 5.12 5.13 5.14 proj

Crag Profile: If you have ever climbed on Creekside, you have probably looked across the road to the south and uphill to see this beautiful, multi-tiered wall that caps the top of the canyon. The Bunker is the crown of this beautiful canyon and holds some seldom-climbed gems and also has a lot of potential. The climbing here tends to be thuggy and overhanging, but there are some vertical routes that are worth the hike by themselves. This wall was mostly developed in the late '90s, then abandoned before a few of the routes could be finished, cleaned, and redpointed. Once you get to the base of the wall, you will see that there is a fixed line about 60 feet up on a fifth class slab. The easiest way to access the routes is by climbing up the middle of the wall to gain the fixed line, then traversing to the left or right. It helps to be on belay. There is also a fixed line on the left side of the wall by the warm ups to get to the ledge above. Once at the base of the routes, clip into a belay bolt that exists at the base of each route.

Approach: Drive 12.5 miles up canyon and park just east of Tunnel 6 on the north (right) side of the road (by Creekside). From here, find a trail across the road to the south, behind the guardrail and to the left of the drainage, that angles up and left towards the cliff. It is important to locate the wall before starting the hike to have a frame of reference. As you hike up and slightly to the left, you will encounter a large boulder about 60 yards uphill; proceed to the left of the boulder. The trail is faint, but there will be a cairn every 50 feet or so. When you see the cliff, approach it from the center and you will be able to access easy fifth class slabs to get to the fixed lines at the base of the overhanging wall about 60 feet up. Alternatively, jug the fixed line on the left side of the wall.

1 **Trench Warfare** 5.11c ★★
The leftmost bolted line on the wall climbs past a hollow flake by the second bolt to the seam on the slightly overhanging face. It delivers a respectable pump if you're not careful with your footwork.
7 bolts, 2-bolt anchor (55')

2 **Trench Foot** 5.11c ★★
This is a great warm up for the wall. Start at the same belay as *Trench Warfare*, but go up the black streaked wall to the right. After clipping the first bolt, move left and mantel up before busting out right to the second bolt on the ledge. From here, fun climbing and sustained movement awaits you.
6 bolts, 2-bolt anchor (60')
FA: Kevin Capps 2013

3 **Saigon** 5.13a ★★★
A juggy traverse takes you up and right into a burly sequence that goes through the steepest part of the route. Once past the fourth bolt, the climbing eases up. Bouldery climbing in a great position! Some may find this one-move wonder soft for the grade. *7 bolts, 2-bolt anchor (60')*
FKA: Kevin Capps 2013

The Bunker approach

The Bunker

fixed lines

4 Apoca-Lips Now!
5.13b ★★★★
Start on Saigon, then traverse up and right after pulling the crux on that route. Meet up with Charlie to climb to the top. This is a must do if you're up here!
8 bolts, 2-bolt anchor (65')
FA: Mark Anderson 06/14

5 Charlie Don't Surf
project
Start at a belay bolt on the right side of the fixed line and climb up the black, water-streaked, overhanging dihedral. A technical and powerful crux (5.14?) hits you quickly with big moves climbing up the seam leading to a large, right-facing corner.
6 bolts, 2-bolt anchor (65')

6 Valkyrie 5.14a ★★★
This continuous and varied line climbs mostly excellent rock up the center of the cave. The shouldery crux hits at mid-height, but burly moves out the capping roof keep the outcome in doubt until the very end.
8 bolts, 2-bolt anchor (70')
FA: Mark Anderson 06/14

Dan Cornella on *Approach Right*, 5.10b, p169.   📷 Dan Gambino

7 Full Metal Jacket
5.13c ★★★
This sustained pumpfest culminates with glorius jug hauling to get to the chains. When the bolt lines diverge, bust up and left through the tiered roofs. *8 bolts, 2-bolt anchor (70')*
FFA: Mark Anderson 06/14

8 14:59 5.13a ★★
A moderate start on *Full Metal Jacket* leads to some 5.12 climbing with a juggy traverse out right and a slight rest before committing to the strenuous underclings in the final roof and pulling over to the top.
7 bolts, 2-bolt anchor (70')
FFA: Jason Haas 05/14

Note: Mark Anderson bolted a project to the right of *14:59* as this book went to press. It will probably be completed before this book is in your hands and will be in the 5.13 to 5.14 range.

Play Pen

2min   A.M.   MOST OF THE DAY   **5 Routes**

≤5.8 5.9 5.10 5.11 5.12 5.13 5.14 proj

Crag Profile: This little wall offers a few fun vertical moderates on decent stone. The approach is minimal – a 200 yard walk on a flat, established trail, making it a great place to get in a few short pitches when you don't have all day. The three bolted routes on the right currently all share the same anchor, so it makes for easy toproping after climbing just one of them. The wall faces northeast and receives plenty of shade on the second half of the day and a little sun in the morning, especially in the summer.

Approach: Park just east of Tunnel 6 on the north (right) side of the road (by Creekside) after driving 12.5 miles up canyon. Take an established trail north of the parking area along the creek for about 200 yards and Play Pen will be just off the trail on your left.

Play Pen

Play Pen approach

1 Toy Box 5.10a ★★

The leftmost line on the wall follows a low-angled, right-slanting slab to some fun stemming in a shallow corner. Climb past the dihedral to find big holds leading to the top.
6 bolts, 2-bolt anchor (65')
FA: Drew Spaulding 2013

2 Old Man's Myth 5.9 ★

A well protected trad climb begins on the left-slanting slab to the right of *Toy Box* to get to a thin crack that climbs straight up the black, water-streaked wall. *Rack doubles to #1, (1) #2 Camalot, 2-bolt anchor (65')*
FA: Drew Spaulding 2013

3 Recess 5.10a ★★

A challenging pull over a bulge and past the second bolt brings you to easier climbing the rest of the way.
6 bolts, 2-bolt anchor (70')
FA: Drew Spaulding 2013

4 Child's Play 5.10b ★★★

Fun and sustained climbing heads up the center of the wall. A tricky mantel towards the beginning starts you out on the steep face with a few more fun sequences before gaining the ledge at the top.
7 bolts, 2-bolt anchor (75')
FA: Drew Spaulding 2013

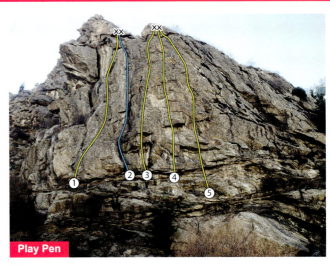

Play Pen

5 Pirate's Bootie 5.10b ★

The rightmost route is extremely dirty, yet still kind of fun. A crux pull over a small roof leads you through a few technical sequences along the way until arriving at the anchor up and left. *7 bolts, 2-bolt anchor (75')*
FA: Drew Spaulding 2013

It's Joe Kinder's prime time to shine. 5.14b, Primo Wall, p191. ⌀ Keith Ladzinski

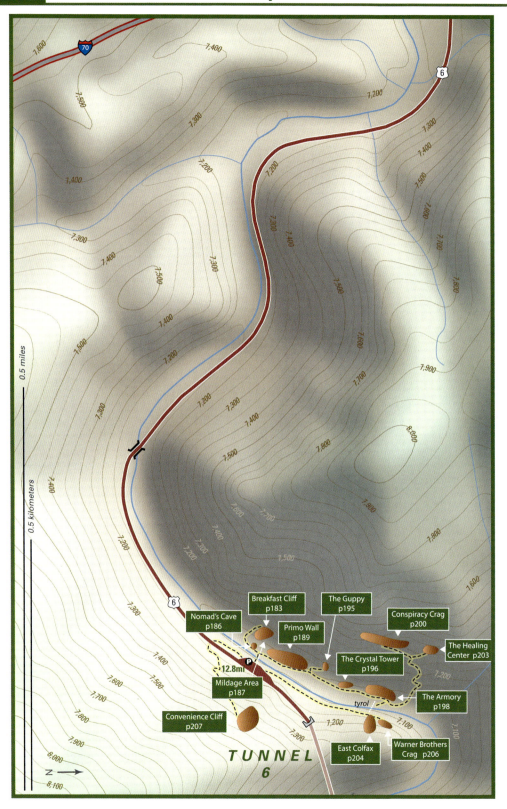

7,600
70
7,400
7,200
6
7,500
7,300
7,300
7,400
7,200
7,200
7,560
7,200
7,400
7,300
1,400
7,300
7,300
7,400
7,300
7,580
7,700
7,500
7,300
1,500
7,200
7,500
1,900
0.5 miles
7,400
7,500
7,200
7,700
8,000
7,300
7,400
1,900
7,500
7,800
7,600
1,700
1,500
7,200
0.5 kilometers
7,400
7,600
1,700
7,400
7,300
1,500
7,200
7,800
1,600

Breakfast Cliff p183
The Guppy p195
Conspiracy Crag p200
Nomad's Cave p186
Primo Wall p189
6
The Healing Center p203
The Crystal Tower p196
P
1,200
12.8mi
Mildage Area p187
tyrol
The Armory p198
7,100
Convenience Cliff p207
1,200
East Colfax p204
Warner Brothers Crag p206
7,600
7,500
7,700
7,300
7,800
7,900
8,000
N →
8,100

**T U N N E L
6**
1,100
1,100

Breakfast Cliff

 15-20min   A.M.   P.M.   ≤5.8 5.9 5.10 5.11 5.12 5.13 5.14 proj   **6 Routes**

Crag Profile: This vertical wall is a nice, sunny alternative to the often-busy Primo Wall. Most of the climbs here are categorized as being short and super crimpy. It is also a good place for people looking to warm up their tendons for some of the harder climbs in the Primo Area.

Typically, the climbs on this wall feel easier with fresh skin because some of the crimps are very sharp. Breakfast Cliff faces west and gets sun from about 11am onwards.

Approach: To approach this wall, use the same approach as Primo Wall (p189) except walk further west, passing Nomad's Cave and taking a faint, uphill trail in the first gully west of the cave. The wall is the first one on your right a couple hundred feet up the trail. If facing Nomad's Cave from the road, Breakfast Cliff is uphill to the left and is west facing.

Parking for every crag in this chapter

Primo Wall →

Breakfast Cliff approach

❶ The Morning Poos
5.8+ ★★★
The leftmost route starts in the right-facing corner and continues with fun, thought-provoking slab climbing with good clipping stances. It's a great beginner lead with a well-protected crux.
8 bolts, 2-bolt anchor (65')
FA: Kevin Capps 2011

❷ Morning Wood 5.10c ★★
Boulder up to gain the ledge, make a clip, rest, and then get ready for a couple of hard moves to get off the ledge. *6 bolts, 2-bolt anchor (55')*
FA: Kevin Capps 2011

❸ Waffle House 5.10d ★★★
Start on the right-facing crack to get established on the ledge. Find a good starting point, and crimp your way to the top. Finish on the anchors to the right, which are shared with *Pete's Kitchen.*
6 bolts, 2-bolt anchor (50')
FA: Kevin Capps 2011

❹ Pete's Kitchen 5.12a ★★★
Thin, technical, and a little cryptic - use a combination of crimps, sidepulls, thumberclings, good footwork, and body tension on this dead vertical crimpfest. It starts out in your face and eases off after the third bolt. If 12a is your limit, it is recommended to stickclip the second bolt.
5 bolts, 2-bolt anchor (50')
FA: Kevin Capps 2011

Gabe Craviero sports some *Morning Wood,* 5.10c, previous page. Matt Lloyd

5 **The Diner** 5.10a ★

This is a fun little climb if you're looking to place some gear. Start in the obvious corner just right of *Pete's Kitchen* and climb the crack up and left to pull onto the face. A .75 Camalot protects this cruxy move. From there, head straight up to the top and belay at a tree or finish on *Pete's Kitchen* for an anchor.
Rack to #3 Camalot (45')
FA: Kevin Capps 2011

6 **Morning Schist** 5.7

Climb the wide, right-traversing crack to the right of *The Diner*. The crack can be protected with a #4 Camalot. Pull around the corner and climb easier terrain to the top. Belay at the tree or use *Pete's Kitchen*'s anchor.
Rack to #4 Camalot (45')

Breakfast Cliff

Jay Samuelson is *My Significant Other,*
5.13d, The Guppy, p195.
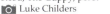 Luke Childers

Nomad's Cave

10-15min

MOST OF THE DAY

7 Routes

≤5.8 5.9 5.10 5.11 5.12 5.13 5.14 proj

Crag Profile: Nomad's Cave is notorious for drilled or chipped sport climbs. Despite that fact, the two best routes in the cave are completely natural – *Pizza Dick* (5.12c) and *Freaks and Geeks* (5.14a). Even though a few routes climb through drilled pockets, they are still fun, kind of like climbing in a gym. The cave is a good place to find shelter on sunny days or in thunderstorms.

Approach: Use the Primo Wall approach (p189). From Primo Wall, head 50 yards upstream to find a large cave. *Pizza Dick* is the route furthest to the right of the cave.

① The Roid 5.13a ★
This route looks like a turd, but it's not. *The Roid* is like sour beer – you either love it or hate it, but no one is in the middle. Climb the overhanging dihedral on the far left side of the cave. Kneebar, shoulder scum, and undercling your way through a full body workout to the single bolt anchor at the lip of the cave.
6 bolts, no established anchors, climb off the slab to the left (30')
FA: Curt Fry 1994

② Express Yourself 5.13b ★
It was 13a, then it broke. Some people call it 13c, some still call it 13a; we take the middle ground. Powerful and manufactured.
4 bolts, 2-bolt anchor (30')
FA: Pete Zoller 1990

③a Hard Day Mining 5.12d ★
Begin on *Predator*, then pull left at the second bolt to finish on *Express Yourself*. It climbs like a route in a gym. *6 bolts, 2-bolt anchor (30')*

③ Predator 5.12c ★★
Power pull on drilled pockets out the center of the cave.
4 bolts, 2-bolt anchor (35')
FA: Pete Zoller 1990

④ Predator X 5.13a
Continue up and right on drilled and chipped holds after the fourth bolt on *Predator*. *8 bolts, no anchor (35')*
FA: Pete Zoller

⑤a Cave Troll 5.13d ★
Start on *Freaks and Geeks*, then go left to pull through a stiff crux and finish on *Predator*.
4 bolts, 2-bolt anchor (35')
FA: Scott Hahn 2005

Nomad's Cave

5 **Freaks and Geeks**
5.14a ★★★
This route can be climbed as a stand start at 13d or add the roof boulder problem intro for the 14a. The crux high on the route revolves around a giant throw to easier climbing above.
5 bolts, 2-bolt anchor (30')
FA from stand start: Tommy Caldwell; FA with boulder problem: Cory French 2002

6a **Caldwell's Groove**
5.13d ★
Climb the overhanging groove to the left of *Pizza Dick*. Make reachy crux moves to a flat edge and finish at *Pizza Dick*'s anchor.
4 bolts, 2-bolt anchor (30')
FA: Tommy Caldwell 1999

6 **Pizza Dick** 5.12c ★★
The rightmost route in the cave has a bouldery crux off the ground on a sloping rail, then big, pumpy slopers to the top. This is one of the few all-natural routes in the cave.
4 bolts, 2-bolt anchor (30')
FA: Fred Knapp 1990; aka Mother Nature

Mildage Area

 15min

 A.M.   P.M.   **4 Routes**

≤5.8 5.9 5.10 5.11 5.12 5.13 5.14 *proj*

Crag Profile: This wall has a couple of routes that are worth heading up the hill to jump on, including *Mildage* (5.11d) and *Inner Gorilla* (5.12d). This is especially true if Primo Wall is too crowded. A lot of crimpers and sidepulls can be expected on this near vertical, east-facing wall.

Approach: Use the Primo Wall approach (p189). To get to Mildage Area, climb easy fourth class terrain 10 feet left of *Halle Bop* (p189) at Primo Wall to find a faint trail that takes you up and left to the base of the climbs. Be very careful on the trail above; any rocks knocked off could make there way to the Primo Wall area.

fourth class

Mildage Area approach

1 **Battle with a Bush** 5.9 ★
Climb the crack in the dihedral just left of *Inner Gorilla*. Belay either from the top of the route and walk off or sketchily clip the anchors on the face to the right.
Rack to #4 Camalot, no anchor (40')
FA: Matt Bolt 2009

2 **Inner Gorilla** 5.12d ★★★
Climb the arête 25 feet left of *Mildage*. Fun climbing around the arête involves small, sharp, and sometimes odd holds.
6 bolts, 2-bolt anchor (40')
FA: Kevin Capps 2011;
Equipper: Luke Childers

3 **Project**
Thin and powerful face climbing.
5.13+? *6 bolts, 2-bolt anchor (45')*
Equipper: Taylor Roy 2011

4 **Mildage** 5.11d ★★
Climb on sharp flakes and small crimps. It's the rightmost line and is worth the hike uphill.
5 bolts, 2-bolt anchor (45')

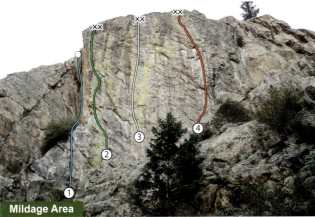

Mildage Area

Christine Liao cruises along in her *Mirthmobile*, 5.10a, next page. Dan Gambino

Primo Wall

15min

MOST OF
THE DAY

EARLY
A.M./P.M.

23 Routes

≤5.8 5.9 5.10 5.11 5.12 5.13 5.14 proj

Crag Profile: This is the classic and always challenging wall in the canyon that will keep you coming back for more. You'll want to make every route your new project with gems like *Moving Out* (5.12b), *Sucking My Will to Live* (5.12c), *Public Solitude* (5.13b), *Squeeze Play* (5.13b), *Primeval* (5.14a) and *Shine* (5.14a). Well, the list could actually be longer with all the fun link-ups like *Flyin' Child* (5.13a) and *Squeezing My Will to Live* (5.13a). Whether it's your first time or you come here a few days a week, it's always a fun time. Primo faces southeast and will get sun in the morning and throughout the day, but is sheltered by trees in certain parts. It's a great early day spot in the winter and a nice evening destination in the summer.

Approach: Depending on what time of year it is, the best approach can vary depending on the depth of the creek.
Tyrolean: Drive 12.8 miles up canyon and park 100 yards west of Tunnel 6 on the north (right) side of the road. From here, hike 200 yards east/downstream on the creekside trail until reaching the tyrolean. Take the tyrol across the creek; Primo Wall will be about 200 yards up stream.

Parking for every crag in this chapter

Wade Across the Creek: From the same parking area described above, you will see Primo Wall across the creek. If it is fall through early spring, put on your waders and walk across the creek in the shallowest spot you see.
Ice Bridge: During the cold winter months, an ice bridge will form across the creek just west of the main parking area about 125 yards past Tunnel 6. It is not recommended to cross anywhere besides the ice bridge because of thin ice.
Hike In: To avoid the tyrolean or walking across the creek, continue another 0.5 miles west of Tunnel 6 and park by the bridge. From here, find a faint, loose trail that hugs the north side of the stream and takes you east (back down canyon) to Primo after a lot of scrambling.

Primo Wall - left side

1 Halle Bop 5.10d ★★
Encounter a sloper sequence on the leftmost route.
4 bolts, 2-bolt anchor (40')
FA: Rich Purnell

2 Mirthmobile 5.10a ★★
A harder start leads to easier climbing on big holds, which makes it a good warm-up for the area.
3 bolts, 2-bolt anchor (40')
FA: Ken Trout 1990

3 Killer Pillar 5.10b ★★
Tackle blocky pinches and big holds in a shallow corner, which becomes slightly overhanging towards the end.
5 bolts, 2-bolt anchor (45')
FA: Alan Nelson 1993

Chris Barlow seeks some *Public Solitude,* 5.13b, next page. 📷 © Adam Sanders

4 Public Solitude
5.13b ★★★★
Classic and amazing! Follow technical climbing up the near vertical face on sloping sidepulls, pinches, and crimps with cryptic footwork.
6 bolts, 2-bolt anchor (50')
FA: Peter Beal 2000; Equipper: Rich Purnell

4a Public Play 5.13c ★★★
A hardman's link-up climbs the crux of *Public Solitude* and finishes with the pumpy, slightly overhanging prow on *Squeeze Play*, making it just a touch harder than *Public Solitude*.
7 bolts, 2-bolt anchor (50')

5 Squeeze Play 5.13b ★★★
A super crimpy lower crux leads to a decent rest and a powerful finish on the beautiful overhanging prow.
7 bolts, 2-bolt anchor (55')
FA: Steve Damboise, Steve Hong 2004

5a Squeezing My Will to Live 5.13a ★★★
A fantastic link-up climbs through the crimpy lower crux on *Squeeze Play*. After the fourth bolt, finish up and right on the super classic, *Sucking My Will to Live*.
6 bolts, 2-bolt anchor (55')

6 Sucking My Will to Live
5.12c ★★★★
This is one of the best 5.12s anywhere! Climbers come from all around to test their ability on this Clear Creek classic. Sustained and technical climbing brings you to a short rest before a final, pumpy sequence to the anchor. *6 permadraws, 2-bolt fixed anchor (55')*
FA: Ken Trout 1992

6a Sucking My Will to Squeeze 5.13a ★★★
Start on *Sucking My Will to Live* and climb past the first crux. From here, spice things up by finishing on the hard upper boulder problem of *Squeeze Play*.
7 bolts, 2-bolt anchor (55')

7 Shine 5.14a ★★★★
This is a hardman's test piece for the canyon. Climb the shallow groove before moving right and up the headwall. Two hard sequences stacked on top of each other lead to one of the hardest moves on the route before easing up a bit. Watch out for temperature-dependent crux holds.
7 bolts, 2-bolt anchor (50')
FA: Peter Beal 1997;
Equippers: Kurt Smith, Mark Rolofson

Primo Wall - middle

8 Grim Aura 5.13d ★★
An obvious link-up climbs the groove through the first crux of *Shine* into the last crux of *Sucking My Will to Live*. This is perfect for those that can't quite bust out the fingery upper crux on *Shine*. Holds have broken recently but the grade seems to have stayed the same.
9 bolts, 2-bolt anchor (55')
FA: Chris Way 2002

9 Primeval 5.14a ★★★★
This is one of the most inspiring lines on the wall. Climb up the crimpy, overhanging face to the prominent arête. Some filled in drilled pockets and glue reinforcement has made the grade of this route a whirlwind of a debate over the years. Even so, it's a great climb!
8 bolts, 2-bolt anchor (45')
FA: Peter Beal 1998

9a Primetime to Shine
5.14b ★★★★
A fantastic link-up climbs the crimpy lower crux on *Primeval* to the sloping ledge, then traverses left through the crux of *Shine* to the top.
9 bolts, 2-bolt anchor (55')
FA: Daniel Woods 2005

10 Eternal Recurrence
5.14a ★★
This route has two strenuous boulder problems on it that are separated by a ledge rest. The upper half gets dirty due to lack of traffic on the route.
8 bolts, 2-bolt anchor (50')
FA: Peter Beal 2002

11 City Slickers 5.12a ★★
This climbs like a V4 boulder problem on a rope and involves a tricky mantel. It's a lot of fun for a shorty.
3 bolts, 2-bolt anchor (25')
FA: Alan Nelson 1990

⑫ Suburban Cowgirls
5.11d R ★   ☐☐
Find this shorty to the right of *City Slickers*. Stickclipping the high and strenuous second bolt is a good idea as you fight through the balancy climbing on sidepulls and crimps.
3 bolts, 2-bolt anchor (25')
FA: Alan Nelson 1991

⑬ Problem Child 5.13b ★★★ ☐☐
Climb *Suburban Cowgirls* to the ledge, rest up, and then climb small holds to a hard-to-clip last bolt (it's better to just skip it).
7 bolts, 2-bolt anchor (50')
FA: Jay Samuelson 2010;
Equipper: Luke Childers

⑭ Flying Cowboys 5.12d ★★ ☐☐
Technical face climbing leads to a plate-like hold where you execute big moves involving a crazy sequence and a mantel to the ledge. It's not over! You still have to do some 5.12- climbing to the anchor. It's harder for short people.
6 bolts, 2-bolt anchor (50')
FA: Alan Nelson 1990

⑭ₐ Flyin' Child 5.13a ★★★ ☐☐
This link-up creates hard and sustained climbing by avoiding any ledge rests that are found on the original lines. Climb through the first crux on *Flying Cowboys* then traverse left on the lip to the pumpy and crimpy upper half of *Problem Child*.
7 bolts, 2-bolt anchor (55')
FA: Jay Samuelson 2013

⑮ Crying Flyboys 5.13a ★★★ ☐☐
Climb the sidepull flake to the sloping rail and tensiony sidepulls above to one hard final sequence to gain the lip. The fun, powerful movement involves a shouldery crux.
4 bolts, 2-bolt anchor (40')
FA: Dave Montgomery, Darren Mabe 2010

⑯ Breakfast Club 5.12a   ☐☐
Climb the seam to the ledge and battle the crux as you pull onto the upper face and arête.
5 bolts, 2-bolt anchor (50')
FA: Alan Nelson, Kurt Smith 1990

⑰ Groan Up 5.11c ★   ☐☐
An intricate opening sequence and mantel brings you to thought-provoking stemming in the corner.
5 bolts, 2-bolt anchor (50')
FA: Alan Nelson, Annette Bunge 1991

Luke Childers is one of the *Crying Flyboys*, 5.13a. 📷 Jay Samuelson

Primo Wall - middle

Primo Wall - mid-right

20 Relative to Standing
5.11b ★★

A short, slightly overhanging route with a couple of big reaches exists just right of *Moving Out*.
5 bolts, 2-bolt anchor (30')
FA: Luke Childers 2009

21 Suspended Sentence
5.12b ★

Begin on *Hangman* but veer up and left at the second bolt to encounter a couple of hard moves revolving around a finger lock.
5 bolts, 2-bolt anchor (35')
FA: Alan Nelson, Annette Bunge 1991

22 Hangman 5.12b ★★

A few thin and technical moves down low leads to a couple of powerful roof moves. *7 bolts, 2-bolt anchor (35')*
FA: Alan Nelson, Ken Trout 1991

23 Tater Tot 5.13b ★

A short and bouldery route climbs up an overhanging boulder on the far right side of Primo. Start on the arête to the right and power your way to the chains; bring a stickclip.
3 bolts, 2-bolt anchor (25')
FA: Taylor Roy 2010

18 River Run 5.13b ★★

Climb the overhanging arête just left of *Moving Out*. Easy climbing brings you to the thuggy moves on the upper boulder problem that consists of slapping at slopers, squeezing pinches, and a high amount of body tension. *4 bolts, 2-bolt anchor (45')*
FA: Peter Beal 1998

19 Moving Out 5.12b ★★★

Technical and powerful moves going up and left out of the dihedral rest halfway up make this route a challenge for the grade. It's one of the better 12b's in the canyon.
6 bolts, 2-bolt anchor (45')
FA: Alan Nelson 1991

Primo Wall - right side

Mark Anderson on the iconic *Skippin' Stones*, 5.11c, p196. Adam Sanders

The Guppy

 15min

 ALL DAY

3 Routes

≤5.8 5.9 5.10 5.11 5.12 5.13 5.14 proj

Crag Profile: Find this wall by locating the impressive prow coming out of the hillside uphill to the west of the Crystal Tower. While the routes here aren't great, it might be a place to escape the crowds for a few minutes. This wall faces south.

Approach: Use the Primo Wall approach (p189). The Guppy is located about 100 yards uphill, between Primo Wall and the Crystal Tower. There is a faint trail heading uphill on the right side of Primo.

to Primo

The Guppy approach

❶ Spinner Bait 5.11d
Start up the slab on the left side of the wall. Move past some bad rock to get to a strenuous mantel move. This sets you up for a few powerful moves to gain a rest before pulling back out right for the jug haul to the chains.
8 bolts, 2-bolt anchor (50')
FA: Luke Childers 2010

❷ My Significant Other
5.13d ★★★
Powerful and bouldery climbing on the overhanging arete makes this a fun testpiece for the area.
5 bolts, 2-bolt anchor (50')
FA: Jay Samuelson 2014

❸ Fish Taco 5.10a ★
The rightmost bolted line has a hard, unsuspecting sequence moving past the third bolt. You feel a bit forced to move left, but the top is more enjoyable. All of the bolts have been removed by the FA party.
5 (chopped) bolts, 2-bolt anchor (40')
FA: Jason Baker, Luke Childers 2010

The Guppy

The Primo Wall tyrolean. 📷 Dan Gambino

The Crystal Tower

 10-15min

 MOST OF THE DAY

 P.M.

6 Routes

≤5.8 5.9 5.10 5.11 5.12 5.13 5.14 *proj*

Crag Profile: If Primo Wall has beaten you to the ground, then head over to the Crystal Tower for *Mineral Museum*, one of the best 5.9s in the canyon. Otherwise test your ability on *Skippin' Stones* (5.11c) and *Quartz Sports* (5.12b). This wall has great stone and a variety of fun, quality rock climbs on it. It faces southeast and gets plenty of mid-day sun.

Approach: Park 100 yards west of Tunnel 6 on the north (right) side of the road after driving 12.8 miles up canyon. From here, hike east on the creekside trail until reaching the tyrolean about 200 yards downstream. Take the tyrol across the creek and the Crystal Tower will be a short 50-yard hike upstream. You may also cross the creek by walking across when the water is low.

Parking for every crag in this chapter

The Crystal Tower

1 Mineral Museum
5.9+ ★★★★

This is as good as 5.9 gets in CCC. Start on the leftmost portion of the wall and climb up and slightly right before busting left under a small roof and up into a dihedral near the chains. *11 bolts, 2-bolt anchor (75')*
FA: Ken Trout 1992

2 Quartz Sports
5.12b ★★★★

Quartz Sports is a true gem for the canyon and one of the best 12b's. Technical face moves get you to a solid shake before reaching for the large piece of quartz on the roof and pulling over. Interesting climbing the whole way. *9 bolts, 2-bolt anchor (75')*
FA: Ken Trout 1992

3 Skippin' Stones
5.11c ★★★★

Fun vertical climbing gets you to a great roof boulder problem and excellent exposure above. Pull through the roof to a juggy finish and the first anchors above.
9 bolts, 2-bolt anchor (65')
FA: Mark Tarrant, Richard Wright 2005

The Crystal Tower - right side

4 Hot Rocks 5.12c ★★★   ☐☐
Powerful moves down low on edges get you mounted onto this beast. The excellent face climbing always seems to be moving left and tickles the arête before blasting to the top. Fight the urge to be suckered around the arête. It's hard for the grade and a crux before the second bolt warrants a stickclip.
9 bolts, 2-bolt anchor (85')
FA: Julian Kinsman 1995

5 Cornered Again 5.11a ★   ☐☐
Interesting climbing takes you through the large corner system and makes you feel almost stuck in the flaring corner at times. Then somewhat easy climbing gets you to a fun, juggy roof to finish things off. It's a pretty cool route, minus the bird poop. **10 bolts, 2-bolt anchor (85')**
FA: Richard Wright, Mark Tarrant 2005

6 Crystallize 5.12c   ☐☐
Climb through choss to get to slightly better climbing by pulling through a few hard cruxes separated by rests. The rock quality and climbing gets a little better towards the top, but only slightly. **10 bolts, 2-bolt anchor (70')**
FA: T. Thomas, Mark Tarrant, Richard Wright 2006

Laura Capps is goood at *Sucking My Will to Live*, 5.12c, Primo Wall, p191.
📷 Kevin Capps

The Armory

10-15min

A.M.   Midday

10 Routes

≤5.8 5.9 5.10 5.11 5.12 5.13 5.14 proj

Crag Profile: The Armory has some of the best looking rock in the canyon, with routes like *Ken T'ank* (5.12c) and *The Gauntlet* (5.12d). We have seen some new routes going up here lately, including *The Overhangover* (5.13a) and *Fully Automatic* (5.12d) and it's finally a wall that you can climb on all day, so long as you're climbing in the 5.12 to 5.13 range. While its approach forces you to cross the creek, the climbing here is well worth it.

Approach: Park 100 yards west of Tunnel 6 on the north (right) side of the road after driving 12.8 miles up the canyon. From here, hike east on the creekside trail until reaching the tyrolean about 200 yards downstream. Take the tyrolean across the creek and the Armory will be just on the other side. You may also cross the creek by walking across when the water is low.

Handicapable

1 Handicapable 5.12b ★★
Walk uphill to the left of *The Diggler* to find this fun little route that is packed with bouldery, fun movement with a bit of a cryptic crux.
5 bolts, 2-bolt anchor (40')
FA: Dave Montgomery, Lisa Stern 2014

2 Off the Couch 5.10b ★★
This recent edition is a good warm up for the area as it is filled with a variety of holds and moves to get your tendons warmed up for *Ken T'ank*. Start just right of *Handicapable*.
6 bolts, 2-bolt anchor (45')
FA: Lisa Stern, Dave Montgomery 2014

3 The Diggler 5.11c ★★
Move 50 feet left of *The Gauntlet* and climb the face past a tough opening sequence. This route was bolted as a much needed warm up for the Armory, but then turned out to be much harder than expected.
4 bolts, 2-bolt anchor (35')
FA: Luke Childers; FFA Kevin Capps 2012

4a Shield of Fate project
A hard, direct start to *The Gauntlet* begins on the blank face (5.14?) just left of the dihedral. After working past two bolts of heinous face climbing, the route merges with *The Gauntlet* and follows easy 5.12 climbing to the top.

The Armory

6 Ken T'ank 5.12c ★★★★

This classic climb ascends the west-facing wall of the Armory on near perfect stone. Climb through a bouldery start to an awkward no hands rest (if you can find it) and into the final boulder problem before clipping the anchors. It's easier if you're tall. *9 bolts, 2-bolt anchor (65')*
FA: Jim Redo 1999; Equipper: Julian Kinsman

Climber: Chris Barlow Adam Sanders

4 The Gauntlet 5.12d ★★★
Stemming and jamming in the dihedral gets you past the first crux. After which, bust out left for some intense finger locking before pulling a couple more hard moves over the upper roof. *9 bolts, 2-bolt anchor (60')*
FA: Darren Mabe 2006

5 The Overhangover
5.13a ★★★
Super fun climbing on the upper section will leave you coming back for more. Climb the first two bolts of *The Gauntlet*, take the ledge rest, then continue up and right. Tackle a short, strenuous, boulder problem that finishes with big moves to jugs.
7 bolts, 2-bolt anchor (60')
FA: Kevin Capps 2012

6 Ken T'ank 5.12c ★★★★
See description on previous page.

6a Project
Climb *Ken T'ank* to the fifth bolt, then climb up and left for a technical sequence before joining back up at the top. 5.13?

Ken T'ank

7 Baretta 5.14b ★★★
Continuous bouldering up the classic, overhanging arête. A burly and slippery start to the fourth bolt on *Fully Automatic* leads to a desperate, dynamic crux at mid-height. Finish with sequential slaps up the prow. Stickclip the second bolt.
7 bolts, 2-bolt anchor (40')
Equipper: Luke Childers 2012;
FFA: Mark Anderson 05/14

8 Fully Automatic 5.13a ★★
Burly moves traversing out right on slopey underclings lead to a difficult transition going to the dihedral. Finish by placing gear on *Semi-Automatic*. This is the natural way to do this route (without continuing up the arête). *4 bolts, rack 0.5 - #1 Camalot, 2-bolt anchor (40')*
FA: Jason Baker 2012;
Equipper: Luke Childers

9 Semi-Automatic 5.11c ★★
Work up the dihedral on the right side of the wall. A slightly overhanging start leads to easier jamming and stemming up higher.
Rack to #1 Camalot, 2-bolt anchor (40')
FA: Alan Nelson, Guy Lords 1990

10 Bar-Stangled Banner
5.12b TR
Toprope the moves to the right of *Semi-Automatic* for an extra bonus.

The Conspiracy Crag

 20-25min

A.M. P.M. ≤5.8 5.9 5.10 5.11 5.12 5.13 5.14 proj **11 Routes**

Crag Profile: This wall holds a few fun sport routes that are off the beaten path and high in the canyon, so the views are phenomenal. Just to name a few; *Designer Genes* (5.12a), *Soma* (5.12a), and *Life is Beautiful* (5.12b) are all great routes that are recommended for a first timer. If you're looking for something easier, than head down to *Martians on Mopeds* for a great 5.9 pitch. The routes here don't get very much traffic, so a brush is nice to make a lot of the holds more friendly. Also, don't be surprised to see a herd of bighorn sheep walking around up here. The Conspiracy Crag is south facing and gets morning sun and nice, evening shade.

Approach: Drive 12.8 miles up canyon and park 100 yards west of Tunnel 6 on the north (right) side of the road. From here, hike east on the creekside trail until reaching the tyrolean about 200 yards downstream. Take the tyrolean across the creek. You may also cross the creek by walking across when the water is low. Once across the tyrolean, hike downstream past the Armory (p198) for a few hundred feet before locating a faint, uphill trail on your left. The trail is littered with plenty of cairns to mark the way, but you should be able to see the cliff as you start to hike up to it following switchbacks.

1 Trail of Illuminati 5.12b
Not worth the effort. A crumbly start and crappy climbing takes you past the third bolt to easier climbing on better rock above. A stickclip is a must for the first bolt.
6 bolts, 2-bolt anchor (60')
FA: Bob D'Antonio, Vaino Kodas 2000

2 Designer Genes 5.12a ★★
A technical and crumbly start pulls over the bulge, heading up and left to some fun jamming in the hand crack for the second half. Good rests are available. *8 bolts, 2-bolt anchor (65')*
FA: Bob D'Antonio, Vaino Kodas 2000

3 Soma 5.12a ★★
Fun and sustained! Like its neighbor to the left, it has a bit of a crumbly start, but then fun and powerful movement on bullet hard stone takes you up the right-facing corner. It's much pumpier than *Designer Genes*. *8 bolts, 2-bolt anchor (60')*
FA: Bob D'Antonio, Vaino Kodas 2000

Conspiracy Cliff

The Healing Center

Conspiracy Crag and Healing Center approach

④ Life is Beautiful 5.12b ★★★   ☐☐
Pull over a roof by the second bolt, then do a small traverse out left before continuing up on edges and small flakes to the top. There are two sets of anchors in case you would like a little extra challenge on this fantastic, pumpy route.
First anchor: 9 bolts (55');
Second anchor: 11 bolts (60')
FA: Bob D'Antonio, Vaino Kodas 2000

⑤ Cyber Leash 5.11a ★   ☐☐
Share the first bolt with *Area 51*, then bust up and left to utilize some liebacking and stemming to get to the top.
5 bolts, 2-bolt anchor (55')
FA: Bob D'Antonio, Vaino Kodas 2000

⑥ Area 51 5.11c ★   ☐☐
Stickclip a high first bolt on the left side of the cave. Climb up and right to gain a short rest by the runout second bolt before pulling some hard moves as you traverse up and left on crimps with bad feet. This route would be better if it cleaned up a bit.
5 bolts, 2-bolt anchor (50')
FA: Bob D'Antonio, Vaino Kodas 2000

⑦ The Space Between 5.10d   ☐☐
Dangerous rock quality, do not climb! This is the first route to the right of the cave. *9 bolts, 2-bolt anchor (80')*
FA: Mike Sheridan 2012

The Conspiracy Crag

8 Frankenfood 5.10c ★

Featured climbing in the left-facing dihedral leads to a ledge where you can either clip the anchor for a decent warm-up for the wall, or climb the challenging extension.
5 bolts, 2-bolt anchor (65')
FA: N. Morrel 2000

8a Frankenfood Extension 5.11d ★★★

A great second half to *Frankenfood* has fun and technical face climbing on great stone. Continue straight above the anchor, pulling on small crimps, edges, and finding a few good holds for rests here and there. There's just enough holds for this thing to have such good movement.
11 bolts, 2-bolt anchor (95')
FA: N. Morrel 2000

9 Martians on Mopeds 5.9 ★★

This is the rightmost bolted line on the main wall. Scramble up some fourth class rock to the first bolt 25 feet up. Fun and moderate slab climbing brings you to an anchor to the left. *5 bolts, 2-bolt anchor (75')*
FA: Bob D'Antonio, Vaino Kodas 2000

9a Martians Extension 5.11c

Climb the 5.9 pitch to a good stance, then continue up and right with featured face climbing on dirty and crumbly rock. A juggy finish takes you back left to the anchor.
11 bolts, slings, 2-bolt anchor (107')
FA: Bob D'Antonio, Vaino Kodas 2000

Alien Autopsy

Note: Find these two remaining routes downhill to the right, a couple hundred feet of the main wall.

10 Iridium System 5.11a ★

A few tough moves get you past the left-facing corner bulge, then a tricky mantel leads to easier and fun climbing on the arête above.
5 bolts, 2-bolt anchor (30')
FA: Mary Zuvela, Vaino Kodas 2000

11 Alien Autopsy 5.12a ★★★

Technical climbing on quality stone starts up the face on the right side of the large dihedral crack. After pulling a quick mantel move at the start, use precise technique to climb up and left on the smooth prow.
6 bolts, 2-bolt anchor (30')
FA: Bob D'Antonio, Vaino Kodas 2000

Crossing the creek to the Primo Wall area.   Dan Gambino

The Healing Center

  25min

  A.M.

  P.M.

≤5.8 5.9 5.10 5.11 5.12 5.13 5.14 proj

5 Routes

Crag Profile: This is a nice moderate wall with some fun slab climbs. Recently developed, this wall is home to some nice seclusion from the ordinary, but is only rewarded to those that choose to venture further up the canyon. The wall faces southeast and receives midday sun.

Approach: This wall is located to the right of Conspiracy Cliff. Use the same approach as for Conspiracy (p200), but when you get towards the top of the hill, locate the low-angled slab to your right.

1 Recovery 5.9+ ★★
Climb the thin and technical face at the start on perfect stone to get to a spicy jug romp towards the top. Share anchors with Ketosis.
6 bolts, 2-bolt anchor (50')
FA: Luke Childers, Josh Brossman 2013

2 Ketosis 5.10b ★★★
Start under the bulge and power your way over to gain a good clipping jug. Work up cool wavy rock to another bulge with an undercling move that leads to more jugs at the top.
8 bolts, 2-bolt anchor (50')
FA: Luke Childers, Josh Brossman 2013

3 Rest & Recovery 5.10b ★★★
This route takes the centermost line up the wall and offers a lot of fun movement and a crux going through a seam. *14 bolts, 2-bolt anchor (115')*
FA: Luke Childers, Josh Brossman 2013

4 AC Separation 5.10a ★★
Pull over a small bulge and climb past some sloper crimps to get to a rest stance. From here, cruise up a slight arête towards the top.
10 bolts, 2-bolt anchor (75')
FA: Luke Childers, Josh Brossman 2013

5 Radial Nerve 5.10a ★★
Start on AC Separation, then bust right after the first bulge to some tricky sequences negotiating a shallow right-facing corner. Share anchors with AC Separation.
10 bolts, 2-bolt anchor (75')
FA: Luke Childers, Josh Brossman 2013

The Healing Center

East Colfax

 5min

A.M. MOST OF THE DAY

≤5.8 5.9 5.10 5.11 5.12 5.13 5.14 proj

9 Routes

Crag Profile: Like east Colfax in Denver, this wall really is a fun place once you go a couple of times. The furthest left route, *East Colfax* (5.11b), offers a variety of slab, overhanging, and awkward climbing, while its neighbors to its right test your slab abilities. This is a northwest-facing cliff and gets sun in the afternoon.

Approach: To get to East Colfax, park 100 yards past Tunnel 6 on the north (right) side of the road after driving 12.8 miles up canyon. Take the creekside trail east/downstream from the parking area for about 200 yards and the wall will be in front of you to the right of the trail. The Primo Area tyrolean is located by this wall.

1 For the Children 5.0
Yes, you read the grade correctly – this is a bolted scramble on the left side of the wall, 20 feet left of *East Colfax*. *3 bolts, 2-bolt anchor (25')*
FA: Greg Hand 2014

2 East Colfax 5.11b ★★
This route may feel a little like east Colfax in Denver, but with less strip clubs. Climb the slab to interesting climbing on overhanging rock. From here, you can clip the first set of anchors and lower, or continue on the fun second half with mixed gear. A 70m rope is recommended.
First anchor: 5.11a, 4 bolts (50');
Second anchor: 5.11b, 8 bolts, rack 0.5 - #2 Camalot (110')
FA: Kevin Capps 2011

3 Fill in the Blanks 5.8
Climb the line of bolts just right of *East Colfax*. A bit of a squeeze.
9 bolts, 2-bolt anchor (80')
FA: Greg Hand, Paul Heyliger 2014

4 Steve's Wild Turkey Day 5.7 ★★
Start on the slab just right of *East Colfax*. A couple of cool sequences gets you to the top of the slab.
10 bolts, 2-bolt anchor (85')
FA: Luke Childers 2011

5 Wild Bore 5.7 ★★★
Like a wild bore, climb the west-facing slab in the center of the wall. Tightly spaced bolts makes for a fun and safe beginner lead.
11 bolts, 2-bolt anchor (90')
FA: Mark and Luke Childers 2011

6 Speeding Ticket 5.6 ★★
Another overprotected parent of a route, but there's nothing wrong with that. Easy climbing through a small right-facing corner leads to some challenging moves and a steep finish. The anchor is awkwardly placed on a ledge behind a bush. This is the rightmost route on the slab.
10 bolts, 2-bolt anchor (80')
FA: Hunt Prothro, Susanna Dent, Greg Hand 2013

7 When I'm 64 5.6 ★★
Begin on the slab just right of *Speeding Ticket*. It's a bit of a squeeze job, but it's a worthy lead for beginners.
7 bolts, 2-bolt anchor (65')
FA: Greg Hand, Kent Lugbill 2013

8 Two Star Six 5.6 ★
Climb the steep but broken rock that joins up with *When I'm 64* at its last bolt. It's easier than it looks.
5 bolts, 2-bolt anchor (50')
FA: Greg Hand, Kent Lugbill 2013

9 Hunting Party 5.10c ★
Just around the corner to the right of the previous routes is a bolted line heading up the vertical face and over a bulge towards the top for a one-move-wonder sequence.
6 bolts, 2-bolt anchor (50')
FA: Hunt Prothro, Susanna Dent, Greg Hand 2013

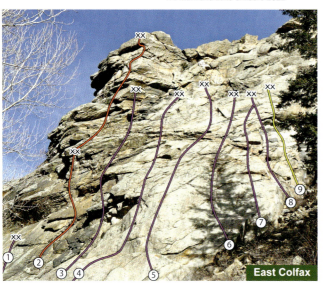

East Colfax

Jay Samuelson on *AC Separation*, 5.10a, p203. 📷 Luke Childers

Warner Brothers Pinnacle

 5min

 MOST OF THE DAY

 Midday

4 Routes

≤5.8 5.9 5.10 5.11 5.12 5.13 5.14 proj

Crag Profile: This nice little crag is newly developed and hosts a few fun moderates and easy climbs. The wall faces northwest and gets a little bit of sun in the middle of the day.

Approach: Use the same approach as for East Colfax (p204), and hike 50 feet past it/downstream/east to find this little moderate crag.

1 Tweety 5.8 ★★
The leftmost route on the wall starts in the right-angling seam on the slab, then shoots up the ledges to the steeper finish.
6 bolts, 2-bolt anchor (40')
FA: Greg Hand, Paul Heyliger 2014

2 I Tawt I Saw a Puddy Tat 5.9+ ★★
A fun route with a few tricky sequences and a final confusing move going to the top. You could finish up and right, or to the left.
8 bolts, 2-bolt anchor (40')
FA: Brian Parsons, Greg Hand, Paul Heyliger 2014

3 Sylvester 5.9
Very mellow climbing brings you to a challenging pull towards the top to get to the anchor. Squeeze job.
7 bolts, 2-bolt anchor (40')
FA: Greg Hand, Paul Heyliger 2014

4 I Did! I Did! 5.6 ★★
This is a great beginner lead and offers plenty of protection while climbing through bulgy ledges. It's the rightmost route on the wall.
7 bolts, 2-bolt anchor (40')
FA: Greg Hand, Paul Heyliger 2014

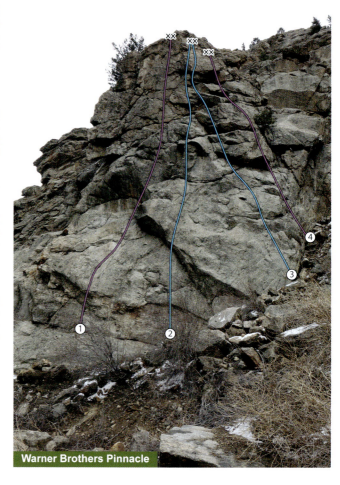

Warner Brothers Pinnacle

Convenience Cliff

20-30min

A.M.   P.M.   ≤5.8 5.9 5.10 5.11 5.12 5.13 5.14 proj   **8 Routes**

Crag Profile: While not named for the easy approach, this crag hosts a variety of fun climbs on beautiful wave-like rock. A lot of the routes here will let your fingertips do the work for you by digging into some of the sharp crimps on routes like *Kum & Go* (5.11d) and *Breaking the Mold* (5.12b). All of the anchors have great toprope access by hiking around to the backside of the cliff. The wall is high in the canyon and gets afternoon sun with its west-facing position.

Approach: Drive 12.9 miles up canyon and park on the north (right) side of the road, going just past Tunnel 6. Walk upstream along the road for 100 yards to a yellow sign indicating a turn in the road. Across the road from this sign, on the south side of the road, is a faint trail and cairn. Walk up the hill trending east and following a trail and cairns to the cliff uphill and to the east. Be careful of loose rocks on the trail as they might end up in the road.

Convenience Cliff approach

① Breaking the Mold
5.12b ★★★★

Fantastic climbing on wave-like rock leads to a stout final sequence through the upper crest of the wave and a big move to gain the top of the wall. Top this route out for extra style points! Leftmost bolted line on the wall. **6 bolts, 2-bolt anchor (45')**
FA: Kevin Capps 2010; Equippers: Kevin Capps, Jay Samuelson, John Garlough

② Kum & Go 5.11d ★★★

Climb the first three bolts of *Five and Dime* to the ledge. From here, traverse left on positive holds to an okay shake before climbing the thin and crimpy upper section. It's not over until wrapping your meat hook over the sharp dinner plate hold at the top of the wall.
8 bolts, 2-bolt anchor (50')
FA: Kevin Capps, Jay Samuelson 2011

Convenience Cliff

3 Five and Dime 5.10b ★★
A good warm up for the crag starts just left of the obvious easy crack. Climb a few steep moves to a ledge and then bust up the face above.
7 bolts, 2-bolt anchor (45')
FA: Kirk Miller 2007

4 Corner Market 5.7
While it's pretty dirty and loose, it's possibly worthwhile. Climb the messy tapering crack located in the dihedral in the middle of the wall.
Rack to #3 Camalot, sling anchor (45')
FA: Vaino Kodas, Mary Zuvela

5 Kwik-E-Mart 5.11a ★★
Consistent fun climbing on thin crimpers follows the bolt line to the right of *Corner Market*. Climb up and right to an anchor below the lip that occasionally has lowering biners.
6 bolts, 2-bolt anchor (45')
FA: Vaino Kodas, Mary Zuvela

6 Thank You, Come Again 5.12a ★
A moderate start leads to a brutal crux at the end.
6 bolts, 2-bolt anchor (45')
FA: Vaino Kodas, Mary Zuvela

7 Self Serve 5.10d ★
The second bolted route from the right on the uphill end of the crag has fun and easy climbing that leads to a stopper crux below the last bolt.
6 bolts, 2-bolt anchor (45')
FA: Vaino Kodas, Mary Zuvela

8 Pump and Run 5.11d ★★
The rightmost route features sustained crimp pulling. Be careful, your fingers might get pumped.
6 bolts, 2-bolt anchor (45')
FA: Vaino Kodas, Mary Zuvela

BRETT MERLIN IS BREAKING THE MOLD. 5.12B, CONVENIENCE CLIFF. P207 ⟨o⟩ ADAM BOVE

Mark Anderson with a *Full Metal Jacket*, 5.13c, p179. Keith North

Matt Lloyd becomes *The Savage*, 5.13a, p64. Keith North

Laura Capps takes a ride with *Officer Friendly*, 5.11c, p70. Kevin Capps

Majka Burhardt takes sight with a *.30-06*, 5.12a, p102.   Keith Ladzinski

5.12c

5.12d

Mike Sheridan has no problem with *Leftover Stuff*, 5.10c, p99. 📷 Dave Montgomery

Kevin Capps on *Apoca-Lips Now!*, 5.13b, p179. 📷 Keith North

Chuck Fryberger cruises the Colorado classic problem, *Mavericks*, V5.
Keith Ladzinski

FIXED PIN

FP promotes climbing ethics that benefit the long-term sustainability of the climbing community by hosting trail days, replacing hardware such as at Anarchy Wall, partnering with local climbing coalitions like the B.C.C. and F.C.C., and collaborating with government agencies including JeffCo to improve raptor closure policies, trail erosions, and general land manager concerns.

FP conducts business in a socially, economically and environmentally sustainable fashion by printing in the U.S. on recycled paper whenever possible, donating to the Access Fund and the American Alpine Club, and local climbing coalitions, and continuing to stay involved with the preservation of areas for which we publish guidebooks.

Kevin Capps
Author

Kevin Capps, a Golden local, spends most of his time leading rock climbing trips in Clear Creek Canyon or the Flatirons of Boulder through his guide service, Denver Mountain Guiding. He has a deep passion for the sport and sharing it with others. He grew up in St. Louis, learning to climb at Jackson Falls in Southern Illinois on the beautiful sandstone the area has to offer. It wasn't long before he made his way out to Colorado to pursue a life in climbing. Since arriving to Colorado, he has developed a desire for climbing and establishing new routes in Clear Creek Canyon. When not climbing in Clear Creek, you might find Kevin hitting the slopes for some skiing or hanging out at a local microbrew. This is Kevin's first guidebook.

Matt Lloyd
Co-author

Born in South Africa, Matt "Eagle Arms" Lloyd is by all accounts a climber. While that title encompasses much, hack author, rock guide, and adventurer are monikers that best describe his exploits. If proximity and a desire for the obscure brought him to Clear Creek, the variety and potential, coupled with his conveniently low IQ kept him here. In the decades since his baptism into climbing, Matt swapped would be bank accounts and steady employment for relentless world travel, though each time returning to climb in Clear Creek.

Jason Haas - Brainchild

Jason Haas is a loving father and husband living in Broomfield, Colorado. However, he is also known for his deep passion for climbing, being a math teacher, and running Fixed Pin Publishing. Jason was the inspiration and psych behind getting this book started as we gathered in Woody's for a beer in downtown Golden in the spring of 2013. He is an all around good guy and was an asset to putting this book together, from climbing routes to taking photos to laying this book out to even replacing old bolts.